THE
OPERATING
MANUAL
FOR THE
SELF

VOLUME ONE

The Big Picture, The Foundation

THE
OPERATING
MANUAL
FOR THE
SELF

Enter the journey of Self-discovery.
Learn how to engage your Self to enrich your life.

VOLUME ONE
The Big Picture, The Foundation

JEFFREY BRYAN
MSW, LCSW, BCD

CONTENTS

CONTENTS

CONTENTS

ACKNOWLEDGMENTS

In deep appreciation and gratitude I want to acknowledge the authors, thinkers, and other people who have contributed to the growth of my own thought, understanding, and development. These people have made *The Operating Manual for the Self* possible.

These include the philosophers, psychologists, and sociologists whom I studied in college, social work school, and in my postgraduate education. They also include current writers and colleagues who have contributed to the explosion of knowledge that we enjoy today. I have listed a small number of these authors in the bibliography.

My clients and patients have taught me what life is all about. They have taught me about the human struggle, what a person encounters and copes with on a day-to-day basis, and about the drive to transcend that struggle.

I offer thanks to my family, Seena, Mark, and Erin, who have challenged me, helped me define my ideas, and have edited some of my writing.

INTRODUCTION TO STUDYING THE SELF

We live in tremendously exciting times, where an explosion of knowledge has taken place. The amount of information and knowledge available to us continues to grow at an ever-accelerating, exponential pace. One area where this is taking place is in the field of psychology, including the academic field of psychological theory. Beyond academic psychologists, people in the helping professions, and individuals, apply this knowledge for the purpose of improving our everyday lives. To enrich psychology and make it more useful, we add in wisdom—the wisdom of 5,000 years of global civilization, and the wisdom of individuals alive today. We therefore have an amazingly rich fund of knowledge to apply when solving life's problems and in making our lives fulfilling.

We Know How to Be Happy

We can no longer claim that we don't know how to be happy. Certain books, teachers, and therapists can show us how. But, we have to make the effort. This book is about the **Self**,[1] about all the parts and aspects of who we are as human beings. We know a lot about the Self and continue to learn more. Since this information is so vast, I hope to make learning about the Self, and how to use the Self, more accessible.

---

1   I use the word Self, with a capital "S," to refer to all the parts and aspects of who we are. A part of the Self, with a small "s," is what we will call the "developmental self."

My Personal Journey

This book has been more than forty-two years in the making. It started during college, when I began my search to understand my Self and the world around me, studying sociology and philosophy. I considered becoming a sociologist, but decided that this field was too abstract. I wanted to actively engage and interact with people, so I pursued a career in social work, specializing in mental health. My career as a psychotherapist began in 1977 with my internship as a social work student, working in the adolescent ward of a psychiatric hospital for children. I left the hospital feeling that I had learned a lot, and that having survived the experience, I could handle anything. I have worked as a staff therapist, supervisor, and clinic director at mental health centers for seventeen years. My private practice as a psychotherapist began in 1984.

In preparation for a career as a social worker in mental health, I began a course of psychoanalysis. This produced considerable deep Self-exploration, insights, and growth. My own practice's orientation has been eclectic and multimodal, including: psychoanalysis, psychodynamic psychotherapy, cognitive therapy, cognitive behavioral therapy, structural and strategic family therapy, couples therapy and marriage counseling, neurolinguistic programming, Ericksonian hypnotherapy, and guided imagery. I have learned to enrich my work by including a person's religious and spiritual belief system as well.

Early on, I came across the phrase CANESI, Constant and Never-Ending Self-Improvement. By adopting this idea and making it a part of my identity, I have grown tremendously, and have made the process of **change** an "ally" rather than an enemy. Of course, I have not always loved what change has brought me.

The exciting human potential movement of the 1960s and 1970s also encouraged me to explore my Self. Tools for my growth have been: extensive reading, attending workshops and seminars, and meditating. Putting into practice what I have learned is a great challenge. My roles as a therapist, husband, father, friend, and son have produced and continue to produce endless "learning opportunities." I have struggled to view every experience in my life as a learning opportunity. Learning to appreciate, and to feel grateful for, difficult life experiences is a "work in progress." I have made some good progress, with more progress yet to be accomplished.

Working with clients of all ages and ethnicities, who have had an amazing variety of problems, has been a privilege, a challenge, and a blessing. My clients have been my biggest teachers about life. Through the process of helping them, I have grown in my understanding about life and in my ability to deal with my own problems. By helping others, one also helps one's Self.

This book is a marker on my personal journey. It marks the moment in my life where I've accumulated enough experience and knowledge to want to share it with others, by writing a book. I feel privileged and grateful to both have this experience and knowledge, and to be able to share it with others. Up until now I've only shared it with clients; needless to say, I hope to share it with others as well.

There is a saying that goes, "When the student is ready, the teacher will appear." This has been my experience, as new opportunities for me to learn continually appear as I'm ready for them. I have had and continue to have many wonderful teachers. I continue to explore my human potential and now, my spiritual potential. I think of myself as a participant/observer of humanity, life, and consciousness, of living and learning. I am pleased to share with you what I have learned so far. Thank you for honoring me by reading this book.

About This Book

The Operating Manual for the Self addresses an immense topic: the Self. I can only cover a relatively small portion of this topic in this book. Yet within these confines, I hope to accomplish some tasks. The first task is to summarize some information that we already have about the Self. The next task is to make a contribution to our knowledge about the Self. This involves exploring many aspects of the Self, showing how they relate to each other, and thus creating "the big picture" of the Self. In other words, formulating the theory of the Self. Some of these ideas are fairly standard and well accepted. Some of these ideas may seem speculative, and indeed some are, but they are based on thirty-five years of personal observation and experience in my capacity as a psychotherapist.

The third purpose for *The Operating Manual for the Self* is to present opportunities for your personal growth by stimulating Self-understanding and by offering "practices" to put theories into action. I hope you will find the practices useful. As a reader, you can enjoy both the theories and practices, or can emphasize one or the other depending on what your needs are and what is of interest to you.

I hope to inspire you to think about your life, your attitudes, and your strategies for getting what you want. On occasion, I will offer alternatives, which you may find useful and beneficial.

Living Life Is an Art and a Science

There are principles and procedures that give predictable results when we act on them. The consequences and outcomes of certain behaviors are almost guaranteed. This makes life a science. For example, if I want to establish a friendship, I need to behave in a friendly manner that makes a potential friend interested in me. If I become hostile and mean, I need to become Self-aware, and see that I am defeating the purpose of establishing a friendship. *The Operating Manual for the Self* contains principles and procedures that you can use to obtain what you want.

Living life is also an art because we can take the principles and procedures and put them into practice, in any way we choose. There are an infinite number of brushstrokes (actions) that we can use to paint what we want to see on the canvas of our lives. How you combine them into your work of art is entirely up to you, and is limited only by your imagination.

> **Point of Empowerment:** *Utilizing our freedom of choice to take any action we want makes living life an art and an adventure.*

So let's be underway as we embark upon the grand journey of living our life consciously, with knowledge and skill, to create happiness and fulfillment for ourselves.

PART ONE: GROUNDWORK

CHAPTER ONE

HOW TO USE THIS BOOK

This chapter contains explanations of aspects of the manual, and some suggestions about how to approach reading it and putting it to work.

A Reference Book, Manual, and Self-Help Book

The Operating Manual for the Self is designed to be a reference book, a manual, and a self-help book. To use *The Operating Manual for the Self* as a reference book and manual, you can turn to a section and read the material for information, clarification, and understanding. There are also some ideas that are developed throughout the book. Each chapter contributes to our understanding of the big picture, and stands by itself as an area of knowledge.

The Glossary

Words that are in **bold** are defined in the **glossary** at the end of the book. The definitions presented in the glossary are important because our everyday usage of these words is often very vague. There are often many meanings to these words, and the meanings of them are not agreed upon. Therefore, there is a lot of confusion about meaning.

The glossary will help you understand new ideas that are not elaborated upon at the time they are introduced, because of space limitations. There may be ideas that seem familiar, but are used in a certain way by the manual and therefore need clarification. The glossary provides this clarity.

Another option is to read the glossary before reading the book. This will give you a basic understanding of some of the ideas in the manual.

> **Point of Empowerment:** *Being clear about what words mean is necessary for understanding.*

> **Practice:** *When you see a word that is in the glossary, please turn to the glossary and read the definition.*

Charts

Charts are a way of organizing a large amount of information. The charts in the manual serve this purpose. However, the boxes of the chart are left blank. In most of the charts, the information in the boxes can fill part of a book. The charts give us a feel for how aspects of the Self relate to each other. It is not possible to explore the content of the boxes at this time.

Book Map, Map of the Self

A listing of the sections of the operating manual is included. This "map" of the manual is designed to help you find a specific section that you are interested in. You can also look the map over to get a sense of the whole book, and a sense of the "whole Self" as outlined in the manual.

Familiar and Complex Ideas

Some ideas in the operating manual may appear obvious and simple. However, there is often something important hidden in the simple and obvious. As we look carefully into the meaning of what seems like a simple issue, a deeper and important meaning often emerges.

Our **Self** is complex. It has many parts and aspects. (I use the word Self, with a capital "S," to refer to all the parts and aspects of who we are.[1]) Since the Self is complex, the manual will be complex. Though this may appear challenging and discouraging at times, the complexity is good news. The complexity creates efficiency, since working with one aspect of our Self can trigger change in a number of other aspects at the same time. For example, if I work to develop a potential ability into a skill that I can use to accomplish a task, I get the satisfaction of accomplishment, I build Self-confidence, and I raise my Self-esteem. For instance, I use my ability to think to learn how to use the word processing program on my computer, not letting frustrations along the way stop me. I use this skill to accomplish schoolwork, which I then feel good about. I build my confidence in my ability to use a computer. I raise my Self-esteem by acknowledging that I persisted in my learning and did not let the difficulty of it stop me.

> **Point of Empowerment:** *Because the Self is complex, you will never get bored with your Self.*
>
> **Practice:** *If you find your Self bored, go deeper into your Self.*

Brief or Deep

One of the goals of this book is to give you the big picture of the Self. In order to accomplish this, we will touch on some topics in depth and on others just briefly. For example, we will explore human needs and the life cycle. This is an introduction to a very vast subject. You can get a feeling for the subject, and begin to

---

1   A part of the Self, with a small "s," is what we will call the "developmental self."

see how it integrates with other topics about the Self. To get the big picture, we will sometimes sacrifice depth for breadth.

A Self-Help Book

RECOGNIZE YOURSELF

As a self-help book, *The Operating Manual for the Self* can function as a catalyst for change. There is useful information as well as new understandings. Practices will help you use the new information to produce change for yourself. As you read the operating manual, ask, "How does this apply to me?"

> ***Point of Empowerment:*** *With recognition, you have created an opportunity for your Self to grow.*

> ***Practice:*** *Think and reflect about an issue. Notice any changes in your Self as you put a practice into action.*

POINTS OF EMPOWERMENT, PRACTICES

The purpose of the Points of Empowerment is to highlight important ideas. You can review a chapter by reading the Points. They are also the basis for the Practices.

The Practices help you understand, digest, assimilate, and use the theory of the operating manual. They suggest ways of putting the ideas into action. You may have heard that "Knowledge is power." Actually, knowledge is power only when you put your ideas into action. The Points of Empowerment and Practices are designed to empower you.

> ***Point of Empowerment:*** *Knowledge is power when you put your ideas into action.*

> ***Practice:*** *Put this Point of Empowerment into practice—act on an idea that you value.*

CHANGE

The Operating Manual for the Self seeks to give us the ability to change, and seeks to inspire us to change. Hopefully, you will feel this inspiration and initiate change in your Self, for your Self. Remember, we are always ambivalent about change, desiring it and fearing it at the same time. Also, there is change that comes as the result of our will, and change that occurs spontaneously, if we allow it.

> *Point of Empowerment: As you read the manual, ideas for change will come to you. It takes initiative, courage, and perseverance to make changes in your Self.*

> *Practice: As ideas for change come to you, write them down and see if you can find a method for accomplishing these changes. If you find a lot of fear about change within your Self, start by making small changes.*

RESISTANCE

As you read *The Operating Manual for the Self*, you may experience some of the following: feeling bored or sleepy, losing interest, feeling discouraged or confused, feeling upset at memories that surface, feeling angry at your Self or another person, and feeling sad, anxious, or depressed. *These reactions are normal.* They are triggered by your thinking and feeling, and by your desire to understand your Self. Some of these reactions are from your resistance to change.

> *Point of Empowerment: You will encounter resistance as you read the operating manual. Resistance can slow or stop your growth and development.*

> *Practice: Notice and become aware of resistance. Try to understand it. But, push through it and continue reading, even if you cannot understand why the resistance is happening.*

SELF-ACCEPTANCE

Please read *The Operating Manual for the Self* with the **attitude** of, and in the spirit of, Self-acceptance. Self-acceptance says, "I am a fallible human being. I am imperfect and make mistakes. *And this is okay.* I won't criticize myself or beat my Self up." As you are reading, when you encounter a moment of painful Self-recognition, Self-acceptance can help you relax and continue to move forward.

Adopting an attitude of Self-acceptance toward your Self may not be easy to accomplish. As children we are automatically Self-critical and psychologically "beat our Self up." Parents also teach us to mistreat our Self by making statements like, "You made so many mistakes on this school project. Don't think you are so great."

> *Point of Empowerment: Self-acceptance will make reading the manual easier. Self-acceptance makes our life easier.*

> *Practice: State the affirmation, "I love and accept myself as I am."*

I DON'T UNDERSTAND. I DON'T KNOW HOW TO DO A PRACTICE.

If you don't understand something in the manual or don't know how to do a practice:

- Consult the glossary.
- Look up some of the words in a dictionary.
- Ask someone what he or she thinks it means or how that person would approach the practice.
- Explain what you think it means to someone or how you would approach the practice.
- Do an Internet search. For example, search Wikipedia.
- Read it and put the book down. Let the material be in your mind. State, "I seek to understand . . . (filling in the blank with the point that you do not understand)."

A response to your request can come from many different places: friends, TV, within your Self. See what comes up over the next three days.

- Put an idea or your version of a practice into action. See what happens.
- Continue reading and come back to the section or practice you don't understand.
- Don't let lack of immediate understanding or confusion discourage you.

Special Contributions of **The Operating Manual For the Self**

The following is a list of the operating manual's contributions to our fund of knowledge:

- A definition of the fundamentals of being human
- A simple yet profound map for personal growth
- An exploration of ability, will, power, empowerment, and choice
- An exploration of the many aspects of the Self
- A precise definition of Self-esteem and an explanation of its importance
- A precise definition of Self-worth
- An explanation of the difference between Self-esteem and Self-worth
- An explanation of the relationship between Self-esteem and the conscience
- An expanded description of human needs
- An exploration of the life cycle and the tasks of each stage of the life cycle
- An exploration of the Self as a system of interacting parts
- The delineation of the major components of the Self

- An exploration of the **developmental self**
- A description of the nature, role, function, use, and misuse of the **Ego**
- A description of the practical use of personality traits and qualities, and an explanation of temperament
- An exploration of the limits of our current conscience and proposals for a new conscience
- A clear and extensive exploration of identity and image, which creates an understanding of how identity and image influence a person's future
- A description of how the resolution of psychodynamic issues is part of our growth
- An explanation of how disturbances of the Self are caused and how disturbances affect a person
- An explanation of how many components of the Self combine into the processes of life

In Conclusion: Wrestling, Persistence, Companionship

Wrestle with the ideas and practices of the operating manual in order to make the material your own. Wrestle with your Self for stimulation, excitement, and a challenge. Remember, the two of you are on the same side. Make wrestling with your Self fun. Make it a lifelong practice.

Many ideas in the manual seem quite straightforward, but there is often a deep complexity to them that takes persistence to understand. On occasion, putting the ideas into practice may not be easy, but with consistent effort, you will succeed. I hope that you will be greatly rewarded for the effort you put into understanding and using *The Operating Manual for the Self.*

Make the manual a companion. Take it everywhere you go. If you don't physically take it, carry it within you. If necessary, take a break from the manual, but make a promise to your Self: set an intention and make a commitment to return to the manual when you are ready.

Our goal is to develop our potential as human beings, while enjoying life. So if you work, love, play, expand, and explore with Self-acceptance, you will get the most out of your Self, and out of life.

CHAPTER TWO

WHY DO WE NEED AN OPERATING MANUAL FOR THE SELF?

In this chapter we will address the question of why we need an operating manual for the self, and talk about what you can hope to see in this manual.

Operating Manuals

What is an operating manual? An operating manual:

- Tells you what the object you have does
- Tells you how to use it
- Lists all the parts
- Tells you how the parts work
- Tells you how to identify a problem
- Tells you how to fix the problem

A manual may or may not tell you how to get the most out of what you have. But we certainly want to know how to get the most out of our Self.

When people have a question about how to be a parent for their children, they often say, "I don't know what to do; there's no manual." On occasion someone says about himself, "I don't know what to do with my Self because I have no manual." Well, now there is a manual you can consult about your Self. If you're a parent, this manual will also help you understand what your children need, and will therefore help you become a more effective parent.

A Manual for My Self

My Self. This is the person in the world I am most intimate with. The two of us are inseparable. Interesting that there are two of us: Me and my Self. To have a Self is to be alive. It is a good idea to learn to work cooperatively with, and to fully utilize, our Self. We want to have the most rewarding, fulfilling, happy, loving, successful, and creative life we can. How can we go about getting the most from our Self to accomplish this? *The Operating Manual for the Self* will tell us how.

> **Point of Empowerment:** *I want my Self to be a friend to me. I want my Self to be an ally in the creation and living of my life.*

> **Practice:** *State the affirmation, "I am a friend to, and an ally with, my Self."*

The Big Picture

The Operating Manual for the Self will show us the big picture of who we are by exploring the components of the Self (the developmental self, ego, personality, conscience, and identity/image) and putting them into a context. We will understand how the parts of our Self fit and work together. We will appreciate our complexity and wonder. We will see the richness of who we are.

If we see how many aspects of our Self there are, we can understand why it takes an entire lifetime to learn to operate our Self. We can become patient with and accepting of ourselves. We will have the information and knowledge that enables us to explore ourselves, and to experience the joy, and sometimes the pain, of discovering who we are. We can become interested in and curious about who we are. We can learn to appreciate our magnificence.

Point of Empowerment: In order to be fully alive, we need to claim and integrate all the aspects of our Self.

Attaining mastery of our Self is a lifetime project. To master something is to develop excellence in our ability to make use of it. If we master the use of our Self, we can use our Self to create what we want.

Point of Empowerment: Our ultimate goal is to develop mastery in utilizing the Self, or Self-mastery.

Point of Empowerment: If we are operating in an unaware fashion, living life on autopilot, we will miss opportunities to develop the best in us and to live life to its fullest.

Conscious Learning

We are born with some knowledge about how to survive. As infants we cry when we are hungry, and cry and cry and cry, until we are fed. Our survival instinct, programmed into our genes, pushes us to do this. We have instructions hardwired into our genes that are the motivators for some of what we need and want to do.

In some ways we are ready to go the moment we are born. However, most of what we need to know about living, we have to learn along the way. Our parents and caretakers are our first instructors. We also learn from siblings, extended family members, teachers, friends, peers, and from the media of our culture. All these are sources of information for learning about how to live and how to accomplish what we want in life.

Beyond learning from others, we want to consciously learn, on our own, what we need to know about succeeding and about developing our Self. We do not have to only rely on what others teach us. We can use *The Operating Manual for the Self* to teach ourselves.

Overwhelmed by Information

The opportunities to learn the art and science of living are endless. We live in the information age, where the amount of information available to us is almost unlimited. This can cause us to feel overwhelmed, to withdraw our interest and attention from learning, and to just run on autopilot. We forget who we are, what we are about, and what we want for ourselves. *The Operating Manual for the Self* can help us move forward by giving us direction and focus.

> **Point of Empowerment:** *The manual gives us opportunities for independent learning, for "Self-study." This empowers us and gives us freedom.*

Stages in Life: The Life Cycle

A person's lifetime, the life cycle, passes through stages. There are *seven stages* to the life cycle. We are: *an infant/toddler, a child, an adolescent, a young adult, an adult, a senior, and an elder.* As we age, change is inevitable, so that we are continually facing something new. *The Operating Manual for the Self* will enable us to become aware of the abilities, tasks, **issues**, challenges, hurdles, and resistances of each stage. This **awareness** can show us what each stage of our life is about and what we need to accomplish during every phase. With this knowledge we can be more effective in accomplishing the tasks of the life cycle.

Each of these stages is distinct in itself, but has residues from previous stages, and anticipates the next stage.

RESIDUES FROM THE PAST

Residues of past stages inevitably exist as we progress from one stage to the next. This is commonly called "unfinished business." We need to know how to identify and finish unfinished business.

For example, in the past, we might have gotten very angry at someone, and held on to that anger for a long time. It may have begun in childhood or adolescence. Let's say it is anger from a friend's betrayal. Years later, we might have doubts about the value of friendship, so we need to release our anger, forgive our friend, and revise our **beliefs** about friendship. Otherwise we will not be able to fully enjoy the friendships we have. The operating manual will help us with this process.

> **Point of Empowerment:** *Letting go of the past helps us be fully in the present.*

> **Practice:** *Try to identify wounds from the past that continue to cause you pain.*

ANTICIPATING THE NEXT STAGE

In anticipation of the next stage in life and what we will face, we can begin to prepare our Self. We can identify and start to develop the new abilities and skills that we'll need, which will make it easier to accomplish the tasks and challenges of the next stage. This kind of anticipation of the future is rarely done in a clear, unambiguous manner. As we grow and develop, the potential abilities that we were born with become the skills we utilize to accomplish the tasks and goals of each stage.

The operating manual will show us what abilities and skills we can focus on as we anticipate the tasks of each stage of our life.

Abilities and Skills

All of us have had moments where we think, "Wow, I never knew I had that in me." We are referring to an ability or skill that we just discovered. We are experiencing the joy of this discovery. If you look at an infant learning to stand for the first time, you can see the joy of mastering a new skill. The infant also experiences the joy of success, finally succeeding at standing after many failed attempts at mastery.

Abilities, Skills, and Stages

Let's look at a few brief examples of the tasks we face and the skills we acquire throughout the life cycle.

- As infants, we have the innate ability to smile. We learn that a smile will get us attention.
- In childhood, we utilize our ability to learn in order to master reading and math. We use our ability to communicate to express our Self and to learn how to negotiate for what we want with our parents and siblings.
- In adolescence, we learn how to make friends and manage peer relationships by using our communication abilities.
- As young adults we explore romantic relationships by using our ability to feel love. Using our ability to think, we consider which careers we are interested in.
- In adulthood, we learn what is required of us at work and in our personal relationships. We use our ability to give of ourselves to fulfill these requirements, in order to reap the rewards of work and relationships.
- As seniors, we integrate the lessons of a lifetime and begin to develop wisdom. We use our ability to experience pleasure to enjoy the fruits of our work life and our loving relationships.
- As elders, we continue to integrate life's lessons into wisdom. We learn how to take care of our health and to fully appreciate the benefits of good health. We use our ability to love our Self. We can call upon our ability to have courage to help us prepare for the end of our life.

The operating manual helps us identify the many abilities that we have and guides us in their use throughout the life cycle.

Human Needs

We, as human beings, are born with needs. The fulfillment of these needs is a powerful motivator, a drive that leads us to take certain actions and to behave in certain ways. There are seven categories of needs. These categories are:

- Survival
- Safety/security
- Belonging/loving
- Self-esteem
- To create, to produce, and to know
- To achieve Self-actualization
- To experience beauty, mystery, and transcendence

There is an order to these needs, which has been called a "hierarchy." The need for physical survival comes first. Without survival, there are no other needs. Once a need is taken care of, we are then free to fulfill the next need. We can't go on to the next need unless we have satisfied the previous need to some degree. We can satisfy one need or all our needs, then circle back to fulfill more of a previous need with greater depth. There are many ways to fill each need. There is no limit to the fulfillment of our needs, if we know what we are seeking and how to find it.

> *Point of Empowerment:* *As we satisfy our needs, our life becomes rich, and we enhance our well-being. We feel happy and content.* The Operating Manual for the Self *will help us understand what our needs are and identify what we can do to fulfill them.*

The Distorted Self

During the course of our lifetime, our Self becomes distorted; we are not who we could be. We do not live up to our potential.

We do not make the best use of our Self. This happens because we do not understand what our potential is, and who we can become. We have limited, and often incorrect, information and knowledge about who we are. We are uninformed and sometimes ignorant. We end up becoming who others think we should be. As children, we unconsciously imitated what we observed others doing because this was the only **choice** we had. We didn't know that there were alternatives. As adults, sometimes we don't understand that we can be different; we also don't understand how to become different.

For example, we have a need for Self-esteem. As children we were dependent on other people, especially our parents, to fulfill our need for Self-esteem. We listened to their statements and comments on our behavior and turned that feedback into good, moderate, or poor Self-esteem. However, as adults we can observe our own behavior, evaluate it according to our values, and turn our evaluation into good, moderate, or poor Self-esteem.

The operating manual will give us the information we need to discover our potential, know what we are capable of, and see a better course of action for our Self. We will come to see how to create the best Self we can be.

Point of Empowerment: We can consciously create the best Self we can be.

Practice: Take some time to think about what your best Self would look like. Write down your ideas.

The Damaged Self

Everyone has had experiences where we are growing and developing in a smooth and comfortable manner; the parts of our Self are becoming more proficient at accomplishing the tasks of our life. But then something happens that injures or hurts us. We feel fear and retreat in pain. Part of our Self has been damaged.

For example, let's say as a seven-year-old I am learning to play baseball. The coach said that I played a pretty good game today. I am feeling confident about my ability to play baseball, and am feeling good about myself because of this confidence. My parents had watched the game as well. My father points out the few mistakes I made and states that I didn't play very well; I should have done better. My Self-confidence gets damaged by his statements, and the good feeling I have about my Self goes away. I experience a setback. The forward movement in my growth and development has slowed.

There are many kinds of experiences that damage our Self. To some degree they are inevitable, and ultimately, they can make us stronger. These experiences also vary in how severely they damage us. Severely damaging experiences are called traumas. All of us have experienced some trauma in our lives. We need to know how to recognize the damaged parts of the Self, and how to repair them. The operating manual can help us do this.

> **Point of Empowerment:** *There are many kinds of experiences that damage our Self. The damage needs* **healing***.

> **Practice:** *Take some time to identify some experiences in your life that damaged your Self. Write them down.*

The Lost Self

As a child, an adolescent, or even as an adult, we start to develop abilities and skills, but run into negative feedback. The negative feedback is a message that says, "Don't do that." These messages are sometimes very intense and forceful. To fulfill our need for survival, and as a response to negative feedback, we may completely stop the development of our Self in some areas. Repression occurs:

we bury—push down into our unconscious mind—aspects of our Self. As a result, we may not have important abilities within our Self to use. In other words, we have lost parts of our Self.

For example, consider the "terrible twos," a developmental stage where two-year-old children say "no" to almost everything their parents tell them to do. If this stage goes well, a child has started to learn the very important skill of saying "no." Saying "no" is our way of protecting ourselves, of refusing something we don't want. It also creates a boundary, a separation, of what does and doesn't belong to us. It takes a lifetime to master the skill of using "no." The two-year-old child has begun that journey. However, if parents or caretakers excessively or severely punish the child for saying "no," he or she will stop developing this necessary ability, and the ability can become lost. At some point in the child's lifetime, he or she will have to recover this aspect of the Self, the ability to say "no."

The operating manual helps us to identify and recover the abilities and parts of the Self that have been lost. We can learn how to reconnect with and reclaim the lost aspects of our Self that we need for our fulfillment.

Point of Empowerment: In order to be healthy and whole, we need to recover aspects of our Self that have been lost.

Practice: Decide to go on a quest to recover your lost Self.

Power and Empowerment

The Operating Manual for the Self will show us how we are powerful, and will empower us to use that power.

Here are two useful definitions:

- **Power** is the ability and willingness to act.
- **Empowerment** is the authority and permission to be powerful.

The elements of these definitions are ability, willingness, taking action, permission, and authority. We will explore how each of these elements is an aspect of the Self, and how to use them all to be powerful and feel empowered.

Point of Empowerment: *With our power, we take charge of our life.*

Practice: *Take a moment to consider the following questions: Where are you powerful? Where do you take charge of your life? Where do you feel powerless? Where do you give up being in charge of your life?*

Change

Change is part of life. It is always occurring, whether or not we notice it. Change is movement. We started out at point A. Now we are at point B. We have moved from point A to point B. We may have decided to go to point B, or life may have pushed us, moved us, there. We may have gone willingly or against our will, possibly kicking and screaming. We can try to slow change down, but we can't stop it. Change is inevitable.

Change can be deliberately planned or can occur spontaneously. We may have initiated deliberate change by using our will to put a plan into action. If change has occurred spontaneously, we suddenly find our Self in a new place. We may be totally surprised, because we didn't think that we did anything to cause a change. Or, we may have prepared our Self for this change. The change occurred spontaneously, "on its own." Spontaneous change terrifies us because we do not, and cannot, control it.

Point of Empowerment: *We are ambivalent about change, wanting and fearing change at the same time. We want positive changes in our life, but fear that the future will bring us negative changes.*

Practice: Think about a change that occurred to you in your life. Use this memory to explore your feelings about change.

The Operating Manual for the Self seeks to give us the ability to change, and seeks to inspire us to change. The manual has many ideas about what to change in your Self, and practical information about how to implement those changes.

Resistance

As change is always present in life, so is resistance. Resistance is the force that slows or seeks to stop change. A useful general definition of **resistance** is: anything that prevents movement from starting, or slows it down once it has started. In the physical realm, friction is an example of resistance. Friction slows down a car when we apply the brakes. As we will want to eventually stop the car, friction—resistance—becomes an absolute necessity. As you can see, there are good reasons for having friction. Similarly, there are good reasons for all types of resistance. It serves a useful and necessary purpose.

In the social realm, for example, someone may be making a promise to us that we want to believe. But we know "in our heart" (our **intuition** talking to us) that we shouldn't believe him. We doubt his sincerity. Our doubt slows down our desire to believe him. Though we may want to believe that the person will keep his word, there may also be good reasons to doubt this. In this situation, doubt is a resistance to desire and causes us to question our belief. It serves a useful and important function.

Point of Empowerment: The message of our experience of resistance is, "Pay attention, there is something important here."

Practice: Learn to notice moments of resistance and tune in to the message of the resistance.

However, resistance can impede our personal growth. It can stop or slow down our forward movement. Resistance can result in avoidance of important parts of our life, and can impede our progress. Resistance can keep us from achieving our goals.

A common resistance is fear. An important example of fear is our fear of change. Our fear of change brings resistance to change. Since growth is change, this fear slows down our growth. Since we tend to avoid what we fear, fear often results in avoiding what we need to face and deal with. In order to move forward we need to face our fears and our resistance.

For example, the person my friend introduced me to asked me out. I want to go out with him, but didn't say yes, because I fear rejection. My fear of rejection is a resistance to my moving forward, to going on a date. It is a resistance to the fulfillment of my Self's need for belonging and love.

> *Point of Empowerment:* Resistance is normal and natural. It is sometimes useful and sometimes a serious blockage.

> *Practice:* Think about a situation in your life that generates frustration because you are not getting what you want. See if you can identify what the specific resistance is to getting what you want. This may not be easy.

The operating manual will help us discover what our resistances are and show us how to resolve them.

The Self in Relationships

Our life is composed of relationships. We cannot be without relationships. We are given family relationships. We create other relationships for our Self. We bring our Self to these relationships; we invest our Self in them. The nature of our relationships is determined by what we contribute to them. As we enrich our Self, our relationships become richer. Since the operating manual helps us to enrich our Self, it helps us to enrich our relationships.

It is through our relationships that we know our Self. As we interact with other people, our behavior shows us who we are. For example, if our relationships tend to have a lot of anger in them, we can conclude we have a lot of anger inside us. We may even be an angry person. This invaluable information shows us where we need to work on our Self.

Point of Empowerment: Our relationships are mirrors, showing us who we are. The desire to make our relationships work can inspire us to become the person we want to be.

Practice: Take a moment to appreciate the value of your relationships.

In Summary

The Operating Manual for the Self helps us know who we are, what we can do, and who we can become. It seeks to inspire us to reach our full potential as human beings. It helps us to explore the richness and complexity of our Self, and to understand our growth, development, and evolution. We can wait until pain pushes us to change, or we can approach our Self with awareness, feeling powerful and empowered.[1]

Point of Empowerment: Nothing changes until you do.

Point of Empowerment: You can explore, discover, understand, utilize, invent, and reinvent your Self with curiosity, excitement, and joy.

Practice: State the affirmation, "I explore, discover, understand, utilize, invent, and reinvent my Self with curiosity, excitement, and joy."

---

1 *The Operating Manual for the Self, Volume I* explains who we are and points the way toward making some changes in our Self. In *OMS Volume II* we go into great detail about how to make changes in our Self.

CHAPTER THREE

A CHALLENGE FOR GROWTH, CHANGE, AND LIVING LIFE

Here are some ideas to challenge you. They are suggestions for action. They are ideals. As we strive toward achieving an ideal, we develop our potential, becoming more of who we can be. We do not expect our Self to reach an ideal, but to strive toward it.

- Think about every thought you have.
- Seek to feel good all the time.
- Give and receive only love.

We do not want to approach this challenge as if it were a demand that we must become obsessed with. We reach for these ideals in a relaxed manner, so that they inspire us. We are not seeking to "hold our Self accountable" or get discouraged.

Think About Every Thought

BE AWARE

Use your ability for Self-awareness to focus on your thinking. The challenge is an invitation to expanded awareness, mindfulness, thoughtfulness, and Self-reflection. We want to create a relaxed awareness, and a focused concentration, for processing our thinking.

ASSESS

Assessing our thinking involves asking the following questions:

- Are these thoughts leading me where I want to go?
- Are they helping me get what I want?
- Do they serve a useful purpose?
- How are they making me feel?

The answers to these questions help us identify thoughts that need changing.

CHALLENGE

Challenge your thoughts. Challenging your thinking means asking:
- Is this thought true?
- Are my thoughts accurate descriptions of reality?
- How objective or subjective is my thinking?
- How clear is my thinking?
- How distorted is my thinking?

Point of Empowerment: As you think, you feel. As you feel, you act. As you act, you create your life. As you think, so goes your life.

Practice: Think about how important your thoughts are.

Seek to Feel Good All the Time

We seek, we desire, to feel good all the time, as a guideline for living. Yet we cannot feel good all the time. Actually, we should not feel good all the time, because discomfort and painful feelings contain important messages for us. We are not looking to fool our Self.

When we don't feel good, we can ask our Self: "Why don't I feel good?" and "What is bothering me?" The answers to these questions point to something that we need to change. We then engage the process of change. Feeling good is restored after we have achieved the change we seek.

There are some people telling us that we need to be happy with less. While there may be some truth to this when it comes to having things, on the whole, this is wrong. We need to seek to have the happiest, most fulfilling, and most joyful life we can create for our Self. Don't allow people to tell you that you should settle for less. Don't believe that you do not deserve to feel good, or that you are cursed, born in original sin, or are a victim caught in circumstances that you cannot change.

Point of Empowerment: To feel good is to have a good life.

Practice: Seek to feel good all the time.

Give and Receive Only Love

You might be thinking that this is impossible. Again, this idea can be an inspiring ideal, not something that we use to measure our success or failure. It is a guideline for behavior, a relaxed standard that we can use for evaluating our behavior. Am I behaving in a loving way? Am I receiving the love that is coming to me?

A crucial point to remember is that we give and receive only love to other people, and also to our Self. *We do not sacrifice our Self, thinking that this is loving others.* If someone attacks you verbally or physically, how can you give and receive only love? *Under attack, love yourself by protecting yourself first.* In addition, allowing another person to hurt you is not giving love. Also, it is not loving toward our Self to constantly put another person's well-being and interests before our own, therefore sacrificing our own well-being and interests.

Point of Empowerment: Self-sacrifice is not love.

Point of Empowerment: The love we give our Self becomes the love we can give to others.

Practice: Give it a try. Give and receive only love.

Challenge for Growth

Point of Empowerment: The Operating Manual for the Self *will give you: ways to think about your thoughts, methods to create good feelings, and approaches to giving and receiving love.*

PART TWO: BEING HUMAN

CHAPTER FOUR

WHO AM I?

The purpose of this section of *The Operating Manual for the Self* is to develop a basic understanding of who we are by considering some aspects of our Self. We will deal only briefly with complex subjects. We will also try to have some metaphysical fun, as we create a context—the big picture—for understanding who we are.

The Universal Question: "Who Am I?"

"Who am I?" is a universal question that everyone asks themselves sooner or later in their lifetime. We are biologically, psychologically, and spiritually programmed to ask this question. Philosophy, religion, psychology, sociology, anthropology, biology, physics, and astronomy have all explored this question.

Our behavior demonstrates how important this question is to us. For example, we constantly test ourselves in various forms of competition to see what we can do and to see what our limits are. We almost constantly seek feedback from others. We compare ourselves to others. We grade ourselves, and value the grades others give us. We look at ourselves in a mirror to discover what we look like.

> **Point of Empowerment:** *"Who am I?" is the question of our identity. At the end of an expansive life, we have 100 answers to this question.*

Practice: Play with the question "Who am I?" Have fun with your answers.

YOU ARE PURE LIFE

Life is pure consciousness and energy.

CONSCIOUSNESS

We are pure consciousness. Consciousness is a characteristic of life. Consciousness is vast and all-inclusive. It has intelligence and creativity, intention and purpose. Human beings have intelligence and creativity, intention and purpose. Consciousness has the ability to be aware. Human beings have the ability to be aware. We could say that we get our abilities from consciousness, and that the abilities of consciousness are expressed by and through human beings.

ENERGY

Energy is. It cannot be created or destroyed; it can only change form (the first law of thermodynamics). Energy is A-LIVE-NESS. A-LIFE-NESS. It sizzles. We experience energy as feeling and **emotion**. We sense and experience our feelings within our body. We sense and experience emotion as E-motion, energy in motion. Our emotion is our impulse to move and our movement once we act on an impulse. Emotion is also the **synergy** (combining into a whole) of a thought and a feeling.

Point of Empowerment: When we feel our feelings and sense our emotions, we feel alive.

Practice: Practice feeling your feelings and sensing your emotions.

SELF-AWARENESS

We are able to be Self-aware. Self-awareness is the ability to stand outside of our Self, and look at our Self, objectively. It is like looking in a mirror and seeing our Self, but the mirror is our consciousness, our mind. We are the observer and the observed.

An infant has consciousness and awareness; it is awake. It can sense and respond to its environment. But it has no Self-awareness. Only when it grows does it start to develop its ability to be Self-aware. People differ in their ability to have Self-awareness. The skill of being Self-aware takes an entire lifetime to develop and to master.

Self-awareness is a profound ability. As we can see who we are, we can change our Self. We can grow, develop, mature, and evolve. We can use our Self to get more out of life, to fulfill our Self.

Point of Empowerment: Self-awareness allows us to take up the challenge of growth. In order to "think about every thought we have," we need to be aware of our thoughts; in other words, be Self-aware. Self-awareness makes it possible for us to know what feels good and what does not. Therefore, it enables us to accomplish the second challenge for our growth: "Seek to feel good all the time."

Practice: To increase the power of your awareness and Self-awareness, take some time to walk around your house saying, "Now I am aware of . . . ," filling in the blank with external perceptions of sights and sounds, and internal perceptions of thoughts and feelings. "Now I am aware of seeing the chair. Now I am aware of looking through the window and seeing clouds. Now I am aware of feeling excited. Now I am aware of thinking that this exercise is stupid."

THE OBSERVER

The observer is an aspect of our consciousness. It is a neutral, non-judging, non-evaluating observer that records everything that we have ever experienced. It records every thought, feeling, and situation that we have ever faced. It creates our memory.

One practical use of the observer is to help us regulate our feelings and emotions. We can shift into being the observer when our feelings and emotions become too intense or too painful for us to handle. This process creates some space between us and our feelings, emotions, and experiences of the moment. This calms us down.

Point of Empowerment: *By becoming the observer, we can better handle our feelings and emotions. This is an alternative to losing awareness and numbing our feelings.*

Practice: *Practice being the observer to cope with overly intense experiences.*

1. *State, "I am now the observer."*

2. *Pay attention to your breathing.*

3. *Use the affirmation, "There is . . . present," while continuing to breathe. For example, "There is anger present." "There is sadness present." "There is the desire to punch someone present." "There is the desire to run away present."*

4. *Breathe and state affirmations of the presence of thoughts, feelings, and impulses until you calm down.*

FOREGROUND AND BACKGROUND

Our consciousness contains a foreground and a background. We are aware of the foreground and unaware of the background. For example, we can be listening to music (the foreground) and be unaware that our leg is falling asleep and becoming numb (the background). When we then try to walk, we become aware of the numbness, and we become unaware of the music still playing in the background. The background becomes the foreground and the foreground becomes the background.

Point of Empowerment: What we are aware of—the foreground—is very small compared to what is in the background of the Self. Aspects of the Self "pop up." They move from the background to the foreground. We need to allow for this and to be aware. These "pop-ups" can be very meaningful and important.

Practice: Practice becoming aware of the flow of something in the background becoming something in the foreground. See if something meaningful "pops up" for you.

"Pop-ups" can be: feelings with messages about our life, insights, memories with unresolved issues, intuitions, creative ideas, and persistent worries, anxieties, or obsessions. All of these deserve our attention.

Point of Empowerment: In the dance of foreground and background is the flow of consciousness. This flow can be pleasurable and even blissful.

Practice: Practice becoming aware of the flow of background becoming foreground, noticing the pleasure of this movement, even if its content makes you feel uncomfortable.

Being, Doing, Having

Let's look at "Who am I?" from other **perspectives**. We say, "I am a human being." Along with being is "doing" and "having." In my "doing," I take action. In my "having," I have things, experiences, and "a life." Being, doing, and having are profound because they describe the entirety of what it means to be human, the entirety of the human experience. Let's see how this is true.

BEING

"Being" words are Am/Is/Are. I am. He/she is. They are. Being implies an indisputable fact, a fact that no one can disagree with.

There is no possibility of arguing with Being. It either is or isn't, black or white. The present moment Is. The now Is. God Is. I Am. We cannot really talk about Being because the realm of Being is beyond description with language. We can try to describe our experience of Being, but this is limited because Being cannot be broken up into parts with language.

We can experience our Being through meditation. Close your eyes. If you can be without a thought or a feeling for a second, you have experienced your Being. If we get good at meditating and experiencing our Being, we can find the calm and peace that exists within us.

Point of Empowerment: *Through meditation we can find the peace that exists within us.*

Practice: *A simple but powerful meditation is to sit, or walk, and focus your attention on your breathing. If thoughts or feelings "pop up," allow them to pass by, not focusing your attention on them. Gently shift your attention back to your breathing.*

Existing

As a human being, I am a fact; my existence is indisputable. I need to be aware of my existence. This seems obvious, but many people are unaware of their Self. They are "asleep," sometimes oblivious to their existence and to their impact on the world.

Our thoughts and feelings exist "in the moment."[1] Their existence is indisputable and cannot, should not, be questioned. Thoughts and feelings are facts. Since we try not to deny things that are facts, we shouldn't deny our thoughts and feelings. Also, since our thoughts and feelings are facts, they cannot be different from what they are, right now. Our

---

1   "In the moment" could mean "in the present moment," "in the now," or "in this second of time."

thoughts and feelings are parts of our Self. As we accept and allow our thoughts and feelings to be what they are, we allow our Self to be who it is.

> **Point of Empowerment:** *Self-acceptance can flow from the fact that, in this moment, our thoughts and feelings cannot possibly be different than what they are. If we can accept who we are, in this moment, we can be at peace with our Self. We will feel peaceful.*

> **Practice:** *Become aware of your thoughts and feelings. Tell them, "I recognize your existence and acknowledge that you cannot be different than who you are in this moment. I accept you exactly as you are."*

> **Point of Empowerment:** *If you want to, you can create different thoughts and feelings for your Self in the future.*

DOING

> **Point of Empowerment:** *We use our power to take action in the world. This is our doing.*

Through our actions we create our life.

Through our actions we express our Self.

What we say, and how we behave, are expressions of who we are inside.

What we do has an impact on our world, on people, and on things.

Since we have an impact, there are always reactions to our actions.

Reactions to our behavior are the consequences of our actions.

Since there are always consequences to our actions, we are always responsible for our behavior.

Practice: As you seek to understand these ideas, and put them into practice, you become empowered.

HAVING

Having means that things exist in our life. Having is the result of doing. As we live, we have relationships with people and with things. We have thoughts, feelings, and experiences. We have the events of our life and the stories that we tell about those events. We have a history—"his story" or "her story."

Ownership, Responsibility

Having implies ownership. In ownership, something belongs to us. An important distinction is "what belongs to me" and "what does not belong to me." We are **responsible** for what belongs to us. We are not responsible for what does not belong to us.

There is often confusion about what belongs to us and what does not, about what we are responsible for and what we are not. We debate, within our Self and with other people, about what we are responsible for. This confusion comes in statements of blame, fault, and guilt, and can cause a lot of pain. Here are some examples of this confusion:

- We are blamed for hitting our sister, and held responsible for her tears. Even though we are innocent, we get punished.
- As a child, I was frequently punished. I blame my Self even though my parents overreacted.
- As an adult I continue to blame my Self if someone mistreats me.
- I feel guilty that our work team failed to reach its goals, even though I am only one member of the team, and the success of the team is not within my control.
- Our spouse blames us, and holds us responsible for, his or her unhappiness. In truth we are not responsible for

our spouse's happiness, since we do not own it. Yet, we may persistently try to make our spouse happy, and agree that we are to blame if he or she is unhappy.

- I blame myself for my friend's anger at me, while the truth is that he is trying to make me feel guilty with his anger.
- I yell at my daughter, "It is your fault that I dropped this glass." The truth is that I am the one filled with rage. My rage caused me to drop the glass.

Point of Empowerment: *It is important to refuse to accept responsibility for what does not belong to us.*

Practice: *Give some thought to situations where you blame your Self for things that are not your responsibility since you do not own them.*

There is, however, great benefit and power in accepting responsibility for what does belong to us. Here are examples of what we are responsible for, and the benefit of taking responsibility for them:

- Our success. We can take credit for our successes and feel good, feel successful.
- Our failures. We learn from our failures.
- Our mistakes. We learn from our mistakes, and can forgive our Self.
- All our feelings. We can listen to our feelings, and honor them by making changes to our life to improve things.
- All our thoughts. We can take charge of our mind and our brain, and develop useful thinking patterns and skills.
- All our behavior and the actions we take. We can:
  - Accomplish our goals as we see what results and effects our actions have.

- Learn to give love as we see what the results of our loving behavior are.
- Learn to receive love as we see how we feel when someone loves us.
- Change our behavior and be more effective in the living of our life.

Point of Empowerment: We can only change what we take responsibility for. Taking responsibility—recognizing ownership—gives us the power to change.

Practice: As you go through a day, practice taking responsibility by saying, "I take responsibility for . . ." Fill in the blank with what belongs to you.

Thinking, Feeling, Acting (Taking Action)

THINKING

We use our ability to think to produce thoughts. Let's identify different thinking processes and their results.

Process	Result
Thinking	Thoughts
Planning	Plans
Analyzing	Analysis, Understanding
Strategizing	Strategies
Processing	Understanding, Meaning
Imagining	Images, Pictures, Stories, Fantasies
Creating	Pictures, Art, Science, Writing
Inventing	Inventions
Dreaming	Dreams, Fantasies
Visioning	Visions
Believing	Beliefs, Belief Systems
Deciding	Decisions

Choosing	Choices
Projecting	Future Plans
Counting	Arithmetic, Mathematics
Speaking (Thinking Out Loud)	Communication

This is an incomplete list of our thinking processes.

Practice: See how you use these processes to produce the various aspects of your life. As you read over the list of your thinking processes and the results, be in awe at how utterly amazing your mind is.

Freedom

Point of Empowerment: Our ability to think gives us freedom. Freedom is a process by which we make the future different from the present. We think about our present, decide how we want our future to be different, and design a strategy to accomplish this. As we put our strategy into action, we make our future different from our present.

Practice: Play with your thoughts and imagination by imagining situations that you would like to experience. Use your freedom to create a different future for your Self.

Errors in Thinking

We sometimes make errors in our thinking processes. Errors in thinking are also known as cognitive distortions. Some of these are:

- **All-or-nothing thinking.** Classifying the world into two categories: all (everything) or nothing—i.e., black or white, good or bad, always or never, and true or false. We fail to see the "in between, the gray, the partial this and partial that." For example:
  - "I always say the wrong thing." This is not true; there are times when you say the "right" thing.

- "I can never do anything right." This is not true; you act effectively ("do it right") at times.
- "You are always late." In truth, you are often late.

- **Overgeneralization:** Making a very broad conclusion based on a single incident or a single piece of evidence. Or, basing our expectations about the future on an event that happens once. For example:
  - I made a mistake. Therefore, "I can never do anything right."
  - I got into one accident in ten years. Therefore I am a poor driver and do not have confidence in my driving.

- **Emotional reasoning:** Thinking that your emotions/feelings reflect the way things really are. "I feel it, therefore it must be true." Thinking that emotions reveal the true nature of things. For example:
  - "I feel stupid, therefore I must be stupid."
  - "I feel angry at you, therefore you must have done something to make me angry."

- **Jumping to conclusions:** Reaching preliminary conclusions from little (if any) evidence. For example:
  - "He was rude to me. He must hate me."
  - "My neighbor parked in front of my house. He must be looking for a fight."

- **Personalization:** Thinking that you are responsible for events over which you have no control. This is also called "self-referential thinking": whatever happens is in reference to you. For example:
  - "My husband has a scowl on his face. He must be angry at me." In truth, your husband is thinking about how his boss yelled at him.

- "Since my child is doing poorly at school, I am a bad mother." The truth is that your child has a learning disability.

- **Filtering:** Focusing entirely on only negative or positive elements of a situation, to the exclusion of the opposite. Applying "all or nothing" thinking to events. For example:

  - "My wedding was perfect." Ignoring the fact that most people thought the band played horrible music.
  - "It rained every day last week." This was not true: there were sunny days too.

Cognitive psychology describes other errors of thinking. These include: catastrophizing, disqualifying (discounting the positive), labeling, restricted vision, imperatives, and mind reading. These errors are defined in the glossary.

> *Point of Empowerment: These errors in our thinking can wreak havoc on our lives.*

> *Practice: See if you can discover an error in your thinking processes. Identify the negative consequences of thinking this way.*

FEELING: OUR EXPERIENCE OF LIFE

Our feelings are a crucial component of our experience of life. Each moment of our life is filled with feeling. Much of the time we are not aware of these feelings. If we direct our awareness to our feelings, we will experience them. We create experiences for our Self to discover what it feels like to be in a particular situation. Does it feel good, pleasurable, or does it feel bad, painful? This is one way in which we learn about life.

> *Point of Empowerment: If we value our life's experiences, we value our feelings. If we are not experiencing our feelings, we are missing out on our life.*

Practice: Spend some time becoming aware of your feelings. Appreciate them as your life.

The Messages of Feelings

Our feelings contain messages for us. They provide us with information about our Self and about our life. Here are some examples of possible messages our feelings send us:

Feeling	Message
Joy	This situation brings me joy.
Happy	This situation brings me happiness.
Sad	This situation brings me sadness.
Anger	This situation brings me anger. I need to understand why I am angry, and decide if I want to change the situation in some way.
Frustration	I am not getting what I want. What do I need to do to get what I want?
Pleasure	This feels good. I want more of this. Or, this feels good; it scares me.
Pain	This feels bad. I want less of this. Or, this feels bad; I want more of this.
Hunger	I need to eat something.
Longing	There is something missing in my life that I need to find.
Anxious	Something that I am not aware of is causing me fear or pain.
Fear	This situation is a threat to me. I need to identify the threat and make myself safe.
Guilt	I did something wrong. Is this healthy guilt or dysfunctional guilt?

Point of Empowerment: Our feelings contain vital information for us. Our feelings will persist until they are heard.

Practice: Tune in to a feeling and see if you can hear the
messages it is sending you.

Defenses Against Feeling

There are times when our experience of our feelings is actually,
or seems to be, unbearable. We fear that we will be overwhelmed
by a painful feeling; that we cannot handle it, cannot cope with
it. We feel that we have to defend our Self against a painful feeling. We need a coping strategy. At these moments we employ
coping strategies that are called **defense mechanisms.**[2] These
strategies take us away from our awareness of our experience and
therefore lessen the intensity of painful feelings. For example,
we deny rage by telling our Self that it does not exist. "I'm not
feeling rage; I'm just a little pissed off." Or we make our Self
numb. "I numb my sadness with alcohol." Or we substitute
one feeling for another. "I'm not angry or anxious. I'm feeling
guilty or upset."

Defense mechanisms help us get through very difficult, or
unbearably difficult, moments.

However, these coping strategies can become habitual and
automatic. We use them without thinking and when they are
not needed.

Point of Empowerment: Our defense mechanisms can dull
our awareness and make us less effective in the living of our life.

Practice: Notice when you react to a painful feeling by push-
ing it out of your awareness. Try to reverse this process by

---

2   The section entitled "Ego Defense Mechanisms" contains a more detailed discussion of defenses.

focusing on the pain. If the pain is too great, you can distract your Self by focusing your attention on something else. Practice controlling your attention/awareness; soon you'll become skillful at effectively experiencing your feelings.

ACTING

There is so much that could be said about taking action, about how we behave. Let's consider three major points.

Behavior Follows Thinking and Feeling

Taking action flows out of thinking and feeling. We think and feel, then act. How does this happen? Thinking and feeling give rise to emotion, which gives rise to a neurological impulse, which moves our body.[3] We take action.

Point of Empowerment: If we want to permanently change our behavior, we must change our thinking and feeling first.

On occasion, we may spontaneously use our willpower to change our behavior. We then need to change our usual thinking and feeling to match our new behavior. Otherwise, our new behavior will not last.

In addition, we can interrupt or stop an impulse to act if we do not like the behavior that it produces.

Point of Empowerment: There is freedom in our ability to interrupt our impulses to act.

Practice: Try it. Identify an action that you do not like. Interrupt the impulse to act in that way. Then, change your thinking and feeling. You have changed your behavior. Repeat this process as often as necessary.

---

3   A neurological impulse is the physical expression of our will.

Our Actions Show Us Who We Are

Since our behavior follows our thoughts and feelings, we can observe our behavior and ask, "What am I thinking and feeling that leads me to this behavior? What does all this mean?" As we answer this question we learn more about our Self.

As an example: My spouse forgot my birthday. I thought, "You forgot my birthday; you don't love me." I felt hurt, afraid, frustrated, and angry. I yelled at my spouse in anger. What can I learn here about my Self? I see the sequence: triggering situation, thoughts, feelings, and behavior. If I consider the meaning of "You forgot my birthday; you don't love me," I will discover that I am afraid, that I have a fear that my wife doesn't love me. I have learned something about my Self.

> *Practice: Observe a piece of your behavior; see yourself acting a certain way. Trace it back to the thoughts and feelings that gave rise to the action. See the connections and the meaning, and understand more about your Self.*

All Behavior Is Purposeful

For the purposes of this discussion, let's say that thinking and feeling, in addition to acting, are behaviors.

> *Point of Empowerment: The purpose of all our behavior is to fulfill our human needs!*

Remember, our needs are: survival, safety/security, belonging/loving, to have Self-esteem, to create/produce/know, to achieve Self-actualization, and to experience beauty, mystery, and transcendence. *Fulfilling these needs is at the root of all our motivations.*

Destructive Behavior

There are times when we behave in a destructive or hurtful manner toward our Self or toward someone else. It is important to recognize that even though our behavior is destructive, we are trying to fulfill a legitimate human need. We can forgive our Self and look for a better way to fulfill our need.

For example, let's say that we're going to buy concert tickets for our friends and are faced with a long line. Since we desperately want to please our friends, we become afraid that we won't get the tickets. We cut the line, making other people very angry at us. We feel guilty about cutting the line. However, our deepest motivation is to satisfy our need for belonging—belonging to our group of friends. If we are insecure, our need gives rise to the fear that not getting the tickets jeopardizes our belonging. We become fearful and impatient. We cut the line.

> **Point of Empowerment:** *Our destructive behavior has, at its root, the intention of fulfilling our needs. This does not excuse our behavior, but can help us understand our intentions and our motivations. This understanding helps us to forgive our Self and to change.*

> **Practice:** *Identify a destructive behavior you want to change. Identify the need that you are seeking to fulfill. Use this understanding as a tool to be kind to your Self, to have compassion for your Self.*

The Mind

To round out our answer to the question *Who am I?*, let's touch briefly on the subject of the mind. The mind is a vast subject because the mind is vast, but we will only cover some of the basics. Most importantly, we have the conscious, subconscious, and unconscious minds.

THE CONSCIOUS MIND

In the previous section on thinking, we listed some of the functions of thinking. These are functions of the conscious mind. Our ordinary day-to-day awareness is a product of a part of our Self (the developmental self, ego, and conscience), using the abilities of the conscious mind. The personality and identity/image tend to operate in the background, in the subconscious and unconscious minds. Additionally, as we make choices for our Self, we are using the conscious mind.

THE SUBCONSCIOUS MIND

Holds Our Belief System; Seeks Consistency

The subconscious mind has important functions. The content of the subconscious mind is ordinarily not in the foreground of our awareness. It operates in the background, but with conscious effort, we can easily become aware of the contents of the subconscious mind. The subconscious mind holds our **belief system**—our ideas about how we and our world work. It seeks to make our thoughts, feelings, actions, and experiences of the world consistent with our beliefs. It tailors and shapes our perceptions of new experiences to fit with our old beliefs.

Seeks Coherence

The subconscious mind also seeks to make our thoughts, feelings, actions, and experiences coherent; that is, our thoughts, feelings, actions, and experiences need to fit together in a way that makes sense to us. Without consistency and coherence we would experience the world as ever changing and chaotic, and be paralyzed with anxiety.

The desire of the subconscious mind to have consistency and coherence alerts us to the presence of inconsistency and incoherence. In that presence we feel "out of balance" and that "something is wrong." When facing inconsistency and incoherence in our thoughts, feelings, actions, and experiences, we have an opportunity to grow, learn, and change. We can identify what is out of balance and what is wrong. We can integrate and be comfortable with what is "new" to us by revising the old that no longer "fits." The subconscious mind can do this automatically.

However, the subconscious mind can also distort and twist our experience of life in order to fit our beliefs and make it coherent. We tend to fit what is new into old boxes and compartments. This can limit us in many ways as we screen out, or ignore, what does not fit with our preconceived ideas, beliefs, and notions about how the world works or should work. In this process of "screening out," we may fail to perceive what is new and novel, and therefore miss what is interesting, exciting, and stimulating, and sometimes very important.

> *Point of Empowerment: In seeking consistency and coherence, our subconscious mind can destroy the new and novel.*

> *Practice: Be aware of the tendency of your subconscious mind to screen out perceptions that do not fit into preconceived ideas and notions.*

Holds, Organizes, and Screens Information

The subconscious mind holds a vast amount of information in memory. At times it is easy to access this information, to recall it from memory, and at times it is difficult. The subconscious mind orders and categorizes information in ways that are useful. It presents information for our conscious use as it is needed, useful, and appropriate. It usually keeps in the background information that is not needed, not useful, or is inappropriate for us at any given point in time. Again, for the purposes of consistency and coherency, the subconscious mind may keep some important information from us.

THE UNCONSCIOUS MIND

The unconscious mind holds the bits and pieces of our Self that we needed to put out of our awareness, out of our conscious mind. We have been discussing how we protect our Self from thoughts, feelings, desires, drives, perceptions, abilities, and memories that are too painful for us to bear. They are stored and held for us in our unconscious mind. The unconscious mind holds these pieces of the Self and returns them to our conscious mind when we can handle them. We reclaim what is lost. We process, "work through," and "come to terms with" what we have buried in the unconscious so that we can be at peace within our Self. If the Self did not do this, our life would be constantly disturbed by the content, the "ghosts," of the unconscious mind.

> *Point of Empowerment: At the end of our life span, as an elder, we can be at peace if we have dealt with the contents of our unconscious mind.*

> *Practice: Learn how to recognize and process the content of your unconscious mind.*

The Mind and the Brain

The mind is different from the brain. The mind and the brain work together, but the mind is vaster, "larger," than the brain. Oversimplifying a bit, we can say that the brain works with the ego to fulfill the needs of survival and safety/security. The mind helps us to fulfill our other needs—belonging/loving, Self-esteem, to create/produce/know, Self-actualization, and to experience beauty, mystery, and transcendence.

The brain brings the mind into our physical reality. We can measure brain activity with scientific instruments. We cannot, yet, measure mind activity directly. Modern neuroscience has provided us with amazing information about the brain. We will continue to learn about how the mind and the brain work together and how they are different.

CHAPTER 5

ABILITY, WILL, AND CHOICE

Abilities and Potentials of the Self

Abilities are aspects of our Self that we use to accomplish a task. We have abilities that lie unawakened, which are potentials. When we activate them, we can use them to accomplish the tasks of living.

When we are born, our abilities are mostly potentials. They unfold as we get older, as we grow and develop. We have many, many abilities, which we might develop into skills as we use them. If we develop confidence in our use of an ability, we have a **capability**. Ability plus confidence equals capability. There are also abilities that we become interested in and choose to develop, achieving some degree of mastery. Beyond mastery is **artistry**. This is the progression of ability: potential, skill, capability, mastery, and artistry.

We often take our abilities for granted. For example, we have the ability to walk. As an infant we couldn't walk. We had the *potential* to learn to walk. This kind of potential is built into our genes. As we got older, we put that potential into action. An infant has the ability to cry when it is hungry, and to scream loudly in frustration if the need to be fed is not being met. So, we are born with several abilities: to sense our basic needs, to feel pain and frustration, and to move our bodies in order to communicate what our needs are.

As we grow, we develop new abilities and become more skillful in using the abilities we have. We say, "I never knew I could do that" when we discover a new ability. An ability that had existed as a latent potential has been brought to life.

> **Point of Empowerment:** *Human beings have many abilities. The progression of ability is: potential, skill, capability, mastery, artistry. Our abilities unfold over the course of our lifetime.*

> **Practice:** *Identify some of your abilities and skills. What skills have you developed into mastery and artistry?*

INHIBITION OF OUR ABILITIES, LOST PARTS OF THE SELF

Some abilities get stunted in their development. Their natural development gets inhibited. For example, a person may say, "When I was a child, I used to speak up for myself. I expressed my unhappiness. However, since I frequently got punished when I did this, I stopped. Even now, I do not speak up for myself. But I may get sick, physically ill, like I did when I was a child, as a way of expressing my unhappiness."

> **Point of Empowerment:** *In growing up—in becoming a child and an adolescent—we inhibited some of the abilities of our Self. They are lost parts of our Self. It is necessary to recover these lost abilities.*

> **Point of Empowerment:** *Some of the pain and frustration that we experience in life comes from lost abilities.*

> **Practice:** *Identify a lost or inhibited ability. Identify situations where this ability would be useful. Try to put that ability into action.*

Another clue that we are dealing with a lost ability is the statement "I can't do that," especially when it is clear that you can if you try. You may lack confidence in your ability, yet you refuse to build confidence by trying to use your ability to accomplish a task. There is usually some fear or anxiety, or both, connected to this ability. As we identify the reasons for our refusal to "try" and push past them, we regain lost pieces of our Self.

Let's look at a hypothetical situation. A person says, for example, "As a child I liked to dance, but was not very good at it. As an adolescent, I became Self-conscious, embarrassed, and stopped dancing. When I was in college I developed a rudimentary ability to dance. This was part of my strategy to meet women. But I was still Self-conscious and inhibited. Over the years I have become more Self-accepting, and willing to take risks. In doing so, I have experimented with different forms of dance and have greatly expanded my skill in dancing. Now dancing has become a source of pleasure and satisfaction."

> ***Point of Empowerment:*** *Lifelong development and expansion of our abilities helps us to lead a rich and fulfilling life.*

TALENT

Talents are abilities that move quickly through the progression of ability: from potential to skill to capability to mastery to artistry.

> ***Point of Empowerment:*** *Everyone has at least one talent, usually several. Our talents are gifts.*

> ***Practice:*** *Identify at least one of your talents.*

Will

Will is the ability to set things in motion, and to keep things moving forward once set in motion. We use our will to do what is necessary, to accomplish a task. Consider driving a car. I use my will to start the car and to drive it. As I do this, it takes me to where I want to go. I also use my will to put my body into motion and to keep it going once started.

What precedes an act of will is a need, drive, desire, intention, or purpose, and a decision to fulfill those things. Wanting to fulfill the need, drive, desire, intention, or purpose is called a motive, the reason we take action. We then make a choice to act on our motives by using our will. Our motives are the fuel for our car.

We generate what is called "willpower." Willpower is the power of movement. A moving object (like my Self) has momentum (the amount of forward movement) and force (the "push" of it). There can be a lot of power, momentum, and force, or a little. A speeding train, for example, has a lot of power, momentum, and force, while a walking turtle has very little power, momentum, and force. Along with thought and feeling, will and willpower are necessary for action. Will and willpower are necessary in order for us to accomplish tasks.

Point of Empowerment: Will carries us along as we take action to fulfill our needs and desires.

Practice: Get a feel for your will by imagining your Self driving the car that transports you toward your goal.

MISUSE OF WILL

Excessive Aggressiveness

The first misuse of will and willpower is when we try to force people into doing what we want them to. We become overly aggressive and "forceful," full of force. In some situations we may get compliance and conformity, but we do not get cooperation and agreement. The person on the receiving end of too much willpower may appear to agree and comply, but secretly and covertly, he or she wants to rebel and sabotage. Two situations prone to this kind of misuse of willpower are parent/child relationships, and supervisor/subordinate relationships at work. Also, in marriage, the force and aggression of too much willpower leads to destructive conflict.

More of the Same, Harder

At times our approach to solving a problem doesn't work. We then resolve to keep trying the strategy that we are using, and to work harder at it. This is "doing more of the same, only harder," using more willpower. On occasion this may solve a problem. More often, doing the opposite of what we are doing, or doing less, in a relaxed manner, are better solutions.

Consider, for example, a parent who is not getting cooperation from her child. Punishment might be seen as a solution to this problem. Sometimes punishment does work, but in this situation, the solution of punishment isn't working. The parent imposes more severe punishments. This makes things worse. A more effective approach is to talk to the child, find out what is bothering him or her, and work together to resolve the disagreement. The parent gives up the force of willpower and uses communication.

Will Is Not the Answer

Some of the goals and tasks we want to accomplish, or changes that we seek to make, are not amenable to the direct use of will or willpower. We mistakenly apply willpower and become frustrated with the lack of results. Here are some examples where the force of will is ineffective in producing the outcome we seek.

- Changing the way we feel.
- Falling asleep.

- Desiring to love another person or desiring another person to love us.
- Developing understanding.
- Being creative.
- Getting cooperation from another person.
- Experiencing happiness or joy.
- Ending depression or anxiety.
- Being sexually aroused.

In the above situations there is a role for will to play, but accomplishing the goal involves a strategy that is not the application of willpower.

Point of Empowerment: There are situations in life where will and willpower do not get us what we truly want.

Practice: Give some thought to this idea. Identify situations where your use of willpower isn't working. Identify an alternative strategy (like verbal persuasion or relaxing and letting go) for accomplishing your goal.

Willingness

Willingness is making a commitment to use our will. We decide to use our will to move us in a certain direction. Willingness is generated by a *motive*, the reason why we take action.

MOTIVES

There are many reasons why we take action. They fall under the categories of need, desire, drive, wish, purpose, and intention.

- **Need:** Something we feel intense motivation to fulfill for our Self, like our human needs.
- **Desire:** These are the "optional" things that we want, which enhance our life.

- **Drive:** An intense desire to accomplish a task. Drives are task oriented.
- **Wish:** A weak desire that we passively fantasize about. We may or may not take action to fulfill a wish.
- **Purpose:** Wanting to accomplish something that will have an effect on something else.
  - For example: eating to satisfy hunger, going to school to get a good job, making friends to avoid loneliness, and dating to find a girlfriend.
- **Intention:** A decision to accomplish a purpose.

Though we are often unaware of our motives, they always exist, especially in our subconscious and unconscious minds. Also, we can have more than one motive at a time. One of our motives may be known to us, but other motives may be hidden. For example, at work we may try very hard at our jobs, telling ourselves that we want to get a raise. Yet an additional motive can be wanting to please our boss, to get his approval so we can feel good our Self and have Self-esteem. Thus our motives can be complicated.

Point of Empowerment: Knowing what your motives are gives you freedom of choice. Change a motive and you change your reason for taking action. Different reasons give rise to different actions or to different results from the same action. Change your actions and you change your life.

Practice: Give some thought to your motives. Identify which ones lead to fulfillment and which ones lead to frustration.

CONFLICTING MOTIVES

Sometimes we have more than one motive at a time regarding a particular issue, and these motives conflict with each other. For example:

- We want to spend time with friends. At the same time, we don't want to spend time with friends because we have studying to do and we want to do well in school.
- We want to complain to our boss about a destructive coworker. At the same time, we do not want to complain because in doing so we will seem disloyal.
- We want to move out of our parents' house. At the same time, we want to live at home because doing so allows us to save money.
- We love our sibling and want to help him. At the same time, we don't want to help our sibling because we are jealous of him.

This is but a small sampling of situations that give rise to conflicting feelings and conflicting motivations.

Point of Empowerment: Conflicting motivations can be painful and can paralyze us, preventing us from acting.

Practice: As you reflect, see if you become aware of conflicting feelings and motivations. Tune in to the pain and frustration that they cause. Try to resolve these conflicts.

Ability and Willingness

POWER

Remember our definition of **power**: "The ability and willingness to act." First comes ability. Once we have achieved the ability, we activate it and bring it to life with willingness. We then act. We are powerful. Our actions may be more or less effective in getting us what we want, but at least in acting, we are being powerful.

Point of Empowerment: To be alive is to have power. Experiencing our power gives us strength and courage.

Practice: As you take action, experience your Self as powerful by noticing the impact of your behavior.

EMPOWERMENT

Along with power is **empowerment**. We have defined empowerment as "the permission and authority to be powerful."

Permission

Human beings of all ages resent having to ask permission to use their will, their power. We have a natural need, desire, drive, and wish to assert our power. When this is thwarted, blocked, or inhibited, we feel frustrated and angry. At times we feel powerless. Feeling powerless can generate a huge amount of anger or rage.

Point of Empowerment: Needing to ask permission is often an illusion. We have the power to give our Self permission.

Practice: Pick a situation in your life and give your Self permission to be powerful.

Authority

Similarly, people feel that they lack the authority that empowers them to act in powerful ways. (In this context we define authority as "having the right to choose to act.") Where does our authority to be powerful come from?

- We are the authors of our life, our life story. As authors, we have authority.
- As human beings, we have legitimate, natural needs. Having these needs gives us authority to fulfill them.
- As human beings we have a sense of justice and fairness. This sense gives us authority.
- Our Self-esteem, Self-worth, and Self-love give us authority.
- The following approach to life gives us authority: "I

am willing to take responsibility for my actions and am determined to act in moral, ethical, and loving ways. I am willing to recognize and to admit when I make mistakes. I feel remorse for any harm my behavior does to others."

Practice: *Claim your authority.*

NO

Feeling a lack of empowerment is often a painful situation for people. It often stops a person from acting assertively, from saying "no" when saying "no" is necessary, appropriate, and important. There are many ways to say "no": "That doesn't work for me," or "No, I can't go along with that," or simply, "No, I will not do what you are asking or expecting." Sometimes we soften "no" with "I can't."

Point of Empowerment: *To advocate for one's Self, to argue for one's rights, requires a feeling of empowerment, along with our power.*

Practice: *Silently, within your Self, say "No." Say "No" out loud. Feel the power of that word. Feel your power as you say "No."*

Choice

There is amazing power in choice.

I choose to look at you.

I choose to say "no."

I choose to go to school.

I choose to watch TV.

I choose to confront you.

I choose to go to sleep.

I choose to experience happiness and joy.

I choose to eat breakfast.

I choose to rebel.

I choose to go to work.

I choose to meditate.

I choose to read.

I choose to love.

I choose to explore my spirituality.

Point of Empowerment: Choice puts us in charge, in control, of our life. Making conscious choices is taking control of our life, consciously, with awareness.

TAKING CHARGE OF YOUR LIFE

Being in charge, in control, of our life means shaping it to be the way we want it. To make conscious choices, we become aware of our needs, desires, drives, wishes, purposes, and intentions. "What do I want?" is the first question to ask in every situation. It is the take-charge question. Other take-charge, take-control questions are:

- "Who do I want to be?"
- "What do I want to do?" and
- "What do I want to have?"

Practice: Make conscious choices.

Being a Victim

If we do not sense the power of choice and do not make conscious choices, then we feel like a victim of life. We feel helpless and powerless. As a victim, we feel at the mercy of the world, and that we cannot change our life's circumstances. This can be terrifying.

Of course, there are events that happen in our life that we do not have control of, and occasionally, we truly are a victim.

Point of Empowerment: No matter what happens, we always have control over, and are in charge of, our reactions to the events of our life.

THE PROCESS OF CHOOSING

Let's say I'm faced with a situation that I need to respond to, or I'm considering how to fulfill a need, desire, drive, or wish. I think about my alternatives. I give consideration to what is in my best interests.[1] I explore my feelings about each alternative. I use my imagination to project a picture, an image, of my choice into the future. What could that look like? I choose one of the alternatives. I use my will to put my choice into action.

Alternatives

Before I can make an effective choice for myself I have to see that I have alternatives. Seeing alternatives is an ability. The ability to see alternatives to choose among is determined by our age and maturity level, and by our ability to be aware.

> *Point of Empowerment:* Choice activates will, sets will in motion. Therefore, before every act is a choice. We may make the choice without awareness or control, but we always make a choice before we act.

> *Practice:* Consider a situation where you are facing choices. With awareness, evaluate the alternatives. Consciously choose an alternative. State, "I choose . . . as my alternative." Feel the power of choice in this process.

WE CANNOT AVOID CHOICE

It is also important to understand that we cannot avoid making choices. If we awake in the morning, we choose whether or not to get out of bed. Our existence forces us to make choices. The fact that our resources, time, and energy are limited forces us to make choices. We cannot avoid making a choice about how

---

1   There are times when we do not choose what is in our best interests. Why do we do this? What are our motives for doing this? Our Self contains the positive and negative, the constructive and destructive. Sometimes the negative—destructive—wins out.

we want to spend our resources. Also, we make a choice about how much awareness we give to the process of choosing.[2]

Practice: Try identifying a moment where you are not making a choice about how to spend your time and energy.

People often say that they "have no choice." What they're really saying is: "Since I don't like the alternatives I have to choose from, I won't look. I will pretend that alternatives don't exist." Or, "I don't want to take responsibility for the consequences of my choices. If things don't go well, I want to have the excuse that 'I didn't have a choice.'" For example, I may confront my boss, while thinking that I don't have a choice. If the confrontation doesn't go well, I can always say, "Oh well, I didn't have a choice." I have "let my Self off the hook," the hook of responsibility.

Sometimes a situation scares us. We may say, "I do not have a choice" and go ahead, despite our fear. We found our *courage*, and took action even though we were afraid. However, we do not acknowledge that we have acted with courage.

Fulfillment and Desire, Ability, Willingness, Choice, and Action

Point of Empowerment: In order to find fulfillment in life, we need: desire, ability, willingness, choice, and action.

Practice: To fulfill a desire, put the following chart into action.

---

2   If we, as the Self, refuse to make a choice, the ego makes the choice, since choices are unavoidable. Much of the time the ego is ill-equipped to make the choices that the Self is responsible for. When we let the ego make these choices, things go badly for us.

Fulfillment and Desire

	Ability	Willingness	Choice	Action
Desire				

For example:

Desire: *To travel for a vacation.*

Ability: *I can think about the various vacation destinations I am interested in.*

I can project myself into those destinations by using my imagination.

I can feel how much fun it is to be in each destination.

Willingness: *I am willing to explore the options I have.*

I am willing to spend the money involved.

I am willing to take the actions necessary to explore, choose, travel, experience, and have fun.

Choice: *I choose a particular destination.*

Action: *I implement my plans. I experience my vacation. My desire to travel has been fulfilled. I feel fulfilled. (I take pictures and show my friends.)*

All of the components have to be in place to experience the fulfillment of a desire. If any are missing, we activate our ability to create the missing components.

We have explored each of these components. Fulfillment of our desires should be straightforward and easy. If this is true, why are we not deliriously happy and intensely fulfilled by our life?

RESISTANCE

As we seek fulfillment, we run into our resistance; the factors that slow us down or stop us dead in our tracks. There are external factors outside of our Self, and internal factors inside of our Self. External factors are hurdles to overcome, like not enough money to go on a vacation. Internal resistances are aspects of our Self that need to be recognized, processed, and resolved. Remember, resistance is normal and natural, but needs to be overcome.

Two major categories of internal resistance are fear and feeling undeserving.

Fear

These examples show how fear can interfere with ability, willingness, choice, and action.

- I am afraid of my ability because I am afraid to see who I could become. If I developed my abilities to their full capacity, I think I would become egotistical and arrogant. I don't want to appear egotistical or arrogant.
- I am afraid of willingness (using my will) because my parents called me "willful" and punished me for trying to get my way. If I use my will, I unconsciously fear punishment.
- I am afraid of my choice because I might make mistakes. I might make the wrong choice. I can't allow my Self to make mistakes.
- I am afraid of taking action, because I might act in a destructive manner, and don't want to hurt someone or hurt my Self.

"I Don't Deserve"

You might say, "I don't deserve to have my desires fulfilled." There are many causes for this feeling. For example:

- I am not good enough . . . so I don't deserve.
- I am unworthy . . . so I don't deserve.
- I do not think much of myself. I have a poor Self-image and low Self-esteem . . . so I don't deserve.
- I am filled with guilt . . . so I don't deserve.

Point of Empowerment: Positive resistance helps us keep what we value. Negative resistance keeps us stuck.

Practice: Identify a fear or feeling of not deserving. State the resistance and say the affirmation, "I now release . . . ," stating what the resistance is. Notice any "resistance to releasing your resistance." Repeat the process with each resistance that emerges until you are free of it.

PART THREE: THE SELF

CHAPTER 6

THE SELF: AN OVERVIEW

Introduction

In these chapters of *The Operating Manual for the Self* we will ask and answer certain questions, from the point of view of the Self.

QUESTION:	ANSWER:
What does our life consist of?	Our life consists of stages.
What do we do as we move through the stages of our life?	We fulfill our human needs.
How do we fulfill our needs?	We accomplish the tasks of each stage.
How do we accomplish the tasks of each stage?	We use our abilities.
Where do our abilities come from?	Our abilities come from the Self.
What are the parts of the Self?	The parts of the Self are described in the perating manual.

This chapter presents an overview of the topics we will later explore in greater detail. We also focus on growing, developing, maturing, and evolving.

Self

We have looked at a person as a human being—a human doing and a human having. From our human being-ness come our abilities. With our abilities we take action; we create. We create a Self. We then live our life having a Self. (Remember, Self with a capital "S" refers to all of the parts of the Self as a whole. Lowercase "s" refers to the developmental self—a component, a part, of the Self.)

At the time of conception, the body begins to form. At birth, the physical body is born, as well as the Self. The Self is a complex entity, with many parts and aspects, all of which have a purpose to fulfill, and the ability to fulfill that purpose. We use the abilities of the Self to accomplish the tasks of life, the tasks that keep us alive and enjoying life.

Parts of the Self

We will eventually explore all the parts, or aspects, of the Self. But now let's have a peek at the fundamental parts of the Self by using a quick list. These parts are the:

- Developmental self
- Ego
- Personality
- Conscience
- Image/identity

Life Span

To help us organize our discussion about the Self, we will trace the development of the Self through the course of a lifetime—a life "span" or life "cycle." The **life span** is divided up into approximate **stages**. These are:

- Infant/toddler

- Child
- Adolescent
- Young adult
- Adult
- Senior
- Elder

Developmental Self

Each stage of the life span gives rise to a **developmental self** (spelled with a small "s"). The Self gives birth to a part of itself to accomplish the tasks of each stage. The developmental self is therefore made up of these stages:

- Infant/toddler (age 0–3 years old)
- Child (3–12 years old)
- Adolescent (12–18 years old)
- Young adult (18–26 years old)
- Adult (26–65 years old)
- Senior (65–80 years old)
- Elder (80 to the end of the life cycle)

The ages listed here are approximations. We do not have a rigid timetable, and there is variation from person to person. Also, there is a beginning, a middle, and an end to each stage, to each phase of the life cycle.

Point of Empowerment: My Self develops over the course of my lifetime.

Practice: Say to yourself, "I am a . . ." and fill in the blank with your particular developmental self. You have increased your Self-/self-awareness.

The characteristics of each component of the developmental self are determined by the age of a person—i.e., where he or she is in the life span. However, this is not the only determining factor. Other influential factors include: maturity level, having successfully completed the tasks of the previous stages, the presence of disturbances of the Self, and the influences of the other aspects of Self.

Self and the Life Span

The chart on the next page shows how each part of the Self exists throughout the life span. The chart is a way of organizing a vast amount of complex information. For example, you could consider the ego line, move into the adolescent stage, and ask: What is the adolescent ego like? What are the strengths and weaknesses of the adolescent ego? Or, how does the ego develop during the course of a life span? The questions and areas of investigation and exploration are almost unlimited. Our purpose here is to illustrate the complexity of the Self as it moves through the life span.

In the coming pages, the operating manual will provide more information about aspects and stages. After reading this material, you will be able to better explore the contents of each box.

Practice: Examine the aspects and stages chart. Allow your Self to take in the amazing complexity.

Human Needs

The Self uses its abilities to accomplish the tasks of each stage of life. The purpose of accomplishing these tasks is to fulfill our needs.

Our needs:
- Survival
- Safety and security
- Belonging/loving
- Self-esteem
- To create, to produce, and to know

Stages of the Life Span

Aspects of the Self	Infant	Child	Adolescent	Young Adult	Adult	Senior	Elder
Developmental Self							
Ego							
Personality							
Conscience							
Identity/Image							

- To achieve Self-actualization
- To experience beauty, mystery, and transcendence

Self and the Mind

We have briefly reviewed the aspects of our mind. The chart below shows that each part of the Self has and utilizes each aspect of the mind. We cannot explore the content of each box at this time, but we can see the relationships that exist in complicated ways.

Mind and the Self

Aspects of the Self	Conscious	Subconscious	Unconscious
Developmental Self			
Ego			
Personality			
Conscience			
Identity/Image			

Growing, Developing, Maturing, Evolving

The Self, as well as each part of the Self, grows, develops, matures, and evolves as it moves through the stages of the life cycle.

GROWING

To grow is to become larger in size. The growth in our size allows us to contain the new parts of our Self that become available to us as we get older. Our capacity to function physically, emotionally, mentally, and spiritually/religiously grows. "Larger" automatically generates more power. We become more powerful as we grow. Developing and maturing helps us to use our power effectively.

Point of Empowerment: *We can feel our Self becoming larger over time.*

Practice: Take a moment to sense how each part of your Self becomes larger over time. Notice how your Self has more substance and power as compared to a point in your past.

DEVELOPING

To develop is to increase our ability. With practice, we develop confidence in our abilities. Our abilities become capabilities that we can rely on. For example, consider how we develop our ability to move our body. There is a sequence: as infants we lift our heads; then we turn our bodies over; then we crawl, stand, and walk; then we run, jump, skip, and hop; then we learn to sing, dance, and play sports. We progress from basic, simple movements to complex movements that can bring us **capability**, **mastery**, and **artistry**.

Point of Empowerment: The development of our ability to move our body can bring us pleasure and joy.

Practice: Remember a moment of pleasure and joy in moving your body.

MATURING

To mature is to age in a way that enhances who we are and increases what we are capable of achieving. Maturing is seeing the world in a new way, different from the way we previously saw it. It is having a new perspective. In seeing the world from a new perspective, we respond to it in a new way. We also act in new ways. These changes in our Self are observable to others.

Parents often wish that their children were more mature, but there is no way to force or speed up maturing. It happens on its own.

We can use our experiences in life to mature. To do this we need to be learning from our life's experiences. If we do not learn the lessons of our experience, not only do we not mature, but we repeat the mistakes connected to those lessons.

Maturity accompanies our achievements. We can define accomplishment as the process of fulfilling tasks to accomplish a goal. Achievements are accomplishments that change who we are. For example, I graduated from college. Looking back, I see that I learned to deal with frustration, learned to delay gratification, and increased my Self-discipline. I see that my understanding of the world has dramatically increased. I have a new perspective on life. All these achievements made me a different, more mature person after graduating college than I was when I first started.

Maturing also involves getting all the parts of our Self to work together in unison.

Parts of our Self can fight with each other, can even be at war with each other, causing us internal conflict. If we do not have all our parts sharing the same purpose and working toward the same goal, we will sabotage our Self, and experience frustration, anger, and pain.

Point of Empowerment: *Growth and development are almost automatic. However, they do not guarantee that we will become mature adults. To become mature adults, we need to be aware of our growing, developing, and maturing, and take responsibility for these processes.*

Practice: *Bring awareness and responsibility to your processes of growing, developing, and maturing.*

EVOLVING

To evolve is:

- To expand our consciousness, awareness, and Self-awareness
- To become more complex, differentiated, and capable
- To Self-actualize
- To increase the richness and depth of our being

Evolving combines growing, developing, and maturing. It is a synergy, a process where the whole is greater than the sum of its parts. Toward the end of a life span, we can look back at the entirety of our life, and see how we have evolved. Also, we can see where we have not evolved—where we have not grown, developed, or matured.

Point of Empowerment: The Operating Manual for the Self *will help us understand what we need to accomplish and achieve in order to reach our full potential. As we reach our potential, we evolve.*

Practice: Put that understanding into action by choosing to grow and develop. Appreciate your maturity, and become aware of where you lack maturity.

CHAPTER 7

HUMAN NEEDS

A need is a hole, an emptiness, that we experience as a drive for fulfillment. It is a motivator. When we satisfy a need we experience pleasure, and we can feel contented, satisfied, relaxed, happy, and joyful. One source of happiness is fulfilling our needs. Fulfilling a need is "filling a hole," and we feel a sense of "wholeness," of completeness.

Our human needs are:

- Survival
- Safety and security
- Belonging/loving
- Self-esteem
- To produce, to create, to know
- To achieve Self-actualization
- To experience beauty, mystery, and transcendence

The two words that generally apply to needs are satisfaction and fulfillment. As each need is different, satisfying different needs brings different feelings and different experiences. For example, satisfying our need for safety and security is very different from experiencing beauty. Yet both are needs.

Our ability to satisfy our needs grows as we grow, develop, and mature. As we satisfy one need, we open up possibilities for satisfying the next need. Beyond survival and safety/security, we can also go up and down the list in any order we want. However, we tend to progress through the needs as listed above, before returning to seek greater fulfillment of a previous need. The fulfillment of each need enriches the experience of fulfilling the other needs.

> *Point of Empowerment: The fulfillment of our needs, in ever-increasing degrees of depth and satisfaction, is a lifelong process that brings ever-increasing intensities of happiness and joy.*

Not Knowing How, Doing Our Best

At times we do not know how to fulfill our needs. Our knowledge may be extremely limited. In using the limited means at our disposal to get what we need, we sometimes behave badly. If our Self has become very distorted, damaged, or lost, our approach to fulfilling our needs can be extremely destructive. However, most of the time, we are doing the best we can to fulfill our needs, using what we know at any given moment.

> *Point of Empowerment: Remember, all behavior—our thinking, feeling, and acting (taking action)—has the purpose of fulfilling our needs, no matter how destructive or distorted the means of fulfillment may be.*

Unfulfilled Needs

Needs seek their own fulfillment with a driving force that is sometimes very intense. Unmet needs can stay with us for an entire lifetime. Unfulfilled childhood needs can seek satisfaction well beyond childhood. But this seeking distorts people of all ages—adolescents, young adults, adults, seniors, and elders—as it distorts the Self. When we are no longer a child, we cannot fulfill the child's needs. But the child inside us may desperately press toward the satisfaction of its needs. This creates havoc in our life.

In addition, our methods of seeking to fulfill the child's needs are the child's methods. As an adolescent or as an adult, using the child's methods to get what we want guarantees failure. For example, if a child does not feel that he belongs and that he is unloved, he will spend his entire lifetime seeking to fulfill these needs. He will use excessive force, or passive/dependent[1] manipulation, to get other people to give him what he wants, so that he can feel that he belongs and that he is loved. These efforts are doomed to failure, yet the unfulfilled need continues to press for satisfaction.

> **Point of Empowerment:** *Everyone has some unmet childhood needs. We need to identify the unmet needs and put them to rest. We can then focus on fulfilling the needs that are appropriate to our developmental self/stage of life.*

> **Practice:** *If you have serious unfulfilled childhood needs, get help to resolve and release the desire or pressure to fulfill them.*

Let's explore our needs.

Survival Needs: Physical, Emotional, Mental, and Spiritual

PHYSICAL SURVIVAL

The first goal of survival is to preserve our physical life. We have a powerful survival instinct that we're born with, that's programmed into our genes. If our physical survival is threatened, we automatically and instinctively respond to the threat. We will take almost any action to diminish and eliminate that threat in order to preserve our survival. This is our "fight or flight" survival mechanism.

---

1   A person can pretend to be needy (dependent) in a helpless manner (passive) to assert pressure on another person.

To illustrate the instinctive nature of our survival needs, consider how an infant behaves. An infant knows when its survival needs are being met; when this happens it feels satisfied, relaxed, and happy.

When they are not being met, the infant feels immense discomfort and cries. Mother Nature has made the crying of an infant almost intolerable to its mother. A mother instinctively feels the discomfort of her infant, and wants to respond immediately to its crying. The infant instinctively knows this and uses its crying to get its needs met.

Point of Empowerment: *Physical survival is our first priority.*

Practice: *Was your physical survival ever threatened? What did you do? Sense how powerful you became in order to stay alive.*

EMOTIONAL SURVIVAL

When emotional stress is so intense that our emotional survival is threatened, we instinctively respond to the threat. If the emotional threat is external, we may verbally or physically defend our Self against it, using our "fight" response. For example, if someone is harshly and constantly critical of us, we will defend our Self and fight with the critical person, arguing that the criticism is unjust. Or we may withdraw emotionally—the "flight" response—to a place inside our Self where we feel that our emotional survival isn't threatened.

If the threat to our emotional survival originates from within our Self, we utilize our emotional defense mechanisms to protect us. We have many defense mechanisms. For example, if we are faced with chronic, overwhelming sadness or anxiety, we may become depressed. The depression numbs our feelings. This numbness preserves our emotional survival by preventing us from becoming emotionally overwhelmed. In this situation, depression is a defense mechanism. Similarly, depression can be an emotional defense mechanism in situations that we perceive as dangerous, and in which we feel powerless to protect our Self. Its numbing effect protects us from overwhelming, paralyzing fear.

Point of Empowerment: *We use defense mechanisms to stabilize and to protect our emotional life.*

Practice: *See if you can notice a defense mechanism in operation. When you feel a frightening emotion, is there something that occurs that diminishes the intensity of that feeling or distracts you from it?*

MENTAL SURVIVAL

Mental survival drives us to create and maintain order and meaning in our life. We experience disorder, chaos, and meaningless as threats to our mental survival, threats to our well-being. If something threatens meaning or order, we feel anxious. We respond by taking action to change the situation. If we cannot be effective in creating this change, we may employ the defense mechanism of denial. We simply refuse to recognize the existence of the threat. We deny its existence and then feel that we can hold on to our sense of meaning and order. Eventually the denial breaks down. We are compelled to search for an effective way to deal with the threatening situation.

Point of Empowerment: *We need order and meaning in our life.*

Practice: *Were order and meaning ever threatened in your life? What did you do to reestablish them?*

SPIRITUAL SURVIVAL

Spiritual survival is the preservation of human dignity and of our spirit. When we are robbed of our dignity, we can become enraged (full of rage) or depressed. Enraged or depressed behavior can appear wild and irrational. It may be hard to understand, but violence can be a way of restoring our dignity. It is an extreme, yet powerful, protest against real or perceived oppression. In the face of situations that crush our dignity, depression is a way of shutting down. By shutting down, we conserve the dignity that remains.

People say, "My spirit has been crushed." By spirit, they are referring to their sense of aliveness, their willingness to actively live life and to take on life's challenges. If a person's spirit has been crushed, it must be restored. A crushed spirit is a human tragedy that takes time to heal and restore, but the healing and restoring must be done.

> **Point of Empowerment:** *If human dignity and the human spirit are threatened, our spiritual survival is threatened.*

> **Practice:** *Was your dignity or spirit ever threatened? How did you respond to the threat?*

SURVIVAL THROUGHOUT THE LIFE SPAN

As a need, physical survival stays the same throughout the life span. The way we assure our physical survival changes. The child is dependent on his/her parents for survival. The adult works, is productive, and therefore provides for his/her own physical survival.

Emotional, mental, and spiritual survival mean different things to us as we progress through the life cycle. For example, emotional survival to an adolescent is having friends. Emotional survival to an adult may mean using one's power to deal with a situation involving extreme emotional stress. Emotional survival to an elder may mean having interaction with other people to avoid isolation.

Safety and Security

We feel **safe** when we are free from threats to our well-being. With safety, we can relax. We don't need to be on guard or afraid. We feel **secure** when we feel confident that what we need will be there for us when we need it. We know that what we have will not be easily lost.

We know that support for our well-being will be there when we need it. A child feels that he can depend on his parents to be available when they are needed. An adult feels secure in the continued presence of his spouse's love.

Safety and security provide us with feelings of comfort. When safety and security are well established, they fade into the background as needs. They move into the foreground of our awareness when they are threatened. We then take action to reestablish them.

A young child continually seeks safety and security from her parents. When these are present, the child feels free to explore her environment. She can leave her parents' side, go exploring, without feeling anxious, without feeling what is called "separation anxiety." The child knows she has a home base, the parent, to return to. The absence of safety and security is debilitating for a child. The worry and anxiety about the parent's absence can be pushed into the child's unconscious, and can last for a lifetime. There can exist a fear of abandonment; this in turn constantly creates anxiety and depression. If these worries, anxieties, and fears exist for a person, they need to be resolved and healed.

If a person feels safe and secure throughout the life span, he or she can explore the limits of the Self, seeking Self-actualization. If there is fear and anxiety, and if a person feels unsafe and insecure, the ability to expand, grow, and explore is diminished.

> ***Point of Empowerment:*** *Feeling safe and secure is a necessity. It is the basis for moving forward in life. If a person is*

provided with an emotional home, a support, that person can leave this home to explore life.

Practice: *Think about your safety and security. In what areas of your life do you feel safe and secure? In what areas of your life do you feel that your safety and security are threatened? What steps do you need to take to feel more safe and secure?*

Point of Empowerment: *Our needs for survival and safety/security give rise to a part of the Self called "The **Protector**."*

Belonging and Loving

BELONGING

Belonging involves being a part of something outside of our Self. Belonging is about relationships and connections, both of which are vital to our well-being. We are driven, by need, to establish relationships and connections with others. The pain of being or feeling isolated from others shows how important these connections are to us. We deeply value "family," in whatever form that takes. We sometimes hold on to very unsatisfying relationships in order to be in a family. The statement "I don't feel like I belong" is profoundly painful. Not belonging can cause severe anxiety, depression, and loneliness. We fear loneliness. Some people are terrified by loneliness and pursue belonging, relationships, and connections with others at any cost.

Point of Empowerment: *The pain of isolation shows us how important our connections to others are. In "be-longing" there is "be(ing)" and "longing." Part of our being is longing for connection.*

Practice: *Take a moment to feel how important your relationships are to you. Feel grateful that you have these relationships.*

The first group that we belong to is a family. The universal image that we have of a family consists of a mother, a father, and a child (or children). However, the modern family takes many diverse forms. There is also the "extended family" of grandparents, aunts, uncles, cousins, in-laws, and whoever else is close enough to be considered "family." All these family configurations can satisfy our need to belong.

As we reach adolescence, we develop a peer group, a group of friends that become very important to us. We may join a club, or feel very connected to our school. Adolescents begin to establish romantic relationships. As adults, romantic relationships, love relationships, are crucial ways to fulfill the need for belonging. "I belong to (belong with) my boyfriend/girlfriend/husband/wife." As adults we may establish our own family, separate from the family we grew up in. We may expand this family by including children.

Beyond these personal relationships, there is our community, city, state, and country. We might consider our Self to be a member of the "Family of Man," the human family. We may belong to clubs and organizations. We may be a member of a profession or work at a company. If we feel connected to them, all the groups that we participate in give us a sense of belonging.

> *Point of Empowerment: As we mature, our sense of belonging becomes deeper and richer, bringing us more fulfillment.*

> *Point of Empowerment: Belonging can give us a feeling of safety and security. It can assure our survival.*

> *Practice: Give some thought to the groups that you belong to. Sense how membership in these groups fulfills your need for belonging.*

LOVING

The family is where our first loving relationships form. Our first bonding, or attachment, is with our mother. All human beings expect to be loved by their mother. It is a "fact of life" that your mother is supposed to love you. The absence of this love feels devastating. A father's love becomes more and more important as an infant, a toddler, or a child grows. Not having our mother's and father's love creates a lifelong longing. The unfulfilled longing for a parent's love needs to be resolved; otherwise, our ability to love is crippled. In order to give love as an adult, we have to first receive love as a child. We cannot give away something that is not first given to us. We depend on our mother's and father's love to start us on the road to loving. Once on the road, there are many opportunities to love and be loved. If we have not experienced a parent's love, we have the great challenge of finding other sources of love to fulfill our need. This can be a formidable challenge because we will feel unlovable, that no one could love us. If we approach relationships with this belief in mind, we will "be proven right." We will not find someone to love us.

> *Point of Empowerment: Without love in our life, we feel empty and lost.*

Being loved, *receiving* love, feels wonderful and is vitally important. However, it is loving, *giving* love, that is a more profound experience. In loving, we call upon, develop, and use, our Self. We challenge our Self. In loving, our Self becomes more. The more loving we are, the richer our Self is. Love is like a flowing river. We stand in the river and become awash in, surrounded by, love. Filled with love, we give love.

> *Point of Empowerment: Love can be built on the foundation provided by safety, security, and belonging. It can grow and flourish.*

Loving is an activity. There are actions that we can take to love someone. In loving we:

- Give to our beloved
- Respond to our beloved
- Respect our beloved
- Seek to know who our beloved is
- Care for and about our beloved
- Are willing to be intimate
- Are willing to commit and connect

In taking the actions of love, we are giving gifts to the person we love. As the beloved receives these gifts, he or she can feel loved.

In being loved, feeling loved, and receiving the gifts of love, we:

- Feel safe and secure
- Experience pleasure
- Feel trusting
- Feel cared for
- Feel known
- Can allow our Self to be vulnerable
- Can feel confident in the love, so that we are not afraid of losing it

Learning to love and to be loved is a lifelong task. We have considered some possible approaches to loving, but there are an infinite variety of subtleties to loving and being loved. This makes love a challenge. Deep within us is the knowledge of how rewarding the activity of loving is. This knowledge drives us to keep trying to love—even in the face of failure, rejection, and disappointment—until we succeed, and find the rich rewards we seek.

Practice: *Practice the actions of loving until you are a great lover. Enjoy the feelings and the experience of being loved. Deepen your experience with awareness.*

Self-Esteem

WHAT IS SELF-ESTEEM?

There are two components to Self-esteem.

Liking and Valuing Our Self

Having Self-esteem is a need. It is hard to experience our need for Self-esteem because it is so much a part of our life, like the air we breathe. We cannot separate our Self from our Self-esteem. Being unable to separate our Self from it, we have a hard time seeing it objectively. Yet everyone seeks to "feel good about themselves." This is the phrase that is most often used when a person is referring to his or her Self-esteem. People say, "I feel bad about my Self." They are experiencing low Self-esteem. Self-esteem is about liking and valuing your Self.

> *Point of Empowerment: Self-esteem is having a fundamental and deep, good feeling for and about your Self, and also having a deep, positive regard for your Self.*

> *Point of Empowerment: When you feel good about your Self, you are experiencing your goodness. Your goodness is a quality that is innately you.*

Knowing and Feeling Your Right to Exist

There are people who have had so little Self-esteem that they have committed suicide. This shows us how necessary Self-esteem is, and how devastating its absence can be. Their thought is, "I have no right to exist." Self-esteem is connected to our right to exist. It is the knowing, conviction, and certainty that accompanies the statement "I have the right to exist." Our existence is a fact, but we may not be certain about, and feel, our right to exist. (We will see that our right to exist is given to us by our Self-worth.)

Point of Empowerment: Self-esteem is the knowing, conviction, and certainty of your right to exist.

Our Self-esteem changes from moment to moment, but has a relatively constant level.

Practice: What is your current level of Self-esteem? Take a moment to rate your Self-esteem, on a scale of one to ten. This is an impression of your Self-esteem at this moment.

Permission and Authority: Ability and Willingness to Assert Your Rights

Point of Empowerment: Self-esteem _provides_ an _empowerment_ (permission and authority) to use our _power_ (ability and willingness) to claim, assert, and exercise the rights of our existence.

If we have high Self-esteem, we have lots of authority, as well as permission, ability, and willingness. When we have low Self-esteem, we have little empowerment and little power.

Point of Empowerment: There is _strength_ that comes with Self-esteem.

Practice: See if you can feel the empowerment, power, and strength of your Self-esteem.

Let's think about some of *the rights of our existence.* As stated in the United States Declaration of Independence, human beings are given the "inalienable rights of life, liberty, and the pursuit of happiness."

- Life: The right to have our survival needs met. We could add "the right to have the *opportunity* to meet all our needs."
- Liberty: The right to freedom.
- Pursuit of happiness: The right to pursue, to seek, happiness. Along with happiness, we could include, "all good

things in life." (We have the right to *pursue* happiness. We do not have the right to happiness. We are not *entitled* to happiness. Happiness is up to us to create, for our Self.)

The rights of our existence also include the right to be, do, and have whatever we choose for our Self, *as long as we do not infringe on the rights of others.*

> *Practice: Say, "I have the right to exist, and I deserve to assert that right." Search your feelings. How certain do you feel about this statement? What does this tell you about your level of Self-esteem?*

HOW DO WE GET SELF-ESTEEM?

We give Self-esteem to our Self. We do this through our own evaluation of our behavior, motivations, and attitudes. *We evaluate our behavior, motivations, and attitudes according to a set of criteria that we hold. These criteria are made up of our values, ethics, principles, and ideals.* (A shorthand version is, "doing the right thing, for the right reason, and feeling good about it.") True Self-esteem is given by us to us, by the Self to the Self. It does not come from external sources. If we look for Self-esteem from external sources, often in the form of approval from others, we will never have true, lasting, or meaningful Self-esteem.

> *Point of Empowerment: Our Self-esteem comes from our own evaluation of our Self. We cannot have Self-esteem based on seeking approval from others.*

> *Practice: Think about how profound this statement is. Also, as we approach Self-esteem in this way, we are truly empowered.*

A child is dependent on his parents for Self-esteem. Parents build a child's Self-esteem with love, acceptance, guidance, appropriate praise, and accurate feedback. Children need kind but accurate, objective, and constructive criticism. False praise, inaccurate feedback, and a lack of constructive criticism create a false Self-esteem that is shaky and crumbles easily. Brutal or constant criticism destroys a child's Self-esteem.

In addition, in order to have good Self-esteem, we need to have a healthy conscience. If our conscience is constantly "beating us up," we cannot have Self-esteem. If our conscience is harsh and filled with unrealistic and perfectionistic expectations and standards, we will not know how to evaluate our actions, motivations, and attitudes appropriately. We will not create Self-esteem for our Self. A dysfunctional conscience will destroy your Self-esteem. (Self-esteem can actually be a component of a healthy conscience.)

Point of Empowerment: To have good Self-esteem, we need to have a healthy conscience.

Practice: Read the chapter of The Operating Manual for the Self *on conscience.*

Children evaluate themselves with their parents' ideas about what they should or shouldn't feel good about. Adults take responsibility for their own Self-esteem. As a person enters adulthood, she needs to develop her own ideas about which behavior, motivations, and attitudes she can feel good about. Without one's own ideas, one cannot evaluate her Self. Developing and having one's own values, ethics, principles, and ideals is part of the process of maturing and developing **autonomy**.[2]

Point of Empowerment: In order to have true Self-esteem, the adult needs to attain a healthy level of maturity and

---

2   Autonomy: being a separate and unique individual. Being in charge of one's life. Having and exercising freedom of choice.

autonomy. Otherwise he remains a child, dependent on the approval of others for his Self-esteem—a Self-esteem that is temporary and unsatisfying.

SELF-WORTH

Related to Self-esteem is Self-worth. Self-esteem and Self-worth are different. We have many misconceptions about what Self-worth is. We think that we have to earn Self-worth through good deeds and accomplishments. We have the phrase "our 'net worth,'" or how much money we have. Is our Self-worth related to how much money we have?

Our Self-worth comes to us by the simple fact of our existence as human beings. *Human beings are born with, and have innate, worth.* The word innate means "inseparable from." Our worth is inseparable from our existence. Additionally, *our existence itself, and our worth, generate the automatic right to exist.* Also, if it is your belief, you could say, "God made me. God does not make anything that is worthless. Therefore, I am worthy." Worth is given, and is not related to any of our behavior. It is important to understand where our Self-worth comes from.

> *Point of Empowerment: Self-esteem is earned. Self-worth is given.*

> *Practice: Realize that you have Self-worth by virtue of being human. Claim that worth by stating the affirmation, "No matter what I do, I am worthy."*

> *Point of Empowerment: Our existence itself, and our worth, generate the automatic right to our existence.*

You may ask, "How can I be worthy if I behave in destructive ways?" The paradox is, if you see and experience your worth, you will not behave in destructive ways.[3] If you behave in destructive ways, you will have difficulty discovering and experiencing your worth.

How do we know if we have low Self-worth? We frequently associate deserving with Self-worth. The thought or feeling of "I do not deserve" is a clue to low Self-worth. We can also directly experience our feelings of low Self-worth, of worthlessness. Sometimes feelings of apathy and low motivation are an indication of low Self-worth. "I should, but I don't care" sometimes means, "I should, but I'm not worth it." Along with Self-esteem, we need to know and feel our Self-worth. Otherwise, we can never fully enjoy our life.

To Produce, to Create, to Know

TO PRODUCE

We want to feel productive. This is our need to produce. It is often expressed as our need and desire to work. We want to feel useful. For many people, feeling useless, not having anything to contribute to a situation, can feel very frustrating and painful.

The desire to produce leads to accomplishing and achieving. Accomplishing is completing a task or a goal. Feeling a sense of accomplishment can be very rewarding. As we accomplish a number of tasks that go together, we achieve something. Achieving involves developing our abilities, strengths, and talents. It is a rich and deep experience. Achieving enriches and develops our Self.

> **Point of Empowerment:** As we fulfill our need to produce, accomplishing enriches our life.

---

3   Along with this is the paradox, "If I truly love myself, I will not behave in selfish or narcissistic ways."

Practice: What are some of your accomplishments? Have you acknowledged them for your Self?

Excessive Pressure to Accomplish

At times we overemphasize accomplishing. It can become an obsession, always on our minds, or a compulsion: "I *have to* spend my time accomplishing this task or goal." We can't relax. We put too much pressure on children to produce accomplishments. This creates stress and anxiety for children. Excessive pressure to succeed through accomplishing can create stress and anxiety for adults as well. It can lead to "burnout," to being depressed and without motivation. In placing too much importance on accomplishing, we invest too much of our Self into it, and neglect other important aspects of our life.

TO CREATE

Our need to create is expressed in many ways. Artists, musicians, dancers, actors, photographers, writers, and composers are clearly seeking to express their creativity through their work. Yet everyone is creative, and creates in some way. Whenever we respond to a new situation, a situation that we haven't encountered before, we create something new for our Self.

Some examples of being creative are:

- A conversation where we communicate our ideas.
- Working out a conflict with another person.
- Finding "win-win" solutions, where differing points of view combine to find a creative solution to a conflict.
- Finding a new, alternative route to avoid traffic. ("The road less traveled.")
- Seeking to be understood in a heated discussion with a family member.

- Cooking a new meal. Decorating your home.
- As a parent, finding a new way to discipline a child because the old way isn't effective.
- Planning a new way of celebrating a birthday, holiday, or occasion.
- Solving any kind of new problem. The problem can be as mundane as fitting extra dishes in a seemingly full dishwasher, and as lofty as finding a cure for a disease.
- Dreaming, fantasizing, and imagining.
- Finding a way to fit two pipes together, as plumbers do, when the circumstance is very uncooperative.
- Adapting to change.
- Initiating change.

The list is endless. These examples show how creativity is expressed by a wide range of activities, from mundane, simple, common activities, to activities that are complex and demanding.

Point of Empowerment: *Each day, we are creative in some way.*

Practice: *Take some time to think about the ways in which you are creative. Think about new ways that you could express your creativity.*

TO KNOW

Our need to know is usually experienced as a desire or drive to understand. This desire or drive can be very intense. Knowing and understanding are the first steps toward effective action. They are necessary for us to succeed.

Our drive to understand can be motivated by other needs. For example, people want to understand other people. Knowing and understanding other people helps us feel connected to them, fulfilling our needs for belonging and loving.

A common complaint is that we are not understood. We want to be understood, but in a deeper way, we want to be known. We want to be known from the depths of our soul, for who we truly are. To be known is to be loved. In a marriage, the desire to be known by a spouse is very strong. Children, no matter how old they are, want to be known by their parents. There can be a lot of pain in the feeling of not being known. A person can feel invisible, that he or she doesn't matter.

When there is difficulty in a relationship, we seek to resolve the problem through understanding. We want to understand the other person's motivation, why he or she behaves in a certain way. At times, we think that knowing a person's motivation allows us to control him or her, and to control the relationship. Through control, we are trying to protect our Self, to feel safe and secure. We sometimes experience anger, fear, or panic when we do not understand another person. We feel threatened. We don't feel safe or secure.

Over a lifetime of experiences, knowing develops into wisdom. We eventually have a deep understanding of what life is all about, and of what works and what doesn't work, in fulfilling our needs.

> **Point of Empowerment:** *Effective living begins with knowing and understanding. Ultimately our knowing gives us mastery of our world. Eventually our knowing can become wisdom.*

> **Practice:** *Cultivate your knowing.*

Self-Actualization

ACTUALIZATION OF PARTS

As we have been discussing, the Self is a complex entity with many parts. Each part (the ego, developmental self, personality, conscience, image/identity, and sub-parts) wants to be actualized. That is, it wants:

- To be utilized
- To be active
- To express itself
- To have its voice be heard
- To participate in the living of our life
- To grow, develop, mature, and evolve
- To have an impact on both our inner world and our outer world

ACTUALIZING POTENTIAL: ABILITY, STRENGTH, AND TALENT

Human beings are full of potential. We want all that potential to be actualized. We want it to move from being potential to being an active, real participant in our lives. We have a need, a drive, to utilize our potential.

We can get immense pleasure out of mastering a new skill. For example, we can see the determination and joy of a toddler as he or she learns to walk. This is the joy that is present when we master a skill. We are actualizing a part of our Self, using and developing our abilities.

Everyone has strengths and talents. We may literally experience an ache that drives us to make use of them. Using and developing our strengths and talents can bring us joy. However, we can miss this joy if we use our talents to over accomplish, or, if we become overly competitive, by excessively investing our Self into winning some imaginary contest.

Point of Empowerment: Whatever we accomplish, using our strengths and talents will bring us satisfaction.

Practice: Think about an accomplishment where you used your strengths or talents. Feel the satisfaction that is there.

SEEKING WHOLENESS

We seek the wholeness of our Self. As we identify, use, develop, and therefore experience all the parts of our Self, we feel more and more whole. Until we have achieved the experience of wholeness, we feel incomplete. We search for completeness.

We feel a specific kind of loneliness and longing. The longing is to know all of our Self. The loneliness is the pain that leads us to search for our Self. Yes, we need to have relationships with people. When this is missing, we feel lonely. But there is a certain kind of loneliness that is misinterpreted. We think that this feeling means we should search for another human being. What it actually means is that we should search for our Self.

Sometimes we try to establish this completeness through others, specifically a romantic partner of the opposite sex who has characteristics that we unconsciously seek for our Self. (Same-sex partners function in similar ways, having characteristics we want for our Self.) For example, generally speaking, men take action, using will. Women allow and receive. So men seek the receptiveness of women. Women seek the willful action of men. Both are necessary for completeness, wholeness.

Another aspect of seeking wholeness is that we put our Self into situations so as to experience aspects of our Self. Here are examples of this.

- I want to experience myself as loving, so I establish loving relationships.
- I want to experience my Self as knowledgeable, so I learn everything I can about a topic and teach others.
- I want to experience my Self as angry, so I look for situations that trigger my anger.
- I want to experience my Self as sad, so I look for situations that trigger my sadness.

Point of Empowerment: Life affords us opportunities, and we create opportunities, to experience all the parts of our Self.

Practice: Give some thought as to the ways you seek to experience aspects of your Self.

THE DISTORTED, DAMAGED, AND LOST SELF

The drive for Self-actualization and the desire for wholeness drive us to:

- **Correct the distorted Self.** These are parts of the Self that function, but not to their full potential, because we do not understand how to use these parts and their abilities. We lack information and knowledge.
- **Repair the damaged Self.** These are parts of the Self that still function, but not to their full potential, because they have been damaged by attacks. These attacks have also hurt and wounded us. Our wounds need healing.
- **Search for and recover the lost Self.** These are parts of the Self that do not function. We have banished them from our awareness because they got us into trouble when they made their presence known. We got punished for using their abilities. They are stored in our unconscious. We need to make them conscious and learn to utilize them.[4]

Point of Empowerment: As we seek to actualize our Self, life becomes an exciting adventure, full of discoveries.

Practice: Commit yourself to actualizing your Self. Identify and take on challenges that will lead you to that actualization. In addition, be aware of the distorted, damaged, and

---

4   For examples, please see the chapter "Why Do We Need an Operating Manual for the Self?"

lost Self. Seek to clarify, repair, and recover these parts of your Self as you search for wholeness and completion.

Beauty, Mystery, Transcendence

We have a need, a drive, to experience beauty, mystery, and transcendence.

BEAUTY

Beauty deeply nourishes our sense of well-being, bringing us happiness, joy, and inspiration. Beauty connects us to deep parts of our Self. There is the beauty of art, of nature, of landscapes, of women, of men, of children, of babies, of dance, of laughter, of tears. Almost anywhere you look there is beauty. In seeing and experiencing beauty you can bring pleasure into your life.

MYSTERY

Mystery comes in many varieties and forms. It intrigues us and captures our attention. It challenges us and surprises us. It stimulates us.

Where do we find mystery? In the unknown. In adventures into the unknown. In exploring the unknown. In things that we can't figure out. In puzzles. In scientific exploration. In mystery stories. In the future.

Some people are so drawn to mystery and the unknown that they risk their lives to explore and experience it. And, some have lost their lives seeking it.

TRANSCENDENCE

Pursuing transcendence is the pursuit of life beyond the boundaries of the Self. We seek to know and to experience transcendence. The experience of transcendence takes us from where we are now, to another place. It can be a momentary experience that passes by almost unnoticed. Or, it can be an experience that is so profound, it changes us forever.

Seeking to know and to experience The Divine/God is an expression of the need for transcendence. We need to know that there is something greater than our Self. As we sense our own limitations, we know that we need support, inspiration, and love from a source greater than our Self.

We seek to experience transcendent states of consciousness. Human beings have always, for thousands of years, sought non-ordinary states of consciousness. Meditation, prayer, music, art, the exhilaration of physical activity, and using substances of all kinds are some of the ways that we reach for transcendence. We want to go beyond the limited parts of the Self, the ego, and the small self. Everyone seeks this in one form or another.

Point of Empowerment: Beauty, mystery, and transcendence enrich our life in beautiful, mysterious, and transcendent ways.

Practice: Seek beauty, mystery, and transcendence.

CHAPTER 8

THE LIFE CYCLE, LIFE STAGES, LIFE TASKS

Stages, Tasks, and the Developmental Self

Point of Empowerment: *Each stage of the life cycle has associated with it an aspect of the Self that we call the developmental self. Each stage of the life cycle or life span contains tasks that the developmental self seeks to accomplish. Through accomplishing these tasks, we fulfill our needs.*

The chart on the next page shows our needs as we progress through the various stages of our lives. The horizontal axis lists the life stage and the overlapping aspect of the developmental self. On the vertical axis are our human needs. We seek to fulfill each of the needs as we progress through the life span, while at the same time experiencing the developmental self.

This chart organizes an immense amount of information. For example, as you view the horizontal line, Self-actualization, consider the following question: How is the need for Self-actualization expressed and experienced through the stages of the life span, by each part of the developmental self? Since the answer to this question could fill a book, we will not be able to answer this kind of question or explore this chart at this time.

Stages of the Life Span ~ Developmental Self/Years

Human Needs	Infant/ Toddler 0-3	Child 3-12	Adoles- cent 12-18	Young Adult 18-26	Adult 26-65	Senior 65-80	Elder 80+
Survival							
Safety and Security							
Belonging/Loving							
Self-Esteem							
Create, Produce, Know							
Self-Actualization							
Beauty, Mystery, Transcendence							

Point of Empowerment: The complexity of human life and activity is enormous.

Practice: Try to appreciate what you accomplish each day, just by being your Self.

Tasks of the Life Cycle

In this chapter we will look at an overview of the tasks of the life cycle. There are a vast number of tasks for us to accomplish during our lives, and each task is a complex challenge in itself. Sometimes we are aware of our purpose as we seek to accomplish a task. Yet often we are on autopilot, acting automatically, behaving with limited awareness. When we wish to initiate change we become more conscious. When things are not going well, we become more conscious. The Self lives some of our life without much help from us.

Point of Empowerment: We accomplish many of life's tasks almost automatically.

Practice: Take a moment to acknowledge this, and to appreciate the wonder of your Self.

With few exceptions, *each task is a lifelong endeavor.* We start to accomplish a task, but rarely fulfill it completely. Often we fall short. Yet we can be satisfied in knowing that our accomplishments have been "good enough." Over time we develop the skills necessary to further fulfill a task, eventually completing it. Sometimes we develop mastery in using our capabilities to accomplish the tasks of life.

In the following section we'll explore a list of tasks. For each task, we will give the need that is fulfilled as we seek to accomplish that task. Some tasks are oriented toward our outer "social" world. Some are concerned with our inner psychological world. Due to space limitations, the description of each task is brief.

Our purpose here is to give you an orientation to the subject of the tasks of the life cycle.

Point of Empowerment: *Since you have a lifetime to accomplish tasks, there is no need to feel overwhelmed, so be patient with your Self. Also, in knowing that we accomplish many of these tasks automatically, you can start to develop confidence in your Self.*

Practice: *Ask, "Where do I want to take conscious control over my life by focusing my awareness on a specific task?"*

Practice: *As you read, ask yourself, "What does this mean to me personally?" Be curious. What are you learning about your Self? Use this list as a reference to return to periodically.*

Infant/Toddler, Years 0–3

A. Communication
   1. Beginning to make his needs known through communication
   2. Survival, safety/security

B. Self-expression
   1. Learning communication skills
   2. Survival, safety/security, belonging

C. Relationships
   1. Establishing and developing family relationships. Beginning to find his or her place in the family.
   2. Safety/security, belonging

D. Attachments
   1. Establishing secure attachments—bonds that give strength to relationships—with caregivers
      a. By feeling and knowing that survival needs will be satisfied
      b. By feeling safe and secure
   2. Safety/security, belonging

E. Trust
   1. Establishing trust
   2. Repeated experience of needs being met, on a consistent basis, builds trust
   3. Survival, safety/security, belonging

F. Boundaries
   1. Beginning to establish the boundaries of the Self
   2. Beginning to establish emotional separation from one's mother
      a. Using "no" to set boundaries
   3. Survival, safety/security, Self-actualization

G. Exploration
   1. Exploring the environment through experimentation
   2. Conforming to the limits of one's exploration
   3. Developing a tolerance for frustration
   4. Survival, safety/security, belonging, knowing

H. Conscience
   1. Beginning to establish a conscience
   2. Safety/security, belonging/loving, Self-esteem

I. Love, receiving
   1. Receiving love from parents
   2. Survival, safety/security, belonging, loving, Self-esteem

J. Love, giving
   1. Giving love by giving affection, showing concern
   2. Loving

Child, Years 3–12

Point of Empowerment: *Accomplishing these tasks is a lifelong process. The child begins to learn about them and to make some initial progress in accomplishing them.*

A. Self-expression

1. Developing communication skills
2. To know oneself. We know our Self as we talk to others, and as we act in the world.
3. Belonging, to know, Self-actualization

B. Emotions

1. Feel feelings. Understand the messages of feelings.
   a. Survival, safety/security, belonging/loving, Self-esteem, to know
2. Moderate and modulate the intensity of emotions
3. Safety/security (within one's Self), belonging, Self-esteem, Self-actualization
4. Control the expression of feelings
   a. Belonging

C. Thinking

1. Learn the skill of thinking, using logic and reason
2. Survival, safety/security, belonging/loving, create/produce/ know, Self-actualization

D. Boundaries

1. Establish healthy boundaries that separate me from not me
2. Survival, safety/security, belonging/loving, Self-esteem, to know, Self-actualization

E. Trust

1. Continuing to develop realistic trust
2. Distinguishing who can and who cannot be trusted
3. Survival, safety/security

F. Self-love

1. Developing healthy Self-love
2. Modifying Self-centeredness, narcissism, and selfishness
3. Belonging/loving, Self-esteem

G. Coping

   1. Develop coping mechanisms to handle, manage, and respond to threats to the child's well-being

   2. A threat is a challenge to the fulfillment of human needs. Threats can be mild, moderate, or severe.

   3. Coping mechanisms are varied. Some examples are: withdrawal, aggressiveness, Self-inhibition, Self-punishment, Self-blame, repression (not allowing one's Self to think or feel), denial (not allowing one's Self to see, think, or be aware), fearfulness, and compulsive behavior.

      a. These coping mechanisms are normal and functional for children. These are the tools at a child's disposal.

      b. These mechanisms need to be revisited as an adult to see if they still work.

   4. Survival, safety/security, belonging/loving, Self-esteem, Self-actualization

H. Impulse control

   1. To control behavior. To not act on every emotion that is felt.

      a. Necessary to function in the relationships that we have

   2. Belonging, Self-esteem

I. Frustration tolerance

   1. To feel frustrated without getting uncontrollably angry and taking this anger out on others

   2. To understand that frustration means "not getting my way"

   3. To accept that we do not always get our way

   4. Safety/security, belonging/loving, create/produce/know

J. Delayed gratification

   1. Learning to delay experiencing the pleasure of gratification from now to a future time

   2. Safety/security, belonging/loving, create/produce/know

K. Self-discipline

1. The ability to act, to accomplish a task, even though you do not feel like it

2. Safety/security, belonging/loving, create/produce/know

L. Conscience

1. Develop a healthy conscience

2. Know right from wrong

3. Safety/security, belonging/loving, Self-esteem

M. Self-esteem, Self-worth, Self-love, and Self-confidence

1. Beginning to develop these aspects of the Self

2. Survival, safety/security, belonging/loving, Self-esteem, create/produce/know, Self-actualization

N. Roles

1. Fulfilling what is expected of a child within roles that the child plays as a: son or daughter, student, friend, brother or sister, cousin

2. Safety/security, belonging, Self-esteem, create/produce/know, Self-actualization

O. Future

1. Start to deal with the future. Have dreams and fantasies about, and make plans for, the future.

2. Create/produce/know, Self-actualization

P. Identity

1. Start building an identity through identification

2. Identification. The process of building a Self and becoming a person, by becoming like another person. Usually done unconsciously.

   a. Self-actualization

3. Answer the question, "Who am I?"

   a. Belonging, knowing, Self-actualization

Q. Image

  1. An image is a picture that contains thoughts, feelings, memories, and beliefs.

  2. Developing a Self-image

    a. Pictures about who I am

    b. Belonging/loving, Self-esteem, Self-actualization

  3. Developing images about our environment and the people in our environment

R. Love

  1. Learning to love and be loved

  2. Belonging/loving, Self-esteem

S. Leaving the family

  1. Learning to participate in the world outside of the family

  2. Accomplishing separation from parents

  3. Create/produce/know

Adolescent, Years 12–18

A. Relationships

  1. Maintain current relationships

  2. Establish new relationships

  3. Belonging/loving, Self-esteem, knowing, Self-actualization

B. Schoolwork

  1. Learning what is taught at school

  2. Taking pride and pleasure in accomplishments

  3. Create/produce/know, Self-actualization

C. Physical development

  1. Cope with explosive physical development

  2. Self-esteem, Self-actualization

D. Sexual development

  1. Cope with sexual feelings

2. Self-esteem, Self-actualization

E. Needs and Desires
  1. Recognizing and seeking to fulfill needs
    a. All seven categories of need
  2. Recognize desires
    a. Knowing what I want for myself
    b. Seeking to fulfill my desires
    c. Self-actualization

F. Recognizing and respecting the needs of others
  1. Developing empathy
  2. Belonging/loving, Self-esteem, Self-actualization

G. Emotions
  1. Experiencing a wide range of new feelings
  2. Emotional regulation
    a. Managing and moderating intense emotion
  3. Expressing feelings appropriately
  4. Belonging, Self-esteem, Self-actualization

H. Thinking
  1. Continue to develop the skills of thinking
  2. To know, Self-actualization

I. Conscience
  1. Conscience becomes more sophisticated and more flexible
  2. Self-esteem, Self-actualization

J. Trust
  1. Continuing to learn who to trust, who not to trust
  2. Learning to trust one's Self
  3. Survival, safety/security, belonging/loving, Self-esteem, Self-actualization

K. Future
  1. Look toward, plan for, a future

2. Find motivation, excitement, and hope in the future
3. Begin to have goals for one's Self
4. Create/produce/know, Self-actualization

L. Past

1. Resolving emotional issues resulting from past threats to one's well-being
2. Beyond coping, an adolescent now has the ability to deal with painful feelings that are left over from past problems that were unresolved at the time.
3. Safety/security, belonging/loving, Self-esteem, Self-actualization

M. Identity

1. Explosive growth in the formation of identity
2. Belonging/loving, Self-esteem, Self-actualization

N. Image

1. Explosive growth in the formation of Self-image
   a. Adding and expanding upon mental pictures of who I am
2. Expansion of images
   a. Images about who others are
   b. Images about what my life is about
   c. Images about what my life should be
   d. Images about what life is in general
   e. Images about what the world is, how it operates
   f. Self-actualization

O. Learning to love and be loved

1. May or may not have a first love relationship
2. May "fall in love"
3. Feeling passion
4. Belonging/loving, Self-esteem, Self-actualization

Young Adult, Years 18–26

A. Moving out into the world beyond the childhood and adolescent home
   1. Self-actualization

B. Furthering education
   1. Knowing

C. Establishing work and career
   1. Create/produce/know, Self-actualization

D. Developing independence and Self-reliance
   1. Self-esteem, Self-actualization

E. Developing Self-confidence
   1. Replacing false Self-confidence with real Self-confidence
      a. Initially, the young adult has little real Self-confidence
   2. Safety/security, Self-esteem, Self-actualization

F. Developing romantic relationships, attachments, and bonds
   1. Loving

G. Exploring sexuality
   1. Within one's Self
   2. In relationships
   3. Self-Actualization

H. Learning to love and be loved
   1. Beginning to develop depth in one's love feelings
   2. Expanding one's capacity to give and receive love
   3. Loving, Self-actualization

Adult, Years 26–65

A. Becoming an adult
   1. Outgrowing childish and adolescent attitudes and behaviors such as: Self-centeredness, Self-importance, selfishness, and narcissism

2. Letting go of childhood and adolescent fantasies, dreams, and activities
3. Developing the abilities of an adult as they become available, with age
   a. Thinking, feeling, planning, understanding, loving, caring, empathizing, etc.
4. Becoming capable—having an ability that you can use with Self-confidence
5. Self-esteem, Self-actualization

B. Evaluating the effectiveness of childhood coping mechanisms
1. Adults have power, and intellectual and emotional abilities that children do not have.
2. Adults can find alternative ways of coping with threats that were not available to them as children.
3. Knowing, Self-actualization

C. Understanding power
1. Recognizing the power you have as an adult that you did not have previously
2. Learning the effective use of your power
3. Self-actualization

D. Establishing adult relationships
1. With family, spouse/partner, children, coworkers, Self
2. Learning and practicing the skills of relationships
   a. Communication, listening, understanding, empathizing, giving, receiving
3. Belonging, Self-esteem, Self-actualization

E. Correcting childhood deficiencies
1. Teach your Self, learn what was not taught to you in childhood.
   a. Examples: How to assert your Self. How to value your Self. How to have Self-esteem and Self-worth. How to manage money, etc.

   2. Self-actualization

F. Learning to love and be loved

   1. Greatly expanding the ability and willingness to love and be loved

   2. Belonging/loving

G. Sexuality

   1. Deepening one's sexuality

   2. Experiencing pleasure and ecstasy through sexuality

   3. Integrating love and sexuality

   4. Belonging/loving, Self-actualization

H. Work and career

   1. Being productive in work and a career

   2. Feeling fulfilled by making a contribution

   3. Create/produce/know

I. Conscience

   1. Incorporate knowledge, experience, and wisdom into the conscience

   2. Seeing the ambiguities of life—"the gray areas"—and using this knowledge to create a more flexible, sophisticated conscience

   3. Self-esteem, Self-actualization

J. Self-esteem

   1. Learning to create Self-esteem for your Self

K. Personality development

   1. Develop and use the resources of one's personality

   2. Self-actualization

L. Know one's Self. Know another. Know the world.

   1. Knowing is an aspect of loving

   2. To know

M. Self-actualization
1. Pursue Self-actualization

N. Creating happiness and joy
1. By fulfilling needs
2. By fulfilling desires
3. By creating and meeting challenges
4. Self-actualization

O. Healing
1. Resolving emotional issues resulting from past threats to one's well-being
2. Healing traumas, serious threats to one's well-being
3. Repair the disturbances of the Self caused by traumas and "just living"
4. Safety/security, belonging/loving, Self-actualization

P. Consciously create your Self
1. Understand your Self
2. Identify areas for growth and development; implement change
3. Create beliefs and attitudes that enhance your life
4. Teach others about the conscious creation of the Self
5. Expand your consciousness
6. Participate in the evolution of the consciousness of humanity
7. Create/produce/know, Self-actualization

Q. Pursue beauty, mystery, and transcendence

R. Taking responsibility for the development of the next generation
1. Having children, if that is your choice
2. Being aware of the next generation and letting this awareness influence your actions. For example, knowing that

air pollution affects a child's ability to breathe. Taking some action to leave a healthy environment for future generations.

3. Belonging/loving, create/produce/know

Senior, Years 65–80

A. Continuing the tasks of the adult

B. Expertise, teaching others
   1. Utilizing career/work expertise to teach others
   2. Using expertise in child rearing and family building to teach others
   3. Teaching others in whatever area of expertise a person has acquired
   4. Create/produce/know, Self-actualization

C. Completion
   1. Finishing "unfinished business"
      a. Making peace with your Self
      b. Putting to rest internal conflict and inner turmoil that has resulted from painful life experiences
      c. Forgiving
      d. Forgiving both our Self and others for creating hurt and pain
   2. Loving, Self-esteem, Self-actualization

D. Conscious creation of the Self
   1. Continue working with one's personality
   2. Improve your disposition; become a pleasant, nice person
      a. Improving your disposition sets the stage for satisfaction as an elder, having happiness instead of unhappiness
   3. Developing Self-acceptance
   4. Identity/image

    a. Defining and refining identity and image to gener-
ate happiness and further success (see chapters about
identity and image.)

  5. Self-actualization

    a. Grow, develop, mature, and evolve all aspects of the Self

E. Spirituality/religion

  1. Developing and deepening spirituality and/or religion

  2. Deepening one's relationship with the transcendent

  3. Appreciating beauty

  4. Belonging/loving, Self-esteem, Self-actualization, mystery,
beauty, transcendence

F. Maintain good physical health

  1. Exercise, exercise, exercise

  2. Good diet and good sleep habits

  3. Self-actualization

G. Learning to love and be loved

  1. Deepening Self-love and loving others

  2. Accepting that human beings have strengths and weak-
nesses/limitations. Loving another, along with that person's
weaknesses/limitations.

  3. Belonging/loving

H. Wisdom

  1. Integrating a lifetime of experience and knowledge into
wisdom

  2. Self-actualization

I. Learning about the end of life

  1. Beginning to think about death and mortality

  2. Questioning one's beliefs

  3. Revising dysfunctional beliefs and adopting beliefs that
enhance life

    a. Self-actualization, beauty, mystery, transcendence

Elder, Years 80+

A. Wisdom

  1. Continue to integrate experience and knowing into wisdom

  2. Knowing, Self-actualization

B. Courage, determination

  1. Finding courage and determination to deal with health challenges

  2. Self-esteem, create/produce/know

C. Completion

  1. Seeing and appreciating all the positive and negative experiences of one's life

  2. Seeing the value of one's life

  3. Understanding and integrating the lessons of one's life

  4. Self-esteem, knowing, Self-actualization

D. Spirituality/religion

  1. Deepening one's spirituality/religion and one's relationship with transcendence and the divine

  2. Appreciating beauty

E. Preparing for death

  1. Clarify one's belief system about death

  2. Face one's fear of dying

     a. If a person's belief is that there is no life after death, he or she must face the terror of nonexistence

     b. If a person's belief is that there is life after death, clarify what he or she expects will happen after death

  3. Talk to family and friends about the ending of one's life and what that means

  4. Share with others, reminiscing about the past, remembering joyful and sad events

  5. Within one's Self, reconcile relationships where disruptions

have taken place. This may or may not include talking to the other person.

6. Belonging/loving, Self-esteem, Self-actualization, mystery, transcendence

F. Learning to love and be loved
1. Enjoying the love that is, and has been, present in one's life

Uncompleted Tasks

As I mentioned, most of these tasks start in childhood and continue as challenges to be accomplished throughout the life cycle. However, if a task, particularly in childhood, has been poorly accomplished or partially accomplished, or not accomplished at all, it will seek our attention and press for completion at a future time.

> *Point of Empowerment: An uncompleted task manifests in our lives as failure to accomplish our roles and goals.*

> *Practice: Ask, "What is stopping me from succeeding in accomplishing my goals and in fulfilling my roles?" Identify the unfinished task. Seek to make progress in accomplishing this task.*

People: Similar and Different

We have traveled through the stages, through the life cycle, and have begun to consider the tasks that every human being faces. As with human needs, every person faces the same tasks. However, tasks vary in emphasis and in importance from person to person and from culture to culture. Yet as this exploration of the tasks of the life cycle shows, at the core, human beings are more similar than different. Our differences are expressed in the ways that we accomplish the tasks that fulfill our needs.

Point of Empowerment: At the core, human beings are more similar than different. We all have the same needs.

Practice: As you consider your tasks and needs, feel in awe of the challenges people face, and appreciate the Self who rises to the challenge.

CHAPTER 9

THE SELF IS A SYSTEM

Self as a System

The Self is a system. It has many parts, components, or aspects. These parts all exist at the same time, simultaneously, and are constantly interacting with each other in a tremendous variety of complex ways. At any given moment in time, no aspect of the Self is in charge. No part is "running the show." Though it may go against our ideas about our Self and may be hard to believe, we will see that this is true. However, one part may be more prominently in our awareness, the foreground, while the other parts are in the background of our awareness. (You, the adult, may take charge and "run the show.") As we understand the various components of the Self, we will learn to recognize the role that each part plays in our life. Each part has a presence, a voice, and a part to play, with its own function, its own job. Each part contributes to the **functioning** of the whole Self.

> **Point of Empowerment:** *As we see the big picture of our Self, the Self as a system, we can appreciate the elegance and beauty of the Self. We can start to feel good about our Self.*

> **Practice:** *As you read further, try to have curiosity about your Self and enjoy discovering who you are.*

Systems

A **system** is a collection of parts that work together to accomplish a task. The parts are surrounded by, and contained within, a **boundary**, the boundary of the system. Each part also has its own boundary. The parts work together, function as one unit, but each part retains a separate existence because it has its own boundary.

An excellent example of a system is the human body. The body has parts—organs (the heart, brain, liver, stomach, etc.), muscles, nerves, bones, etc. Each organ has its own boundary and function. They live together, within the boundary of the skin. The organs work together to accomplish the tasks of the body. Each part (organ) has an essential and important role to play, job to do, in the functioning of the whole (body). And, the whole is different from each of the parts. The whole accomplishes tasks that each part cannot accomplish on its own. Each part makes its contribution, so that the whole can carry out its functions.

Another example of a system is a city surrounded by water, like Manhattan is in New York City. The outer boundaries of the city are the rivers. All the component parts—buildings, houses, people—have their individual boundaries. Each part contributes to the functioning of the whole.

Another characteristic of a system is that *the whole is greater than the sum of its parts.*

If you dismantle the whole, and put all the parts in a box, you have all the parts, but they do not function as the whole does. The whole is a special arrangement of the parts. There are special relationships among the parts that allow them to combine, to make the whole. The body can think, feel, walk, talk. None of the parts separately can accomplish these activities, but the body as a whole can.

A city has a government that enables the city to accomplish tasks, like providing police and fire protection. None of the parts of the city—its citizens, buildings, or government—can perform these functions for themselves. Yet without the citizens, buildings, and government, there would be no city.

Systems exist within systems. A person/Self exists within a family. The family is also a system. The family may live in the city. The city may be in a state. We can see the truth of the saying, "No man is an island."

Point of Empowerment: Our system, the Self, is composed of ego, personality, developmental self, conscience, and identity/image.

Practice: Start to think about your Self as made up of components. You will immediately begin to understand your Self more clearly.

The Self as a System, a Metaphor

To help you get a feel for the Self as a system, and to visualize it, let's look at the following diagram. It is a map of the Washington, DC, subway system. It has five lines, each of which, for our purposes, represents one of the five major components of the Self. There is a line around the system; this represents its boundary with the outside world. It is a metaphor for the Self. As a metaphor, let's see how it can help us understand some aspects of our Self.

131

"You," your **consciousness**, activates all the lines, parts of the Self. You are the electricity that powers the trains.

Each station that we pass through represents a moment or an event in our lifetime. There are small, insignificant stations and large, important stations. Actually, we have an immense number of stations, moments in our lives.

A passenger, you, may travel along any of the lines. You have a choice as to which line you want to focus on, which line you pay attention to. As you focus on the various lines, or parts of the Self, you get to know your Self.

We can consider the subway lines as representing the lines of development of a part over an entire lifetime, with a beginning, middle, and end. Each stop then represents a point in time in the development of the part, progressing from infancy to being an elder. Over time each part of the Self grows, develops, matures, and evolves.

We can get stuck at a "station" along the way. This represents a point in time where there is a disturbance of the normal developmental process. We do not progress, or our progress is slowed down.

You can also travel along the line in either direction. If we take our "train" (part of our Self) backward, we are regressing to an earlier stage. If we decide that we are going to "repair a station or a section of track," this is a positive decision. If we go in reverse without thinking, we may be acting as a previous, less mature, version of our Self. Generally, this is not a useful approach, but it may show us where we need to work on our Self.

There are places where the lines intersect, and sections where the lines run parallel, side by side. When the lines run parallel to each other, they are working together. They are functioning harmoniously. But, let's say the intersections of the lines represent moments when there is a conflict between parts of the Self. They are both trying to occupy the same space at the same time. They are fighting each other. We have an inner conflict.

As our train travels through its line, stopping at stations, we hope they are pretty stations, and that we have good memories of our visits to them. Of course we can hit the station on a bad day. We then move out of the station, on our way to the next station. If we have acknowledged the "bad day," we can let go of the unpleasant memory of our visit to that station.

If we enter a station that is "under construction" or "under repair," we have work to do in this area of our Self.

In observing the map of our subway system, we see that the lines do not disappear after the train has passed by. The stations do not cease to exist because our train has passed through and moved on to another station. They live in our memory. This is our past. Our memories of the stations will usually fade and contain "fuzzy" details. However, it is possible to close your eyes and to imagine that you are visiting a previous station, at an earlier point in your life. These memories can be so vivid that we can feel like our past is still alive within us. This is particularly true if we experienced a trauma at a "station."

Communication and Feedback

Within a system and between systems, there is communication and feedback. Communication is the flow of information from one part to another, or from one system to another. Information comes in many forms. Within the body, it is electrical impulses that travel along the nerves. Between people, it is verbal communication (words) or nonverbal communication, like facial expression or tone of voice. A system, like the Self, needs to be effective in sending, receiving, and interpreting information.

Any system, like the Self, needs to know how well it is functioning, how well it is fulfilling its tasks. Feedback is information about the effectiveness of a system's functioning. Feedback occurs within a system, among its parts, or between systems. People (the Self) ask, "How am I doing?" in order to obtain feedback from other people. The question then becomes, "How open to feedback is a system/person?" and "How accurately can a system/person interpret the feedback that he or she is getting?"

Point of Empowerment: Success in life is a form of feedback. It means that we are acting effectively and getting what we want. Failure, as feedback, means that we are not acting effectively to get what we want in life.

Practice: Ask yourself, "How open am I to feedback: feedback from others and from life?" Are you willing to use feedback effectively to change and to become more effective at living life?

Boundaries

A **boundary** is a barrier that separates. A system needs boundaries to exist. Without boundaries, a system (such as the Self) ceases to exist. The skin separates what is outside a body from what is inside the body. Without the boundary of our skin, our insides would become outsides, and our body would cease to exist. Within the skin, each organ of the body has its own boundary, a barrier that separates it from every other organ in the body. The barrier guarantees that the organ remains whole.

The boundaries of our Self keep us separate from other Selves. Also, the components that comprise the Self (ego, personality, conscience, developmental self, and image/identity) have their own individual boundaries, making it possible for them to keep their "selves" separate and stable.

Point of Empowerment: For the Self, a boundary separates me from not me. Throughout our lives we face the challenge of clearly seeing and understanding what is me, and what is not me. Our boundaries define who we are and who we are not.

Practice: *Take a moment to close your eyes. Sense your skin as the boundary that separates the inside of your body from what is outside of your body.*

OPEN BOUNDARIES AND EXCHANGE BETWEEN SYSTEMS

While systems have boundaries, no system can exist by itself. It must exchange energy with other systems in order to stay alive. There must be openings in the boundaries for the purpose of exchange with other systems. The body has the mouth to take in food. There are openings in the skin through which sweat flows out to help the body regulate its temperature. The skin can also take in sunlight to produce Vitamin D.

In our city example, cities trade with other cities. Farmers who live near the city provide it with necessary supplies. Trucks deliver essential goods across bridges and through tunnels, the openings in the city's boundaries.

BOUNDARIES PROTECT

Another important function of boundaries is protection. The skin protects us from environmental threats that could destroy us, like viruses and bacteria. The boundaries of the Self protect us from being overwhelmed by threats.

We can easily see our physical boundaries. We project our physical boundaries into the space around us. We can feel when someone has crossed into our "space" and "violated our boundary." We recoil and back up to regain a protective distance between our Self and another person.

Point of Empowerment: *Ideally, our boundaries open and close in a flexible manner, appropriate to the situation.*

*They can be partially open and partially closed, to vary-
ing degrees.*

Practice: *As you go through your day, notice when you are
more open and when you are more closed. We open and close
to the external world, and to our internal world of thoughts,
feelings, and experiences.*

When Parts of Our System Conflict

There are times when parts of our Self are in conflict, fighting each
other. This is actually a fairly frequent occurrence. The feeling we
have in this situation is confusion—confusion about what we feel,
and confusion about what we should do. There is also ambivalence—wanting and not wanting something at the same time. If
our inner conflict is intense, and about something important to
us, it can be very painful, frustrating, and exhausting.

Consider the fact that our physical body, which is composed
of our parts and organs, can be fighting against itself. This condition is called an autoimmune disease. One part of the body, the
immune system, is attacking another part. Autoimmune diseases
can be deadly.

Point of Empowerment: *When aspects of our Self are oppos-
ing each other, we experience frustration, anger, exhaustion,
anxiety, or depression. We are being "Self-defeating" and need
to resolve this as quickly as possible. We need to establish
peace, balance, and harmony within our Self.*

Practice: *See if you can identify where you may be experiencing this kind of inner conflict. Write down what you have
discovered. As you continue to read the operating manual,
you will have a clearer picture of which parts might be in
conflict with each other.*

CHAPTER 10

BOUNDARIES OF THE SELF

To help us organize our discussion about boundaries, we will discuss the development and maturing of boundaries throughout the life span, with reference to the developmental self.

The chart below helps us organize the information presented on boundaries.

Stages of the Life Span ~ Developmental Self/Years

	Infant/ Toddler	Child	Adole- scent	Young Adult	Adult	Senior	Elder
	0-3	3-12	12-18	18-26	26-65	65-80	80+
Boundaries							

In addition, we will answer the following questions:

- What are boundaries?
- How do they form?
- What part of the Self creates our boundaries?
- How do healthy boundaries for the Self greatly enhance our life?
- What is the healthy functioning of a boundary?
- What are the dysfunctions of boundaries?
- How do we correct the dysfunctions of boundaries?
- How do we maintain healthy boundaries?

The Self Creates and Defends Our Boundaries

The developmental self and the ego are responsible for (have the job of) creating our boundaries. They are also the defenders of our boundaries. As we go through the developmental stages, we will see how this happens.

We have seen that boundaries are an aspect of a system, and that boundaries need to be flexible in their opening and closing, as appropriate. We have been discussing physical boundaries. We also have emotional and mental boundaries. Remember, a boundary is a barrier that separates.

INFANT AND TODDLER BOUNDARIES

Let's start with the human being as an infant. The boundary that an infant is born with is its skin. This distinguishes "him" from "not him." *Again, we are recognizing the crucial function of a boundary, the separation of me from not me.* The infant does not have emotional or mental boundaries. It only has a physical boundary. The infant controls—opens and closes—its physical boundary with statements such as: "Yes, I will eat this." "No, I will not eat this." He or she makes these statements nonverbally, through gestures. These are sometimes very insistent and powerful.

NO: The Boundary-Setting Word

Around age two, the child—now a toddler—starts to develop an emotional boundary. An emotional boundary is about "These feelings are my feelings" and "These feelings are not my feelings." Up until this point, in the child's experience, there was no distinction between the child's feelings and the mother's feelings.[1] The tool

---

1   This can be hard to see due to the toddler's lack of communication skills. One can observe a mother's emotional sensitivity and her connectedness to her child, her attunement. This connection, attun-

that the child uses to begin to establish an emotional boundary is "NO." (Sometimes parents hear "No, no, no, no, no." We can sympathize with the frustration of a parent who hears this twenty times a day.)

"No" is the boundary-setting word. It is what we use to establish and defend a boundary. We use our power to say no. We draw our "line in the sand." There are many forms of "no" that are "diplomatic" and suited for situations that require tact. For example: "That doesn't work for me. I can't agree to that." "No" communicates "This is my boundary and you may not cross it."

"Yes" is the word that lets things pass our boundary. If we agree, we say yes. We actively take something in, or we give permission to "come in," and allow things to pass our boundary.

- I breathe, saying yes to air. I hold my breath, saying no to air.
- I eat, saying yes to food. I do not eat, saying no to food.
- I look, saying yes to seeing. I refuse to look, saying no to seeing.
- I attend school, saying yes to learning. I refuse to go to school, saying no to learning.
- I do not say anything when you yell at me, therefore saying yes. I allow you to yell at me. I loudly say "Stop," insisting that you stop yelling at me, therefore saying no. I will not allow you to yell at me.

Point of Empowerment: *No is the boundary-setting word. It is a powerful word when used effectively. We spend our lifetime learning the art of saying "no."*

ement, is in two directions—mother to child, and child to mother. Experimenters have demonstrated this. See http://www.youtube.com/watch?v=apzXGEbZhto.

Practice: Say *"no"* and feel the power that is in that word.

Practice: Say *"no." Say "yes." Feel how they are different. Feel how these are both "power words"—how "no" keeps unwanted things out of your life, and how "yes" brings desirable things into your life.*

The Autonomous Self

Age two is also the approximate age when we start to create the autonomous Self and the separate Self. The autonomous Self is capable of interacting with the world in such a way as to take charge of its life. It has the ability to fulfill its needs, and to be aware that other people also have their needs. The autonomous Self honors and defends its own boundaries and respects the boundaries of others. This awareness and ability increases as the Self grows and matures throughout the life span.

The Separate, Unique Self

The separate Self consciously recognizes that there is me and not me. It is increasingly aware of its boundaries and utilizes them to accomplish the tasks of Self-definition, defining "who I am" and "who I am not." The separate Self defines itself as a unique individual. This process has been called individuation, and continues throughout the life span.

CHILD AND ADOLESCENT BOUNDARIES

Mental (Thinking) Boundaries

At around age seven the child begins to create a mental boundary. The child begins to experience and understand that "These are my ideas. These are *not* my ideas." This process continues well into adolescence and throughout the life span. A child becomes "argumentative" and "disagrees." (Again, this process can be very wearing on adults.) Yet what is happening is that the child is defining what he or she thinks, what his or her own thoughts are.

Different

Disagreement and arguments are also part of the process of differentiation. The child or adolescent is beginning to establish himself as a person, as "different" from other people: "This is what I think." "I am different and this is who I am." "It doesn't matter what you think, Mom and Dad." "It doesn't matter if I'm right or wrong. I just want to be different by having my own ideas." Paradoxically, the weaker the sense of Self, the more strongly an adolescent clings to his ideas.

Opening Boundaries

Along with "being different," the child or adolescent begins to learn how to open boundaries so as to include others in his or her internal world. One of the purposes of children having friends, and adolescents having a peer group, is to learn to "allow others in." We start to pay attention to what others think, feel, and want.[2] This process can go easily, or can proceed with great difficulty.

If a child or an adolescent is very resistant to the process of opening boundaries to allow others in, there can be intense conflicts with parents or other authority figures, and with siblings and friends. Children and adolescents can isolate themselves in

---

2   The process of "allowing others in" starts with using our five senses—sight, hearing, touch, smell, and taste. As we see or hear others, these perceptions are registered and organized in the brain. They start to form images (pictures) of others. Over time these images become very complex. They are filled with thoughts, feelings, memories, beliefs, and attitudes toward others. In psychology these images are called "objects." They have powerful effects on our lives.

order to avoid interacting with others. If they have experienced boundary violations, their boundaries can become overly rigid and closed. They resist the process of opening up their boundaries to let others in.

Point of Empowerment: Our inner boundaries are formed by our thoughts and our thinking. They are reinforced (made stronger) by the power of our feelings.

Point of Empowerment: Our external boundaries—those between our Self and other people—are formed and defended by saying no, and by our actions.

Practice: Identify something that causes you pain. Sense if the pain is caused by allowing something past your boundary that is not you, that does not belong to you. Say to yourself (think), "This . . . (anger, for example) . . . does not belong to me. It is not me. I now reject it." See and imagine your Self free of what does not belong to you. Imagine your Self feeling better.

YOUNG ADULT AND ADULT BOUNDARIES

The young adult and adult continue the process of strengthening and developing their boundaries. The adult seeks to develop flexible, not rigid, boundaries. These are boundaries that can flexibly adjust the degree of being open or closed, as appropriate, to current circumstances. Learning the skill of consciously opening and closing our boundaries is a lifelong process.

Healthy Boundaries

Point of Empowerment: Healthy boundaries are flexible, opening and closing easily, as appropriate. They allow a flow in both directions, in and out. Unhealthy boundaries are rigid, and are either excessively open or excessively closed.

Unhealthy boundaries can alternate between being excessively open or excessively closed.

Practice: *Your eyes and mouth open and close. They take in light and food. Your mouth opens to express your ideas. Open and close your eyes and your mouth. Feel how you are in control of this process. Sense what it feels like to open and close your boundaries.*

Boundaries and Romantic Love Relationships

Natural Blurring of Boundaries

In romantic relationships there is a natural blurring of boundaries as a "we" is formed. Without this relaxing of boundaries, there is no "we." Instead there is isolation, disconnection, and alienation. If there is to be intimacy in a romantic relationship, flexibility in a person's boundaries is necessary. This is symbolized by the sexual relationship. Sex is a metaphor for blurring boundaries. The man crosses the woman's boundary. He allows himself to be "taken in," physically and emotionally. The woman allows a man to cross her physical and emotional boundaries. She "takes the man in." This process can be quite stressful if a person has experienced boundary violations and has therefore rigidly closed or excessively opened his or her boundaries.

Point of Empowerment: *In romantic love relationships, there needs to be a sense of mine, yours, and ours. This is a reflection of healthy boundaries.*

Boundary Confusion

The ability to understand "what is me" and "what is not me" is an ability and skill that becomes more sophisticated over time. This skill is especially useful, and sometimes severely challenged, in romantic love relationships. One person says, "It's you, not me." The other person responds with, "No, it's not me, it's you." There is confusion and conflict about: What are my thoughts and feelings? What are your thoughts and feelings? What thoughts and feelings do we both have? In a relationship, this argument (conflict) can be painful, and can go on for years.

Point of Empowerment: Healthy Self-boundaries are essential for healthy relationships. In every relationship there is some boundary confusion.

Practice: Where in your relationships is there some boundary confusion? Through introspection, try to clarify what belongs to you and what belongs to the other person.

SENIOR AND ELDER BOUNDARIES[3]

Love

Hopefully a senior has become more and more skillful and knowledgeable about love. At this stage of life, a person may have achieved considerable mastery in adjusting his or her boundaries within a love relationship. If this knowledge and these skills have not been developed, this is a good time to begin. Some form of counseling or psychotherapy, or intense personal growth, might be necessary. If growth in this area is not addressed at this time, the opportunity for this kind of mastery may not happen again.

Opening Mental and Emotional Boundaries

The experiences of life may have taught a person that life is ambiguous, full of contradictions and paradoxes. Hopefully opening the boundaries of one's mind has resulted in an "open mind." This is a mind that is open to new ideas, to understanding another

---

3   Please don't skip these sections, no matter what your age.

person's point of view. It is open to the excitement of seeing how the world changes and develops.

An open emotional boundary can exist within one's Self. A person is capable of feeling a wide range of emotions, as well as the emotional states in between—frustration, sadness, and anger, and happiness, joy, love, and ecstasy. Our goal in life is to eliminate defensive walls (closed emotional boundaries) between our Self and our emotions.

> **Point of Empowerment:** *To have a rich life is to experience all the emotions that a human being is capable of experiencing.*

> **Practice:** *Notice where you block your emotions. Open up your emotional boundaries by becoming aware of and dissolving your defenses, your blockages. State, "I now open my Self up to all my emotions."*

Boundaries and Dying

If a person has worked throughout his lifetime to create healthy, secure boundaries, he can now allow those boundaries to soften as an elder. The "I" is secure and is not afraid of letting go of its boundaries. Letting go of boundaries is part of preparing for death. The total dissolution, dissolving, of boundaries, occurs during death. Without some preparation for this experience, death becomes terrifying—if not consciously, then unconsciously. The ego is a strong guardian of our boundaries, and our sense of being a separate person. Unless the ego has been strengthened and has matured throughout the life span, it faces the thought of dissolving its boundaries with intense terror. It fears that it will "cease to exist." We may then compulsively hold on to life, out of the fear and terror of nonexistence. We therefore miss the pleasure and the joy of continuing to live life.

As we have been learning about love, we have been learning how to relax our boundaries. We have, at times, totally released our boundaries (for example, when we have an orgasm or fall asleep).[4] This ability will help us in dying, so that when the time comes to appropriately let go of life (the death of the body), we can do so with comfort and ease.[5]

> *Point of Empowerment: We learn to use our boundaries throughout our life span (our life cycle). The infant comes into life with limited boundaries, and the elder leaves life with sophisticated, but relaxed, boundaries. This is the ideal progression in the development of boundaries.*

> *Practice: Strive to become a master in the art of using your boundaries. Start by learning to assertively say "No." Finish with secure yet relaxed and flexible boundaries.*

Respecting the Boundaries of Others, Self-Respect

If parents respect their child's boundaries, they are teaching the child to respect the boundaries of other people. This is being a good role model, or "setting a good example" as a parent. Respecting another's boundaries begins with keeping a respectful physical distance, and with entering his or her physical space only when invited in, or given permission to enter.[6] Permission is granted when another person does not object as we approach him.

We also recognize that other people have thoughts and feelings that are different from our own. When we recognize their *right* to

---

4 Falling to sleep is "releasing into nothingness, no-thing-ness." This terrifies some people and keeps them awake.

5 The belief that a person, as a soul, exists after death is a comforting thought. Many people believe in some form of an afterlife.

6 Parents often ask, "Is corporal punishment effective?" Maybe, maybe not, but it is definitely disrespectful and a boundary violation.

have those thoughts and feelings, we are recognizing and respecting their boundaries. If we recognize our right to our thoughts and feelings, we are strengthening our boundaries and creating Self-respect. If we respect our boundaries, others will also respect them.

Point of Empowerment: When we respect the boundaries of others, we create Self-esteem. Out of that Self-esteem we feel powerful and strong, and can defend our boundaries.

Boundary Violations

Boundary violations occur when one person crosses the boundaries of another person with some degree of force, aggression, or violence. Boundary violations are disrespectful and devalue the other person. Sometimes they are extremely destructive and damaging. Examples of boundary violations are:

- Telling another what she "thinks or feels," and refusing to hear what she has to say.
- Telling a person what he should do, and putting coercive pressure on him to conform to our wishes.
- Refusing to see or hear about another person's perceptions of an issue.
- Manipulative, controlling behavior, including using guilt or intimidation.
- Manipulating and controlling another person with rewards or seduction.
- Forcing another person to live up to our expectations of him through our aggression, intimidation, or manipulation.
- Punishing another person with rejection, disapproval, or the withdrawal of love. (We are not referring to the appropriate parental disciplining of children.)
- Imposing limits on the freedom and Self-determination of another person (excluding situations where another person is abusing us).

- Physical, emotional, or mental abuse and violence.
- Murder, rape.

RESPONDING TO A BOUNDARY VIOLATION

A person on the receiving end of a boundary violation can recognize it by feeling the pain of the violation. Typically, a person then says "NO" and takes action to end the violation. An adolescent or adult has the power to take this step. The child's power is limited. He or she may be punished for saying no. Often a child will hurt him or her Self (be Self-destructive) as a way of responding to a boundary violation. Self-destructive behaviors can be: failing at school, overeating, drug and alcohol use, suicidal behavior, Self-cutting, isolating one's Self from friends, obsessions and compulsions, fighting with siblings, or fighting with parents about issues seemingly not related to the violation.

Boundary violations cause shame in children. When a child feels the pain of a boundary violation, often he doesn't understand it. The child blames himself, thinking, "I caused this pain" and "I did something wrong, am a bad person, a defective boy." This is shame. Also, there is the thought, "I am worthless." Healing this shame and worthlessness can take many years, depending on the severity of the violation.

Boundary violations cause a person's boundaries to fluctuate between the extremes of being excessively open or excessively closed. People are unable to defend themselves in assertive ways, when this is appropriate. Their boundaries are too open. Or, they cannot open their boundaries to allow others to come in. They cannot establish satisfying and intimate relationships, which require open boundaries. Their boundaries are too closed.

Recognizing and Repairing Boundary Violations

The first clue that a boundary violation has occurred is emotional pain. Emotional pain is often first experienced as physical pain. Once this pain is felt, then the search for its cause can begin. Knowing what boundary violations are, we can connect the pains with a violation.

If a boundary violation is occurring now, the first step to repairing the violation is to end it. A person needs to claim his power, and see what he can do to stop the boundary violation. This involves taking action: either the person should say no immediately, or get help with a situation that may be too much for him to handle on his own.

Once the boundary violation has stopped, healing becomes possible and necessary. True healing cannot occur until the boundary violation has stopped.

> **Point of Empowerment:** *If a person has experienced severe boundary violations or abuse, or both, a personal journey of healing is necessary. The journey can include psychotherapy, reading, workshops, getting support from family and friends, and seeking spiritual or religious support.*

Boundaries Are Sacred

Over the course of a life cycle, the following processes take place regarding boundaries: creating, strengthening, opening, establishing flexibility, softening, and dissolving. As we develop our awareness of and appreciation for our own boundaries, we can see that the boundaries of a human being are sacred, and that they're worthy of our respect, honor, and love.

> **Point of Empowerment:** *Boundaries are necessary to maintain the integrity, the wholeness, of life.*

CHAPTER 11

THE DEVELOPMENTAL SELF

Ability, Stages

As we have said, the Self gives birth to the developmental self (small "s") during the life cycle. As our genes carry instructions for the development of our body throughout our life, the Self has a plan for the emergence of the developmental self. Each aspect (self) of the developmental self will provide us with what we need, when we need it.

> **Point of Empowerment:** *The developmental self is intimately related to the tasks of each stage of the life cycle. It has the abilities we need to accomplish the tasks of each stage.*

In earlier chapters, I have listed the approximate ages for each self. Each stage of the developmental self has a beginning, a middle, and an end, and a transition period into the next stage. Since there is a transition, the end of one self overlaps with the beginning of the next self.

The "Inner Self"

There are usually parts (aspects) of a previous self that have not grown, developed, or matured. Since they still need to grow, develop, and mature, these parts are carried forward, and continue to be an active part of the next aspect of the developmental self.

For example, if a forty-five-year-old man persistently acts like an adolescent on a particular issue, going out with the guys several times a week to get drunk, we could say that his "inner adolescent" is "alive and well," and motivating his behavior.

Another example: A seventy-year-old woman thinks that her mother did not love her enough, and has felt angry about this for sixty years. Her anger has become a seething resentment, which poisons her current relationships. Her "inner child" experiences an unresolved issue that dramatically affects her life.

As an elder we have the: inner infant, inner child, inner adolescent, inner young adult, inner adult, and inner senior as parts of our Self. Those past "inner selves" contain negative aspects of the developmental self that need to mature, but they also contain positive characteristics that we can enjoy. For example, we can retain and enjoy the child's playfulness or sense of wonder throughout our lives.

> *Point of Empowerment:* Our developmental self becomes more complex as we age, having "inner selves" as part of its makeup.

> *Practice:* To get a sense of your "inner self," state, "I am an/a . . . ," filling in the names of all the previous selves, up to and including your current self. For example, "I am an infant/toddler, a child, an adolescent, a young adult, and an adult." Notice how you feel when you say that.

Tasks Not Accomplished, Unfulfilled Needs

As we have mentioned, when the developmental self did not accomplish an important task of the life cycle, this task continues into the next stage, still needing to be accomplished. For example, if as a child I have not learned to respect the rights of others, I will not be able to fully love a partner as an adult. Respecting another's rights is now something I need to learn as an adult.

As an adult, we may have a more difficult time completing a task than as a child. One reason for this is that along with completing the task, we are often dealing with the painful, negative consequences of the unfinished task. In our example, having lacked respect, we experienced the negative consequences of our disrespectful behavior, and need to repair the damage to our relationships that we have caused. Yet as an adult we have abilities that we did not have as a child. We have the ability to learn from our experience, and therefore can understand the importance and benefits of respecting the rights of others.

The unmet needs that we carry forward from one stage of the life cycle to the next continue to press for fulfillment by the developmental self. For example, if as a child my needs for Self-esteem were not met, as an adult, the child part of me still presses for that Self-esteem, but seeks to get Self-esteem in a childish manner. The child's approach to Self-esteem is to get her parents' approval. As adults, our "inner child" seeks approval from parental substitutes, like a teacher, boss, or spouse. If, as adults, we use the child's approach to obtaining Self-esteem, our true need for Self-esteem will never be fulfilled.

> **Point of Empowerment:** *If we do not complete the tasks or fulfill the needs of a stage of the life cycle, we create an agenda for a future aspect of our developmental self.*

> **Practice:** *Think about what might be your agenda for completing incomplete tasks and fulfilling unmet needs. Are the strategies you're using to achieve fulfillment and completion appropriate to your current developmental self?*

Our Focus

There have been many studies of infant, child, and adolescent development. Since the later aspects of the developmental self have received less attention, we will seek to learn more about them. For each aspect of the developmental self, we will focus on:

- Unique aspects and defining characteristics
- Limitations and vulnerabilities
- Abilities
- Opportunities and challenges

In the section on the adult, we will also shed a little light on "what life is all about."

Begin with the End in Mind

Something to consider before we begin our exploration of the developmental self is Habit Number 2 in Stephen Covey's *The 7 Habits of Highly Effective People*: "Begin with the end in mind." For our purposes, this suggests the question, "How can we make being an elder the most rewarding stage of development?"

> *Point of Empowerment: The tasks that make being an elder the most rewarding stage of life, and the tasks that help us make the most out of the life we are living now, are the same.*

One of the most profound examples of this is the task of learning to love. If we spend our entire lives learning the skill of loving, as an elder, we have mastered much of this skill. We can then reap the rewards of this mastery: we can fully, joyfully, and richly love and be loved.

Infant, Toddler (0–3 Years Old)

TOTAL DEPENDENCY

Infants and toddlers are totally dependent upon their parents for their survival. Infants and toddlers have ways of communicating their needs, but cannot fulfill their needs by themselves.

If an infant's or toddler's needs are met, there is relaxation, contentment, and a feeling of safety and security. If they are not met, there is frustration, anxiety, fear, and ultimately panic and depression. At this stage, there is little tolerance for frustration, and great need.

BELIEF SYSTEMS

The infant and toddler are beginning to create a belief system about life and the world, and about "me-in-the-world." The system is composed of meaningful sensations and feelings, because language is very limited. Experiences are beginning to accumulate. Out of the toddler's experiences, and throughout childhood and adolescence, comes a belief system that will have a profound influence on a person's life.

> *Point of Empowerment: We have a system of beliefs about how the world operates and what life is all about. We create this system out of the experiences of infancy, toddlerhood, childhood, and adolescence.*

> *Practice: Think about your early years, and about what your early experiences taught you about life. How are the beliefs that formed during this period of your life influencing you now? What do you need to change in your belief system to get more fulfillment out of life?*

THE TODDLER

The toddler is developing the ability to communicate with the people in her life. There is immense curiosity, and an immense need to explore the world. There is a tenacious and determined drive to master certain skills, like walking. There is the start of the ability to love and express affection. There is pure joy, wonder, innocence, and delight. The toddler's ability to think is helping her start to understand cause and effect; she is beginning to see that there are consequences to one's actions. Motivation is based on fulfilling survival, safety, and security needs. This is accomplished by expressing one's needs, and by pleasing one's parents and caretakers.

> **Practice:** *Experience the pure joy, wonder, innocence, and delight you had as a small child.*

Around age two, the toddler begins what has been called the process of separation/individuation. The toddler's willfulness is intended to create an emotional separation between her Self and her mother. The process of establishing an independent emotional life makes a person an individual, and continues throughout childhood and adolescence.

Child (3–12 Years Old)

SOCIALIZATION

The child continues to learn the basics of "how to participate in the world." This is the process of socialization. The child's world consists of the family, school, and neighborhood.

The child uses his ability to think, feel, understand, and act to participate constructively in these environments. Adults want the child to respond with cooperation to the increasing expectations of parents and other important people in the child's world. This can happen with relative ease and some difficulty. When the fit,[1] or compatibility, between the child and the environment is poor or extremely poor, the process of learning and socialization can be very difficult.

---

1   Fit, as in, "Does the child 'fit in' with? Is the child compatible?" Or, "Does the child 'stand out' with excessive willfulness and rebellion?" This makes the life of the child and parents easier or more difficult.

ENOUGH

The child's ego is forming and beginning to develop. Unconsciously, the child self and the child's ego ask a question. *Am I having, doing, and being enough to fulfill my needs?* If the answer is no, anxiety emerges and motivation increases to have, do, and be more.

"Enough" is an important criterion of measurement. Other criteria of measurement, beyond "enough," are: well, good, excellent, or the ever-illusive perfect. This is important because almost all adults struggle with feelings of "not good enough." These feelings begin in childhood. They can haunt a person just below his or her everyday thinking and feeling, or they can be quite conscious. The desire to feel "enough" is profound, and motivates a variety of behaviors. This whole idea of "enough" is filled with the notions of success and satisfaction, as well as feelings of failure, ambivalence, and anxiety.

The child's approach to feeling "enough" is to get his parents' love and approval by living up to their expectations. The conversation between the child and parents often centers on "Is the child doing enough?" But "Am I doing enough?" gets generalized and converted into "Am I being enough? Am I enough?" The child feels anxious because his belonging, loving, and esteeming needs are not met if he does not get "enough" love and approval from his parents.

> *Point of Empowerment: Feeling "enough" helps us fulfill our needs for safety/security, belonging/loving, and esteeming.*

> *Practice: Identify feelings of "not being good enough." Understand the origin of these feelings. Decide that you are enough. (Ultimately, being enough is a decision.)*

POWERLESSNESS

Children are relatively powerless. Their ability to assert their will, so as to have an impact on their world, depends on getting permission from their parents and other authority figures. Needing this kind of permission causes frustration, which can be intense and hard to manage for the child. If a child's will is constantly thwarted, defeated, and disallowed, the child will assert his power through self-destructive means, and will hurt himself. This is a child's way of trying to influence his parents. The child's desire for revenge can also be present.

THINKING AND FEELING

The child's intellectual abilities are developing, but are limited. The child tries to understand and explain his world, but misinterprets the meaning of events due to these limitations. Unnecessary pain can be generated, and false beliefs about the Self and the world can be created or reinforced. These beliefs affect us throughout our lives, as they generate our "approach to life."

> *Point of Empowerment: A child's misinterpretation of an event can create false, dysfunctional beliefs that affect him his entire life.*

> *Practice: Has this happened to you? Are you holding on to any of your child self's outmoded beliefs?*

The child's ability to manage his feelings is developing, but is limited. As we say, "This is a work in progress." We recognize the child's limitations and continue to teach him the ability to deal with feelings. One way that parents teach this is by being a role model, by handling their own feelings constructively. Children learn by imitating their parents.

STRENGTHS

Children experience and express pure: happiness, joy, delight, spontaneity, curiosity, deep feeling, action, imagination, play, hopefulness, innocence, intensity, and passion. Since a child is usually protected from adult anxieties and worries, he can at times experience the world in a pure, uncontaminated fashion. His pleasure is not "spoiled" by anxiety and worry. When adults are free of worry and anxiety, they can have moments where they have this kind of experience. By observing children at play, adults can learn how to "live in the moment."

NEEDS

Children need nurturing, love, guidance, limits, discipline, feedback, **empathy**, and good role models. Parents can give a child what he or she needs. However, there is no perfect environment for a child to grow up in. Children need frustration in order to learn how to deal with frustration. Children need to be allowed to express their thoughts and feelings, but need to be taught how to do this in an appropriate manner. Children are self-centered, selfish, and aggressive. They experience worry, fear, and anxiety. Parents help children deal with all these attitudes, emotions, and behaviors.

PERFECTIONISM

Children use a common strategy to cope with life, called perfectionism. Perfectionism is the demand and expectation to be perfect. Being perfect means: never making a mistake, *always* being and doing the best in comparison with others, *always* knowing the right answer to questions, and *always* knowing what to do. Children think, "If I am perfect, I will get the love and approval I want." If there is an absence of parental guidance and direction about what to do or how to be, children resort to perfectionism as their way of making up for what is missing.

> *Point of Empowerment: We can carry a child's perfectionism into adulthood, with disastrous results. The demand to be perfect creates tremendous anxiety and depression.*

Practice: Do you demand perfection from your Self or from other people? See how painful this is.

SHAME

Shame is a complex, universal feeling experienced in childhood. If constructively handled by parents and authority figures in a child's life, shame helps the child develop a conscience.

The feeling of shame is accompanied by the thought, *I have done something wrong. I feel ashamed of myself.* An accepting and forgiving attitude by parents toward the child helps mitigate this kind of normal shame. Through the use of empathy, parents teach a child to feel remorse and sorrow for behavior that hurts others. Remorse and sorrow are healthy components of a healthy conscience.

However, shame is usually carried to the next step of, "There is something wrong with me. I am flawed, defective." Behavior-related shame is generalized and becomes shame of the Self, shame of one's existence, shame of one's being. Here is when a parent's love helps the child to develop feelings of worthiness, of Self-worth. Self-worth is the antidote to feelings of shame about my existence, shame about my very being.

A child experiencing severe and/or chronic punishment, mistreatment, neglect, or abuse by a parent experiences intense hurt, pain, anger, and rage, along with the devastating terror of, "I could die, my very existence is threatened." The needs for survival and safety/security feel threatened. Belonging and loving are also at risk. These feelings are diminished if the child blames himself for the parent's behavior. "My parents are not monsters. I am being punished (mistreated, neglected, or abused) because I did something wrong. I am flawed and defective. *And,* if I become *perfect,* I will survive, feel safe, belong, and be loved." Thus shame and perfectionism are comforting, as they help the child cope with threats to his needs.

Point of Empowerment: By learning empathy, normal child-hood shame becomes remorse and sorrow, aspects of a healthy conscience. Excessive childhood shame is a devastating state of being that needs to be healed.

Practice: Give some thought to the role of shame in your life. Seek help if you've experienced excessive amounts of shame.

ISSUES AND LIFE LESSONS

The limitations and experiences of childhood and adolescence automatically generate "issues." Issues are made up of misunder-standings, confusions, false beliefs, dysfunctional attitudes, and internal conflicts. What causes issues? What are some examples of issues?

- My parents demanded a lot from me before they would show me love. My issue: "I think that in order to get love I must constantly please other people."
- My father lost his job. My mother continued to spend money. My parents fought about money. Hearing them fight, I felt scared and insecure. My issue: "Spending money will create problems and put you in danger."
- My parents worked long hours. I felt alone and neglected. My issue: "I am not important. I do not matter."
- The first person I fell in love with did not want to have anything to do with me. I was ten years old. My issue: "Love is disappointing. Love hurts."
- My mother was frequently disappointed with me, and she'd send me to my room for hours. My issue: "If I disappoint a person, I will be rejected and alone."

Issues are set up in childhood and take a lifetime to unravel, correct, and resolve. Having and resolving issues is part of what life is all about, because in this process we learn life lessons. This learning may not even be conscious. Throughout our lifetime, we have learned about love, authority, power, money, cause and effect, and more.

> *Point of Empowerment: Childhood creates many "issues" for us to work with and to work through. They can take an entire lifetime to unravel, correct, and resolve. They provide an opportunity for lifelong learning.*

> *Point of Empowerment: We can resolve the issues of childhood as an adult, having the capabilities of an adult.*

> *Practice: Think about your childhood experience. Try to identify some of your "issues." Begin to work with them as a path to growth and evolution.*

Adolescent (12–18 Years Old)

TRANSITION

Adolescence is a transitional stage of development. The adolescent is leaving childhood and moving into young adulthood. Early, middle, and late adolescents are very different people. They experience immense changes in their emotional, intellectual, and physical makeup. Adolescents experience increasing maturity, as well as the immaturity of childhood, at the same time.

IDENTITY AND IMAGE

The adolescent is struggling with the question, "Who am I?" This is the question of identity. To shape and build their identity, adolescents become obsessed with finding others to identify with, to become like. Adolescents also ask, "Who do I see my Self as being?" and "Who do I imagine my Self to be?" These are the questions of Self-image. Adolescents are preoccupied with their external image, with how others see them, and are obsessed with their own internal Self-image.

EXTREMES AND ABSOLUTES

Adolescents experience extremes—extremes of thinking, feeling, and doing. These extremes are fueled by: inexperience, desperation, panic, fear, anxiety, limited understanding, projections that the future will be just like the "unhappy" present, intense hormonal changes, and passion. Passion can be very positive, resulting in great dedication, joy, and pleasure. However, passion can also degenerate into an obsession, in which an adolescent focuses on one thing, excluding all other activities. Obsession limits an adolescent's opportunities for having a wide variety of experiences.

Adolescents think and feel in absolutes: "This is the worst day of my life." "I will never be happy again." "Since I lost my girlfriend/boyfriend, I will never love again." "No one will like me unless I wear the jeans that everyone is wearing." These statements are usually the "drama" of adolescence. However, if these kind of statements result from a real or imagined trauma, they become decisions and beliefs that can seriously limit one's future possibilities in life as a young adult and adult.

> **Point of Empowerment:** *The tendency of adolescents to go to extremes and to think in absolutes, combined with a stressful or traumatic event, can give rise to decisions and beliefs that seriously limit future possibilities for a person.*

> **Practice:** *As an adolescent, were there events that were very stressful or traumatic that caused you to make decisions or form beliefs that have limited your fulfillment in life?*

POSITIVE CHARACTERISTICS, UNHAPPINESS

Adolescents can be adventurous, creative, passionate, curious, intense, loving, sensitive, and idealistic. They seek new experiences with aliveness and with the joy of living life. They can also be miserable, unhappy, anxious, depressed, and unable to deal with the stresses of life. They have many "first time" experiences, which are exhilarating and fear inducing at the same time.

SELF-CONSCIOUS AND INADEQUATE

Adolescents experience a Self-consciousness that is sometimes paralyzing. They may have awareness of themselves, their world, their problems, and their limitations, but these perceptions cause anxiety. They may understand their problems, but are unable to do anything to solve these problems. This causes frustration and a feeling of powerlessness.

Adolescents can feel a deep sense of inadequacy. They may feel that they are not up to the expectations placed on them, and to the demands of living. They lack Self-confidence, and their arrogance hides what is missing. There is the feeling of "not good enough." Perfectionism compensates for this feeling.

SEPARATION AND INDEPENDENCE

The adolescent is seeking to separate (create distance) from her family, and to become more independent. This is accomplished partially through friendships and membership in peer groups. These relationships also satisfy adolescents' deep need for belonging. However, the rigid conformity to peer group standards is a way of seeking external controls to tame an adolescent's inner chaos. Separation and independence are also accomplished through an adolescent's experimentation and new experiences.

We see that adolescents face many challenges: adolescence is a developmental stage with many opportunities for growth, as well as difficulties to overcome.

Point of Empowerment: Because of the great challenges of adolescence, we leave this period of development with much "unfinished business"—experiences that continue to have a painful emotional charge attached to them.

Practice: Do you continue to have "unfinished business" from adolescence that you need to revisit and resolve?

Young Adult (18–26 Years Old)

SELF-CONFIDENCE

The young adult ventures out into a world that can be much larger than the world of childhood and adolescence. This world is unfamiliar and stressful, and at the same time enticing and exhilarating. The young adult is largely unprepared for this new world. There are many new experiences and new challenges. Because of his lack of experience, the young adult lacks Self-confidence. There is some Self-confidence, but the need for more is great.

Lacking substantial Self-confidence is a hallmark of this period of development. Since we cannot function without Self-confidence, we often substitute false confidence or overconfidence for true confidence. Sometimes this false confidence or overconfidence actually helps the young adult achieve extraordinary accomplishments and successes. However, it is common that these successes are followed by failures and setbacks. If these failures and setbacks become learning experiences, the stage is set for further accomplishment. Continued experience and success can develop into real Self-confidence.

Crisis of Confidence

There is a vulnerability that the young adult has due to shaky Self-confidence. Failures and setbacks can erode confidence.

Numerous or serious failures and setbacks can diminish Self-confidence, to the point where a person experiences "a crisis of confidence." This lack of Self-confidence results in anxiety, depression, and a paralysis of not being able to take action. This serious condition needs to be recognized as a *crisis of confidence*. Rebuilding confidence is necessary, and can be accomplished by recognizing past successes and accomplishments. This recognition becomes an understanding that the abilities that resulted in these successes are still within the person, and can be counted on to help with future achievements. Confidence is then on the way to being restored.

EXPERIMENTATION FOR SELF-DISCOVERY

The young adult faces choices about work, career, love relationships, and lifestyle. He needs to make room for experimentation, for success and failure, and for mistakes. He may start off with ideas about what he wants to do. If these choices bring him satisfaction and fulfillment, he has made good choices for his Self. If he does not know what he wants to do, he may need time to discover what feels right. Young adults need to allow themselves time to explore and discover.

LOVE AND RELATIONSHIPS

Love relationships become more important. Young adults search for a partner. They experience attraction, falling in love, building relationships, and being intimate. There is the excitement of a new relationship, and hope for the future. There are also the natural fears of rejection and failure, the fear that the love won't last, and the fear of intimacy. With a partner, the young adult fulfills the need for belonging and loving. In addition, since nature has programmed human beings with the drive to procreate, finding a partner becomes a drive.

The young adult may have had successful and rewarding, or unsuccessful and painful, romantic relationships as an adolescent. Previous relationships influence current relationships.

Positive, rewarding experiences build confidence and excitement. Negative experiences result in caution and fear. Some healing of hurt feelings about past relationships may be necessary in order to create the freedom to fully engage in a current relationship. (Actually, healing wounds from a relationship that has ended is always necessary to enable us to be fully engaged and present in our next relationship.)

ABILITIES

Emotional maturity and the ability to think things through without impulsive behavior are developing further. There is the ability to be Self-reflective, to be objective about one's own behavior, and to see the impact of one's behavior on other people. There is increased Self-awareness (knowing what I am thinking and feeling). There is increasing ability to experience feelings and to interpret their meaning.

The young adult is starting on the road to adulthood, beginning to put childhood and adolescence into the past.

Adult (26–65 Years Old)

Adulthood is the longest developmental period. We are adults for most of our lives, approximately forty years. Hopefully, at sixty-five years old we are different people than we were at thirty. Adulthood is a complex period of time characterized by increasing abilities. These abilities enable us to be more and more effective in dealing with the tasks of adulthood, the demands of life, and the fulfillment of our needs.

Along with accomplishing tasks and fulfilling our needs, what are we doing as we live through the life cycle stage of adulthood?

To answer this question, let's add two new categories to our discussion of the developmental self: life lessons and life themes. We can describe adulthood this way:

- We use our abilities to resolve our issues.
- As we resolve our issues, we learn life lessons.
- As we resolve our issues, we explore life themes.
- As we explore life themes, we learn life lessons.
- As we accomplish the tasks of adulthood, we explore life themes.
- As we use our abilities, accomplish the tasks of adulthood, resolve our issues, explore life themes, and learn life lessons, we evolve.[2]

We may automatically resolve issues and explore themes as we "rise to the occasion" and spontaneously live our life. Yet awareness can greatly facilitate resolving and exploring.

We can deliberately choose to develop abilities, and to focus our attention on specific tasks, issues, and themes.

We will present lists of abilities, themes, and issues. This will provide us with the information we need to make informed choices and to bring clarity to our actions. We will then more easily complete the adult stage of the life cycle, while adding richness and fulfillment to our lives.

AWARENESS

Point of Empowerment: Create awareness by intentionally focusing your attention on these sections of the operating manual.

Practice: Put your awareness into action by choosing abilities to develop and issues to resolve.

---

2   A corollary of this process is: as we evolve individually, we contribute to the evolution of humanity.

LIFE LESSONS

Point of Empowerment: Life lessons are about what is effective and what is ineffective in getting us what we want in life.

Point of Empowerment: Life lessons are about <u>how</u> the actions we take and the results we get <u>feel</u> to us. New experiences bring new feelings.

Practice: Give some thought to, "What have I discovered in life that works to get me what I want?" And also, "What have I discovered in life that gets me the opposite of what I want?"

Practice: Evaluate the effectiveness of your actions by using this question: "Are the consequences of these actions what I want, or the opposite of what I want?"

INCREASING ABILITIES

As adults we have increased ability to:

- Think, analyze, and understand
- Feel, and correctly understand the messages and meanings of feelings
- Take/initiate action
- Imagine
- Know our desires, needs, and values
- Use our power and our willpower
- Have clear intentions
- Focus our attention
- Learn from the past
- Plan for the future
- Discern, make distinctions
- Tolerate frustration, delay gratification, and have Self-discipline

- Weigh priorities
- Develop and utilize our intuition
- Use our freedom
- Make conscious decisions and choices
- Give and receive
- Love
- Self-reflect
- Experience pleasure, happiness, and joy
- Expand and utilize awareness of our environment and our Self
- Experience the now, being fully present in the moment
- Focus our actions to accomplish tasks and fulfill needs
- Set goals
- Have dreams for our Self and our life
- Empathize

As we enter adulthood, we have some of these abilities. As adults we develop them further. We develop some of these abilities for the first time.

Point of Empowerment: With awareness, we can identify our abilities. As we use them, we become more skillful. We can eventually achieve mastery in the use of our abilities.

Practice: Think of some of your abilities that you would like to become more proficient at. Practice, practice, practice.

THEMES

Life contains themes that every human being explores. Living involves exploring themes. If we are alive, we do not have a choice—we must deal with these themes, though our choice is sometimes avoidance. People deal with an immense number of themes. Some of these themes are:

*Love, Authority, Cause and effect, Consequences to our ac-
tions, Freedom, Success, Failure, Cooperation, Conflict,
Aggression/War, Peace, Harmony, Balance, Happiness, Joy,
Gratitude, Abundance, Wealth, Knowledge, Wisdom, Fun,
Pleasure, Emotion, Values, Loyalty, Truth,*

*Frustration tolerance, Delay of gratification, Self, Self/Other,
Self-discipline, Self-esteem, Self-love, Self-confidence, Self-
Awareness, Self-respect, Self-acceptance, Self-actualization,
Friendship, The nature of relationships with parental
authorities,*

*The nature of relationships with siblings and other relatives,
Autonomy, Self-determination, Sexuality, Power, Money,
Religion, God, Spirituality, Sameness, Difference, Diversity*

Point of Empowerment: *Life brings themes for us to explore.
We can approach them with curiosity and excitement, or we
can resist dealing with them. If we resist life's themes, we
resist life. This kind of resistance causes us great suffering.*

Practice: *Imagine a situation in your life that reflects a
theme. Imagine your Self courageously and successfully dealing
with this situation.*

We often explore themes through what is called "the duality of
opposites," such as love/hate, rich/poor, pleasure/pain, wanted/
unwanted. Actually these opposites are "two sides of the same
coin." Opposites provide a "contrast" for us to explore. For
example, rich/poor are two sides of the coin called abundance.
Love/hate are actually two sides of the coin called love. We
might call hate the "dark side" of love. We often find our Self
experiencing the unwanted, dark side of a theme. Through the
pain of that experience, we are learning to clearly identify "What
we don't want."

Point of Empowerment: The idea that there are themes in our life is extremely useful.

Practice: Identify a theme. Recognize the positive and negative aspect of that theme. Seek to have less of the unwanted negative side, and more of the wanted positive side. For example, you could say, "I want less hate and more love in my life." Take the steps necessary to create this for yourself.

ISSUES

Issues are aspects of themes. Or "variations on a theme," as musical compositions are sometimes called. Here are just a few examples of issues.

- In order to get love, I must constantly please others.
- Spending money will put me and/or my family in danger.
- I am not important. I do not matter.
- Love hurts.
- If I disappoint a person, I will be rejected and alone.
- I can't stand being alone; it will kill me.
- I can't bear loneliness. I need to always be with someone else.
- It is wrong to love yourself.
- Guilt and suffering are noble.
- Love is Self-sacrifice and worry.
- I need the approval of others to feel good about myself.
- It is wrong to feel anger.
- I am ashamed and feel guilty about who I am.
- I will never be satisfied with my body. It must be perfect.
- I need to worry in order to keep myself and the ones I love safe.
- The world is a dangerous place.
- You have to beat the other guy in order to succeed.

Every person has these kinds of issues. The number of issues is almost unlimited. People experience these issues in their own unique way. Yet there are also universal issues that everyone struggles with. Issues are tied to childhood events and memories. Aspects of issues are: confusion, misunderstandings, and false beliefs. Our issues may also contain contradictions and internal conflicts. Internal conflicts can sometimes lead to "being at war with our Self." This can be extremely frustrating and painful.

Point of Empowerment: At the heart of an issue is a false belief or misconception about our Self, others, the world, or life.

Point of Empowerment: Issues cause us to be ineffective in our behavior. We create areas of our life that are not working the way we want.

Practice: As you identify where your life is not working, try to discover the false belief that underlies your ineffective behavior. What is the "issue" here?

Certain behaviors and attitudes are generated by our issues. For example, we may have a belief that "It is wrong or dangerous to feel angry." Yet we feel angry! In truth, anger can be a healthy reaction to certain situations. It contains important and useful information for us about the situation. Believing that anger is dangerous, we become fearful of our anger and of other people's anger. Our belief about anger causes us to disown our anger. When we naturally, appropriately, and spontaneously feel angry, we have an internal conflict. We want to feel it and not feel it at the same time.

Ambivalence: Wishing for and Fearing at the Same Time

If we believe that "having love in our life is dangerous," we will avoid loving relationships. We will slow our Self down, or sabotage our Self, as we search for a loving relationship. Yet we need loving relationships. If we also believe that "I can't bear loneliness," we will rush into a relationship. We now have an internal conflict—wanting and not wanting a loving relationship at the same time. (Wanting and not wanting something at the same time is called ambivalence, and "having an approach/avoidance conflict.") This internal conflict puts us at war with our Self. If the wish for a relationship, and the fear of a relationship, are both intense, this internal conflict can be very painful.

SELF-ESTEEM, SELF-WORTH, AND SELF-LOVE

Becoming an Adult Through Self-Esteem

Children and adolescents are dependent on their parents, family, and teachers to obtain a sense of Self-esteem, Self-worth, and Self-love. As young adults and adults, we must establish these things for our Self. As adults, we are no longer dependent on others in the way we were as children or adolescents. The abilities and power we have as adults give us the opportunity to develop and experience esteem, worth, and love for our Self.

> *Point of Empowerment: The process of creating Self-esteem for our Self as an adult is the same as the process of becoming an adult. What our parents used to do for us, we now do for our Self.*

Remember, as an adult we still have an inner child and an inner adolescent who pursue unfulfilled needs using the child's or adolescent's strategies. These inner aspects of our developmental self think that they must get the esteem, worth, and love they didn't get as a child or an adolescent. In reality this isn't true, but people spend a lifetime seeking what they didn't get as children or adolescents. As adults, we learn how to give up the child's or adolescent's sense of need.

Point of Empowerment: We can unnecessarily spend our lives seeking the esteem, worth, and love that we did not get as a child.

Point of Empowerment: As you learn to experience Self-esteem, Self-worth, and Self-love, you can give this to your inner child and adolescent.

Practice: Try a meditation to open up communication with your inner child or inner adolescent. Sit quietly with your eyes closed. Imagine your inner child or inner adolescent sitting there with you. Talk to them and teach them how to have esteem and worth, and how to love their Self. As you teach these lessons to them, you clarify and learn them for your Self.

Remember, Self-esteem is the result of our own evaluation of our behavior, attitudes, and motivations, according to our highest ethics and values.

Self-worth is the recognition of our worth, our value, as human beings. It is a given, given to us by the virtue of who we are as human beings. Our worth is innate, contained within us. It is not something that is earned.

Self-Love

Self-love is a great challenge for everyone. It takes an entire lifetime to learn how to effectively love our Self. Many people think it is wrong to love yourself. They confuse Self-love with narcissism, selfishness, and Self-centeredness. The way we love our Self is to take the same actions toward our Self that we'd take as we love others. Love your Self as you would love others. (If necessary, please review the section on how to love in the chapter on needs.)

Other examples of Self-love are:

- Treating our Self with kindness and compassion.
- Seeing our worth and our goodness.

- Giving our Self the freedom of Self-determination.
- Avoiding harsh Self-criticism and judgments.
- Giving Self-acceptance to our Self.

We can see that if we treat our Self with kindness and compassion, we will treat others this way. If we are unkind to our Self and lack compassion for our Self, kindness to others, as well as compassion toward them, is impossible.

Point of Empowerment: *We can only give to others what we already have within our Self.*

As children our Self-love is dependent on the love we receive from others. The process of loving, as an adult, is to love our Self first, and then to give this love to others.

THE CHILD'S AND ADOLESCENT'S COPING MECHANISMS

As children and adolescents we develop coping mechanisms. These are strategies we use to respond to our world—our external world of people and events, and our internal world of thoughts and feelings. We also respond to the consequences of our own behavior. Any strategy that helps us get through a moment of pain or difficulty is a successful coping mechanism. Children and adolescents create coping mechanisms out of the abilities and resources they have at the moment.

Point of Empowerment: *The coping mechanisms that we used as a child or an adolescent do not work for an adult.*

Point of Empowerment: *When used by an adult, the child's strategies result in creating the opposite of what we want.*

For example, children and adolescents use withdrawal or aggression as strategies. They get quiet, pout, and become silent, or they attack, physically or verbally. As an adult these two coping mechanisms are no longer an effective response to the world. Adults need to communicate, to express themselves to others. Some adults think that they will manipulate others through their withdrawal or aggression. Though this may seem to work in the moment, in the long run these manipulations do not get us what we want.

Other examples of a child's approach and the corresponding adult approach are:

Child's Approach	Adult's Approach
Helpless dependency	Constructive assertiveness
Submission	Constructive Self-expression, rebelling, constructive assertiveness
Conforming	Independent thinking and acting
Whining, crying	Constructive Self-expression
Spite	Constructive Self-expression
Withholding our Self	Self-expression and giving
Selfishness	Giving to our Self
Self-destructiveness	Constructive assertion of our power
Self-punishment	Constructive expression of anger
Withdrawal	Communication
Manipulation	Constructive action
Aggression	Constructive assertiveness
Self-blame	Assessing realistic responsibility
Self-numbing	Awareness
Self-criticism/Self-blaming	Self-acceptance
Denying responsibility	Accepting responsibility
Approval-seeking	Having confidence in our Self; knowing and acting on our values

As adults, we can see how the child's or adolescent's way of responding to and coping with the world needs to be revised.

Point of Empowerment: *As adults we have power and the ability to be Self-reliant in a way that we did not have as a child or an adolescent.*

Practice: *Identify some of the coping mechanisms that you used when you were a child or adolescent that you continue to use as an adult. Find the adult alternative and put that into practice.*

Senior (65–80 Years Old)

CONTINUE THE WORK OF THE ADULT: SELF-ESTEEM, SELF-ACTUALIZATION, HEALTH

As seniors we continue with the work of the adult, extending our abilities and capabilities, resolving issues, learning life lessons, and exploring the themes of life. We seek to accomplish the tasks of being seniors, and continue to fulfill our needs. We have learned, though we may not be aware of that learning, how to create Self-esteem. As seniors, we can focus more on actualizing our Self. We know our Self better than we ever have, though again, we may not be fully aware of this knowledge. We can increase our Self-knowledge and Self-awareness if we choose to. Hopefully we have learned many lessons about our Self and about life. We can transform what we have learned into wisdom about how the Self works, and about how life works.

As seniors, we seek to maintain our health: physical, mental, emotional, and spiritual. Keeping healthy involves moving: moving the body, mind, emotions, and spirit. We exercise, think, feel, and pray/visualize/experience God or Spirit, according to our beliefs.

DEEPEN AND ENRICH RELATIONSHIPS: BELONGING AND LOVING

We have experienced romantic relationships, family relationships, and friendships. We may have had close relationships with co-workers and colleagues. We may have participated in groups and organizations. As seniors we can use our experience, knowledge, and wisdom to deepen the relationships we value. We can enrich and expand our sense of belonging and loving.

> **Practice:** *Try on the idea that you are a member of the family of man, that you belong to the family of man. You can enjoy this sense of belonging.*

EXPANSION INTO NEW AREAS

Based on our accomplishments and successes, we have the opportunity to greatly extend our abilities, capabilities, and skills into new, exciting, and expansive activities.

We may:

- Engage in new work areas as an expert or as a beginner. We can look for opportunities to teach what we have learned in the workplace, becoming a consultant or volunteer.
- Find new and expand old pleasures, happiness, and joy. Examples are: traveling, developing creative abilities like painting or writing, gardening, enjoying nature, enjoying sex, exploring new foods, cooking, enjoying sports and being physically active, and seeing more movies. The opportunities are endless, if we seek them.
- Be a grandparent. If the opportunity isn't there right now, become a foster grandparent. Go to the playground and watch the children playing. Be energized by their play and the fun they are having.
- Explore all that the "New Age" has to offer. Take workshops. Read books. Practice yoga.

- Go into therapy, individual or group.
- Develop and strengthen important and necessary attitudes like Self-acceptance and Self-love, for example.

Point of Empowerment: Self-acceptance can bring you peace and the ability to love yourself.

Practice: Look back over your life. See that you could never, ever, have been different than you were in any particular moment in time. State the affirmation, "I accept who I was then, who I am now, and who I am becoming. I am—and am becoming more—Self-accepting."

COMPLETION OF UNFINISHED BUSINESS

Unfinished business refers to past painful experiences that continue to be with us, as they continue to have a "negative emotional charge." The pain of these experiences still exists within us and causes us physical, mental, and emotional distress. Examples of unfinished business usually begin with "I remember." For example, I remember:

- When my friend betrayed me by teasing me along with the other kids.
- When my father humiliated me by insulting me in front of relatives.
- When my wife/husband cheated on me.
- The shame I experienced when I was playing baseball, the team was depending on me, and I struck out.

Point of Empowerment: Everyone carries these memories around within their Self. As a senior, it is time to release and heal these painful memories and feelings.

Practice: Embark upon a personal healing quest to make peace with the past and to release painful emotions associated with the past. Become free.

EXPERIENCING LOSS

This stage of life (65–80 years old), being a senior, often contains many losses that a person needs to cope with. If we have not already experienced the death of our parents, this will most likely occur during this time period. There is also the death of other family members and friends.

There may also be the loss of one's health. Declining health can be devastating for an individual. The loss of health can be sudden or gradual. There may also be the loss of a person's standard of living. As this can be very hard to cope with, a person can become anxious and depressed.

A senior's coping ability may become extremely stressed. Feelings of grief and sadness from prior losses in life can become activated. We cope with loss and grief through the process of mourning. Mourning losses can be a process with a beginning, a middle, and an ending. However, multiple losses can severely tax a person's ability to complete the mourning process. Depression may occur. A person can be overwhelmed by sadness and grief.

Point of Empowerment: Along with support from loved ones, deepening your religion and spirituality can be a way of coping with loss.

Practice: Acknowledge the losses in your life. Look toward your religion and/or spirituality for comfort, support, strength, and inspiration.

BEAUTY, MYSTERY, THE TRANSCENDENT: RELIGION AND SPIRITUALITY, WISDOM

As seniors we can focus on fulfilling our need for beauty, mystery, and the transcendent. We can appreciate the beauty of nature, of art and architecture, of people and humanity. We can enjoy mystery stories and films. We can wonder about the mysteries of life and death. Seeking the transcendent involves deepening our experience of our religion and/or spirituality. Meditation can bring us experiences of the transcendent. We can develop transcendent humor. To do this, we recognize and appreciate the absurdity of life: that life is full of surprises, paradoxes, and contradictions, and often doesn't go the way we expect it to go.

As seniors we have a lifetime of experience and knowledge, even if we are not fully aware of these resources. We can remember, think about, feel, and assimilate and integrate our experiences and knowledge. We then create wisdom. We experience the limitations of being "older" (not old), yet at this stage of life we can have a wisdom that was not possible at a "younger" age.

ENDING SUFFERING

As seniors we do not have to be over focused on the past or the future. We can be in the moment, focused on the present. One of the many benefits of this is that we can end our suffering. We end our suffering by accepting what is in the moment. We end our suffering by letting go of anguish about the past and worry about the future.

> **Point of Empowerment:** *Suffering is caused by fighting what is in the present moment.*

> **Practice:** *Breathe in and out; relax. Say to your Self, "I accept all that is, in this present moment."*

LOOK TO THE FUTURE

A senior may say, "I have no future." This statement is deadly. It will literally kill you. Yes, the long-term future may look bleak, with declining health and death. One solution here is to look forward to the near future and make plans for pleasure and fun. Another approach is to investigate what dying is all about. Do we cease to exist or is there an afterlife? If there is an afterlife, what could that be like? Is there reincarnation? (Billions of people believe in reincarnation.) What could reincarnation be like? What do you want in your next life? Read about people's near-death experiences. Try a past-life regression.

CELEBRATE LIFE

We can acknowledge and celebrate our accomplishments in the areas of family, love, and work. We can "give our Self credit" for our achievements. Occasionally a person may see his Self as largely a failure in life. But everyone has some successes, and acknowledging them can provide momentum for moving forward. Sometimes, just putting one foot in front of the other is a triumph.

> *Practice: Focus on having fun, and on pleasure, happiness, and joy as your way of celebrating life.*

Elder (80+ Years Old)

THE WORK OF A SENIOR

As an elder we continue the work of the senior.

ELDER: THE BEST STAGE OF LIFE

Being an elder can potentially be the best stage of life. As an aspect of the developmental self, the elder stage can potentially be the culmination of the accomplishments of a lifetime. What does a person need to do throughout the life cycle to make this true? What does an elder have to do to make this the best stage of life?

> *Point of Empowerment: The tasks of making "being an elder" the best stage of life, and the tasks of making the most out of the life we live, are the same.*

Here are some of these tasks:

- Maintain our health
- Consciously grow, mature, develop, and evolve (physically, emotionally, mentally, and spiritually)
- Consciously seek to accomplish our tasks and fulfill our needs to our fullest potential
- Resolve our issues, learn life lessons, and explore the themes of life
- Continually push to expand our limitations, taking on challenges
- Love and have loving relationships
- Experience happiness, joy, pleasure, and gratitude
- Learn to tolerate pain and painful feelings
- Learn to hear the messages of our feelings
- Let go; seek closure, completion, and healing
- Connect to the divine with religion or some form of spirituality
- Cultivate wisdom
- Practice the challenge: Think about every thought. Seek to feel good all the time. Give and receive only love.

CONSCIOUS DYING

Today more people than ever are exploring the idea of conscious dying. (Of course, we cannot die consciously if we have not lived consciously.) Conscious dying involves maintaining awareness, alertness, and consciousness before, during, and after the death process. Some people are finding this an exciting prospect. There are certain assumptions here. One is that our consciousness continues to exist after life. You may not believe this, but it can be fun to explore the possibilities.

Practice: Be curious about the process of dying. Learn about dying as a way to overcome our natural fear of dying.

CHAPTER 12

THE EGO

Purpose and Abilities of the Ego

The ego uses its abilities to fulfill its purpose, its job, and its function. The abilities of the ego are to think, feel, perceive, make assessments, make decisions, take action, gather and transmit information, remember, and to be aware of itself.

PROTECTION AND SURVIVAL

One of the jobs (purposes) of the ego is to help fulfill the needs of survival and safety/security. It perceives threats to our well-being and takes actions to protect us. These actions are automatic, immediate, and impulsive, coming from our survival instincts. These actions can be effective, but lack sophistication and thoughtfulness. The ego's impulsive behavior can also be destructive if there is no input from the Self, as the Self needs extra time to think about the usefulness of our behavior.

THE SELF'S INTERFACE

Another purpose of the ego is to be the Self's interface with the external world outside of our Self, and the internal world inside our Self. We could say that the ego lives on the surfaces of our boundaries to the external world and to our internal world.[1]

---

1   There are also boundaries within our internal world that are hard to perceive. We perceive our internal life through our awareness of our

As the interface, it gathers and transmits information. The ego is like the operating system of a computer, its "Windows." The operating system takes in information from the computer's keyboard, mouse, and touch screen, and transmits information through the monitor.

When the ego takes in information from the outside world, it uses our sensory perception system of sight, hearing, touch, taste, and smell. The senses are the abilities of our sensory organs—the eyes, ears, skin, tongue, and nose. For example, our eyes have the ability of sight. The ego uses our senses and the organs of the body (especially the brain) to provide the Self with information.

> **Point of Empowerment:** *Since we rely on the ego for very important information, it is crucial that this information is accurate and undistorted.*

> **Practice:** *Try to notice when your ego is bringing you distorted information.*

> *(We will discuss why this happens.)*

FULFILLING NEEDS

The ego evaluates information from our external and internal worlds, to make sure that there is enough of what we need for survival and safety/security. It can get involved with fulfilling our other, more complex, needs, but fulfilling these needs is primarily the responsibility of the Self. Here the ego can "step on the toes" of the Self by taking over a job that does not belong to it.

---

thoughts and feelings.

FOLLOWING INSTRUCTIONS FROM THE SELF

The Self decides what action we need to take to fulfill our needs and desires, and to accomplish our goals and purposes. The ego then puts into action the behavior that the Self chooses. The ego then gathers information about how the world has responded to our behavior. This is feedback for the Self. The Self interprets the feedback from the external world, and decides upon the next course of action to take. The ego then acts upon these decisions.

The Self initiates action into the world. The ego is functioning properly when it follows the instructions of the Self without changing them. A person may say or do something, then say, "That did not come out right. It was not what I meant to say." Or, "That is not what I meant to do." Here the ego has changed the instructions from the Self. Almost always, these changes get us into trouble.

THE EGO IS ALIVE

Point of Empowerment: The ego is a very important part of our Self. It is always active and alive. It has thoughts and feelings.

Practice: Start to get to know your ego by learning what it does. See if you can hear its voice.

Ego and Developmental Self Are Similar and Different

The ego and the developmental self work closely together, "hand in glove," so to speak. It is often hard to see how they are different. The infant's and toddler's self and ego are very basic, and are almost the same. The child's self and ego are more developed. But again it is very hard to differentiate between the child's developmental self and the ego. The child and the ego both use many of the same strategies to cope with the world, and to fulfill the basic needs of survival and safety/security. An older child is developing more effective strategies for achieving belonging/loving and Self-esteem, for example. The child can give of himself or herself, while the ego is more concerned with "getting" for itself.

We can sense how the child and the ego are different. The ego can feel hard and mean, while the child can be selfish and aggressive. The ego reacts with fear to external threats, a fear generated by the needs of survival and safety/security. Children react with hurt, pain, and fear to external threats, but their fear is the fear of hurt and pain.

Over time the Self and the developmental self become very different from the ego. As we grow and develop, the Self/self becomes more complex, detailed, intricate, and complicated; it naturally has many aspects to it. The ego becomes more effective in fulfilling its functions and its purpose. It becomes a well-functioning part of the Self.

The ego is shallow and limited, living on the surface of the boundaries of the Self. The Self and the developmental self have depth. They are "large" and become larger as we grow, develop, and mature. Think of the ego as a rubber ball, and think of the Self/self as a brain, with all its convolutions, canyons, and crevices. The ego is like the moon, smaller and reflective of light, but important in its own way. The Self/self is like the sun—larger, shining, and giving off light.

Limitations of the Ego

The ego can be very effective at accomplishing its tasks, when it accepts the role it is supposed to play in our lives. Its abilities to think, feel, transmit information, and act need to be developed. The Self has abilities, capabilities, characteristics, and tasks that extend well beyond the ego. For example, consider the ability to love. Clearly the ego's ability to love is very limited. The Self's ability to love can be immense, almost unlimited.

The limitations of the ego are that it is automatic, reactive, and prone to impulsive action; its ability to perceive and to understand are also limited.

AUTOMATIC, REACTIVE, AND IMPULSIVE ACTIONS

The automatic, reactive, and impulsive actions of the ego that originate in our survival instincts, and our need for safety/security, are sometimes shortsighted. This shortsightedness occurs because the ego lacks the deeper thinking abilities of the Self. It may be successful in accomplishing the immediate purpose of Self-protection, but can create other problems in the process. For example, at nine years old we may think that being called a name is a threat to our safety/security and Self-esteem. To protect our Self and our Self-esteem, our ego starts a fight, hitting the kid calling us names. (Hopefully, at sixteen years old, we understand that hitting someone is not the best way of dealing with being called names.)

THE EGO'S TACTICS

The immature ego will use "less than admirable" tactics to get its way. One tactic is control and manipulation through using guilt, anger, helplessness, and inadequacy/inferiority. Using intimidation through threats and attacks, spite, arrogance, and superiority is another tactic. The immature ego will also lie and deceive. These are just a few examples of the ego's approach to life. On the other hand, the Self can be interested in the constructive use of personal power in order to accomplish its desires and goals.

> **Point of Empowerment:** *The ego uses less than admirable strategies to get what it wants. The Self uses constructive personal power as its strategy to fulfill desires, needs, and goals.*

Practice: Identify some of your ego's strategies. See how they often get you the opposite of what you want for your Self.

LIMITATIONS OF THE DEVELOPMENTAL SELF LIMIT THE EGO

The ego's behavior can be ineffective, as it is affected by the limitations of the developmental self. For example, as an adolescent, our adolescent self may feel that our survival is linked to our popularity. "If I am not popular, I will die." The adolescent's way to popularity is by making everyone happy, which of course is impossible. The ego takes the desire for popularity and acts in its own way to make us popular, no matter what the costs are, no matter who suffers in the process. The adolescent, due to his limited thought processes, and the ego, due to its immaturity, both have strategies that will be met with limited success. The adolescent is not capable of controlling or modifying the ego.

LIMITED PERCEPTION, LACK OF UNDERSTANDING

The ego thinks that the only thing that matters is what it perceives through the five senses, while the Self/self is attuned to the world of our feelings, which give us important messages about what is happening in our lives. Using its limited thinking ability, the ego draws many wrong conclusions about the events of our lives. The Self/self, however, uses its greater ability to think, feel, and process information to create understanding. The Self/self then utilizes its understanding to design its approach to the world.

Practice: Understand the limitations of the ego. Don't ask more of your ego than it is capable of accomplishing.

Distortions of Ego Functioning

There are a number of factors that distort ego functioning, making it less effective. A distortion occurs when a factor interferes with the ego's ability to do its job. The job is only partially accomplished, or the ego focuses on the wrong thing, the wrong issue.

Distortions of ego functioning are: perfectionism, ego defenses, wishful thinking, inaccurate and false beliefs, and hidden agendas.

PERFECTIONISM

Children utilize the strategy of perfectionism to cope with their world. For example, a parent may make excessive demands on a child that the child cannot live up to. The child does not know how to live up to these expectations. The child decides, "I will be perfect and therefore be able to fulfill my parent's expectations."

Like the child, the ego also uses perfectionism to deal with expectations, but then the ego applies it to many situations, inappropriately and destructively. If the Self does not help the ego to give up this strategy, the person holds on to perfectionism as an adolescent, a young adult, an adult, a senior, and an elder.

> *Point of Empowerment:* The demands for perfection distort the ego and make a person miserable.

> *Practice:* Are you perfectionistic in many or a few areas of your life? Does this strategy, this habit, cause you pain?

EGO DEFENSES

Protection against Internal Threats

The ego defends us against what it perceives to be threats—"external threats" from outside our Self/self, and "internal threats" from within our Self/self. The "fight or flight" reaction is the ego's response to someone or something that threatens our survival, safety/security, belonging/loving, or Self-esteem. We behave in an aggressive manner toward the threat, or leave the situation.

The ego uses what are called **"ego defenses"** to protect our Self from internal threats to our emotional and mental survival, our emotional and mental safety/security, our need for belonging/ loving, and our Self-esteem.

Internal threats are intensely aggressive and destructive thoughts, feelings, and wishes. For toddlers, children, and adolescents these defenses are necessary and appropriate because they are often the only way we know how to manage our emotions and our aggressive destructiveness. At times they are useful to us as young adults, adults, seniors, and elders.

> **Point of Empowerment:** *Ego defenses help toddlers, children, and adolescents manage and control their emotions and aggressive destructiveness.*

For example, as a child, an adolescent, or even as an adult, we may be feeling intensely angry at an important person in our life. We experience two kinds of threats. First, our feelings of love for this person are threatened by our anger. Secondly, we are afraid that this anger will cause us to behave in a manner that will alienate this person in some way. We fear that we will then lose this person, or lose what this person gives to us, or does for us. Our anger is a threat to our well-being. We fear our anger. Our ego responds with the defenses of denial and projection: "I am not angry at you." (Denial.) "You are the one angry at me." (Projection.) These statements are made consciously, semiconsciously, or unconsciously to our Self. They may or may not be said out loud to another person.

Denial Plus Another Defense

Our ego defenses begin with denial and then add a strategy, an action, to handle the reality we have denied. Denial says, "No, this isn't happening" to the internal threat. (We can deny the reality of external threats also.) But since the threat *is* happening, as part of our life, we must respond to it in some way. For example, we have denial plus:

- **Repression.** We push the reality into our unconscious mind. "I am not feeling guilty. But, since in reality I am, I push it down, bury it in my unconscious."
- **Projection.** We say that someone else has our reality. "I am not feeling angry. But, since in reality I am, I say that you are the one feeling angry."
- **Displacement.** We take our reality from one place and put it somewhere else. "I don't feel guilty about hurting you in some devastating way. But, since in reality I do, I tell my Self that I feel guilty about eating too much."
- **Substitution.** I tell my Self that my reality is not really "A" but is actually "B." I say that I am not angry but "upset." I say that I don't hate my sibling, but convince my Self that I really like him. I substitute liking for hating.
- **Rationalization.** We use our thinking ability to convince our Self that the denial is okay. "I didn't just lie to you. But since in reality I did, I tell my Self that it is okay because I am protecting you."
- **Rationalizing the denial.** "I did not just lie to my Self. But since in reality I did, I convince my Self that it is okay because I think I cannot face the reality and have to protect my Self."

Denial Diminishes Us

When we deny our reality, we diminish our Self. We are diminished because in denial we are making our Self and our life less than it is. We hide our feelings from our Self. We dim our awareness. We disown and lose parts of our Self. We lose the truth about our Self and our world. We lose trust in our Self, and we lose Self-confidence. We become less effective in our actions because we lose the valuable information that our perceptions contain.

> **Point of Empowerment:** *In order to recover our full Self, we need to stop using denial and ego defenses.*

> **Practice:** *Stop using your defenses by claiming your power. You are stronger than you think you are.*

Loss of Perceptions, Loss of the Truth

Once we, our ego, employ a defense, we start to fool our Self. We are denying the *truth* of what we think and feel. We will not be effective in dealing with our world, or our own responses to our world. We simply do not know what is happening. In our example, the child who is defending against his anger cannot deal effectively with what or who caused the anger.

The ego defenses keep our perception system from working accurately. Denial is a refusal to see or hear. "I want to believe that my friends are loyal to me, so I make myself blind and deaf to the fact that they gossip about me." I deny the reality of their disloyal, gossiping behavior. The ego is "deaf, dumb, and blind" to my friend's hurtful behavior. A desire to believe in the loyalty of my friends causes an ego distortion.

> **Point of Empowerment:** *As an adult most ego defenses no longer serve us. They diminish our effectiveness in life.*

> **Practice:** *See if you can identify an ego defense that is no longer useful. Allow your Self to experience the feeling that the defense is hiding.*

WISHFUL THINKING

Effective ego functioning can be distorted by "wishful thinking." We want something so much that we convince our Self that we are getting what we want, even though we are not.

Examples of wishful thinking are:

- "People like me." The truth is that people are tolerating your presence out of politeness.
- "I am popular." The truth is that having one friend is not being "popular."
- "People listen to me." The truth is that no one is listening. You are only hearing your Self talk.
- "My bad-luck gambling streak will end soon." Not really.
- "Eating this will not harm me," even though I am 350 pounds.
- "The doctor doesn't know what he's talking about. I can smoke," even though I have emphysema.

We do not perceive the world accurately. Again, the ego makes us "deaf, dumb, and blind." We pretend that things are or are not happening according to our wishes. We ignore the negative consequences of our behavior.

Point of Empowerment: The wishful thinking of children and adolescents is deadly for adults.

Practice: Are there situations where you are destroying your Self with wishful thinking?

INACCURATE, FALSE BELIEFS

Our beliefs about how the world operates instruct the ego as to how it should perceive the world. They restrict and color the information that the ego gives to us. Consider that once upon a time, people believed that the world was flat. They filtered out any information, which was brought to them by their ego, that contradicted this belief.

Remember—as a toddler, a child, and an adolescent our ability to think and to understand the world is limited. Inevitably, we develop inaccurate, false beliefs about our Self and about how the world operates. For example, a belief that I am unlovable, that no one could love me, will cause the ego to deny any perceptions to the contrary. And, as we deny perceptions that could challenge this belief about our Self, this belief is reinforced. We are stuck in a **vicious circle**.

I am unlovable. I deny perceptions that show that people love me, perceptions that would contradict my belief. In my denial, I am proven right. I am unlovable.

This repeats and repeats.

I am unlovable. I deny perceptions that show that people love me, perceptions that would contradict my belief. In my denial, I am proven right. I am unlovable.

> **Point of Empowerment:** *We can be stuck for a long time in a vicious circle where our false and hurtful beliefs about our Self keep the ego from bringing us perceptions that could change these beliefs.*
>
> **Practice:** *Try to identify some false beliefs about your Self that distort your ego's ability to perceive.*

HIDDEN AGENDAS

The Self may have a hidden agenda. There is something that we are trying to achieve, and we are hiding this fact from our Self or other people, or from both our Self and others. We then ask the ego to pretend, to lie for us. The ego cannot perform its normal functions of accurately bringing us information or truthfully carrying out the Self's wishes if it is pretending and lying.

A common example of a hidden agenda is when we give a gift with "strings attached." Our intention is to induce obligation in the other person. We fool the other person, and our Self, into thinking that we are being generous. We are denying the truth about our gift; our ego becomes distorted. If the other person believes in the generosity of our gift, their Self becomes distorted.

> **Point of Empowerment:** *The antidote to hidden agendas is honesty.*

> **Practice:** *Practice honesty.*

Misuse of the Ego

The ego has specific jobs/functions to accomplish. The Self/self may use the ego for purposes it is not designed to do.

The misuse of the ego occurs with excessive responsibilities and expectations, avoiding responsibility, and using the ego as a substitute for Self-esteem.

EXCESSIVE RESPONSIBILITIES, EXPECTATIONS, AND DEMANDS PLACED ON CHILDREN AND ADOLESCENTS

There are two situations that cause the child or adolescent, and the child's or adolescent's ego, great distress. One situation occurs when a child, or an adolescent, is given responsibilities that he is not prepared for, or that don't belong to him. This can happen when one or both of a child's parents do not fulfill their role properly, or are absent physically or emotionally. The parent is physically or mentally ill, or both. The parent has left the child through death, divorce, moving away, or mental illness. The parent is physically or emotionally absent and unavailable. Under these circumstances, the child or adolescent becomes a caretaker for other children, or for a parent, or for both. The child or adolescent is also his own caretaker, as there is no one taking care of him. We call this child a "parentified child." This situation requires that the child or adolescent takes on responsibilities that are a tremendous burden for him. The child is constantly asked to perform tasks he is not really able to accomplish.

The parentified child and the child's ego appear strong as they take care of others. However, underneath appearances, they are both very weak. Forced to grow up faster than they should, there is tremendous anger, resentment, and rage. There is guilt and shame. The child and the child's ego have been shamed.

The other situation that creates great distress for the child and the child's ego is when the expectations of, and the demands on, a child are too high, unrealistic, or perfectionistic. This results in a deep sense of inadequacy, shame, and feeling not good enough. The ego feels what the child feels, inadequacy and shame.

Since the child can barely cope with these two situations, he relies heavily on the ego, which has to deal with the outside world. The ego is forced to take on tasks and responsibilities, and to make decisions and choices, that it is not prepared or designed for. The ego feels a sense of inadequacy and shame. It feels rage. The ego has been misused, abused.

Point of Empowerment: Sometimes, in order to adapt to a situation that is beyond our control, we inadvertently misuse the ego.

AVOIDING RESPONSIBILITY

There are times when we say "I have to." Or "I can't." Or "I have no choice." We pretend that we truly do not have a choice, that we do not have alternatives. However, it is rarely true that we "have no choice." We almost always have a choice. The truth of the situation is that we do not want to take responsibility for our choices or our behavior. We seek to fool another person or our Self, or both, about the truth. We deny, and create rationalizations and justifications for, our behavior. For example:

- "I can't go out with you. My parents won't let me." Truth: I don't like you and don't want to be with you, but I lack the courage to tell you.
- "I can't go to the movies. My parents didn't give me money." Truth: I don't like the movie you chose, but I don't want to tell you that.
- "I can't leave my spouse because I don't have the money." Truth: I am terrified of leaving and of being alone.
- "I don't have a choice—I have to work at this job I hate, to support my family." Truth: I am afraid of change.
- "I couldn't do my homework. I had to babysit." Truth: I just didn't feel like doing my homework.
- "I forgot our anniversary because I was too busy at work." Truth: I don't really care.
- "It's not my fault that I burned our dinner. I was just watching TV." Truth: I was neglectful and don't want to admit it.
- "I can't do this by myself. Would you help me?" Truth: I don't want to make the effort to act independently.

These situations are so common, to all of us. The individual, the Self/self, is refusing to take responsibility for his or her decisions, choices, and behaviors. Since the ego interacts with the outside world, it then deals with these situations. It is forced to make decisions and choices, and take actions. It is forced to take responsibilities that belong to the Self/self. The ego resents this. If a person chronically avoids this kind of responsibility, the ego is being misused. The ego becomes angry at us, the Self. It turns against us.

Point of Empowerment: The ego resents being forced to take responsibilities that belong to the Self.

Practice: Develop courage and take responsibility for your life.

SUBSTITUTE FOR SELF-ESTEEM

People believe that they have to: "Bolster my ego." "Build my ego." "Satisfy my ego." "Feed my ego." "Stroke my ego." When asked why, their response is, "I do this to feel good about myself." What they are actually seeking is Self-esteem, the good feeling about one's Self.

The ego is not a source for our Self-esteem. This is a serious misuse of the ego, as it has its own functions. Self-esteem belongs to the Self/self. Remember, Self-esteem is obtained when we evaluate our own behavior; when we are pleased or satisfied, we give Self-esteem to our Self.

Some people spend endless hours trying to build the ego to obtain Self-esteem. Here the ego is like a balloon that constantly needs inflating because it is constantly losing air. We say, "A person is full of hot air." We sense what this person is trying to do. It doesn't feel good to us to be around a person who is trying to inflate his ego as a substitute for true Self-esteem. It feels like this person is ego inflating at our expense. When we make this mistake, it brings us constant pain and frustration, and is very Self-destructive. We will lack Self-esteem and suffer because of it.

Point of Empowerment: Pumping up the ego for Self-esteem is a mistake. Actually, proper use of the ego builds Self-esteem.

Practice: Identify actions that you take where you pump up your ego with the intention of creating Self-esteem. Learn the right way to build your Self-esteem.

Though we substitute ego inflation for Self-esteem out of a misunderstanding, it is still a misuse of the ego. The ego becomes resentful and angry at us, the Self/self.

The Malfunctioning of the Ego

If we do not respect the ego's limitations, it malfunctions. If we distort the ego, it malfunctions. And most seriously, if we misuse the ego, it malfunctions. The ego is unable to carry out its proper functions; it cannot do its job. But, worse than that, the ego turns negative and destructive. It "turns against the Self," becoming a source of our Self-destructiveness.

> **Point of Empowerment:** *A malfunctioning ego is negative and destructive. It will seek to destroy others, but primarily it will seek to destroy you, the Self, first.*

> **Practice:** *Consider and take in the idea that some of your Self-destructiveness or Self-neglect is caused by a malfunctioning ego.*

Self-destructiveness is a serious problem. A malfunctioning ego causes Self-destructiveness. Other sources of Self-destructiveness are: Self-hate; low Self-esteem and Self-worth; lack of genuine Self-love; Self-alienation; apathy; repressed pain, anger, and rage; spite; and laziness.

Grow, Develop, and Mature

As a part of the Self, the ego grows, develops, and matures. Remember our definitions: To grow is to become larger in size. To develop is to increase our ability, making it something that we can rely on and have confidence in. To mature is to age in a way that enhances who we are and increases what we are capable of achieving.

As we accomplish our tasks, fulfill our needs, resolve our issues, and explore life's themes, we use our ego.

Point of Empowerment: *As we use the ego properly, it naturally grows, develops, and matures.*

Practice: *Use your ego properly.*

Failure to Grow, Develop, and Mature

If the ego fails to grow, develop, and mature, we say that the ego has been "arrested in its development." If we push the ego beyond its limitations, do not correct its distortions, and misuse it, we will cause its growth, development, and maturing to stop or slow down. Our life stagnates. We will often fail to accomplish what we are trying to do. Under certain circumstances we can develop a mental illness.

The Ego and Spirituality

Many spiritual texts recommend "killing" or "eliminating" the ego. This is impossible. This idea is a misconception. The ego is a part of our Self. No part of the Self wants to die, or is willing to die. We are not interested in "Self-sacrifice." If we think we must "kill off the ego," or "become egoless," we create a war within our Self. This internal war will dramatically slow down our progress along a spiritual path.

The ego is a guardian of our boundaries. It is necessary for us to have boundaries. However, the ego can get carried away, being overly enthusiastic, and at times extreme, about our individuality. It can create rigid, closed boundaries. For example, it can become extremely possessive and guarded about "what is mine." "Mine" can be a constructive boundary. However, the ego is often fearful of losing what it has, and afraid that it will not have what it needs. The ego can hold the belief that "There is never enough." Here is where the ego needs to be reigned in, restrained, and educated by the Self.

If we are on a spiritual path, our goal is to help the ego accept its limitations and to be part of the system of the Self. The ego is an important member of the "team." We can help the ego to "transcend itself" by helping the ego to relax its own boundaries and its need for control.

Making the Best Use of Our Ego, a Healthy Ego

We will be making the best use of the ego if we do everything possible to facilitate its growth, development, and maturity. If we, as a Self/self, take responsibility for our life, the ego is happy. As we let go of perfectionism and hidden agendas, and correct false beliefs, the ego is strengthened. If we do not push the ego beyond its limits, the ego experiences comfort.

If we live with lies, we pass on a certain sickness to the ego. The ego feels like a child who has to keep family secrets and perpetuate family lies and cover-ups. It carries a painful burden. With lies, the ego is sick, weak, and ashamed.

> *Point of Empowerment: The ego thrives and is filled with life if:*
>
> *We live our life in truth.*
>
> *We live authentically, by acknowledging who we are.*
>
> *We live with integrity and therefore build our Self-esteem.*
>
> *We are honest with our Self by acknowledging our weaknesses and our strengths.*

CHAPTER 13

THE PERSONALITY

Our personality is part of our Self. It is important to learn about our personality because:

- We are born with a personality. If we know how our personality works, we can use it as a vast resource to enhance our life.
- Some of the resources that our personality offers us are the strengths, abilities, and talents that come naturally to us.
- We can identify and change some of the weaknesses of our personality. If we are feeling frustration and pain, it might be caused by an aspect of our personality. Because the aspect is part of our personality and therefore may not easily change, we can understand why we need to be patient with our Self and not be Self-critical.

Analogy: You as a House

Let's introduce a new concept here: "You." We will define You as the sum total of your being. A very useful analogy is to think of You "as a house." In dreams, a house is often a symbol for You or the Self. You are born with the foundation of your house already in place. The foundation of your house is made up of your: genetic structure, body, parts of the Self (personality, ego, and developmental self), and family, culture, and country. We include family, culture, and country as part of the foundation, because you will grow up in this environment from the start of your life. These social and cultural influences start to make their impression on You as an infant.

Your personality is an important part of the foundation and the framework of the house. The framework holds the plumbing and electrical wiring. (Pipes and wires are channels by which energy flows around your house.) After You attach the walls of the house to the framework, your house is ready to move into. Over time, You make your house distinctly your own with interior decorating and landscaping (conscience, identity, and image).

You Are Unique

There is no one, absolutely no one, who is exactly like You. Your personality is an important part of what makes You an absolutely unique person. You can see your uniqueness in your physical body. Your uniqueness is also expressed in your foibles,[1] quirks, idiosyncrasies, eccentricities, interests, problems, issues, and challenges.

> **Point of Empowerment:** *Your personality is one of the important factors that makes You an absolutely unique individual.*

> **Practice:** *Identify something that is unique about You. Appreciate your uniqueness.*

Nature or Nurture

There has been a debate in psychology about what is called "nature or nurture." "Nature" is what we are born with. "Nurture" is what we pick up from our parents and family during the course of our childhood experiences. In the past the debate has been either/

---

1   Definition: Foible—a minor weakness or failure in character.

or—nature or nurture. Currently, we think in terms of both/and—both nature and nurture. We are born with a personality. And, through the process of **identification**, we, as children, imitate, pick up, and make our own the personality characteristics of parents, family members, and other people who are important to us.

> *Point of Empowerment: Our personality is formed by nature and nurture.*

Changing Your Personality

You can change your personality. The part of your personality that comes from nature can be very challenging to change, but it is possible. The part that comes from nurture is easier to change. There are also parts of your personality that you must adapt to. They can seem to rule you and be next to impossible to change. Our temperament is an example of this. Certain traits that we possess, such as argumentativeness, or the tendency toward anxiety or depression, can dominate our personality, and be challenging to change. Adapting, which is accepting and working with these aspects of our personality, is a useful approach.

Aspects of Personality

CONSISTENT AND PERSISTENT

Your personality has many aspects that can last a lifetime. There are consistent and persistent thoughts, feelings, and behaviors that are part of your personality. Your personality consistently colors how you fulfill your roles (such as husband or wife). It pushes you to accomplish certain tasks and goals, and influences how you go about accomplishing them. It colors your moods and feelings.

Ask parents about how their children are different. They will describe the differences, and tell you that their child was this way from birth. "He was like that as a child." And, "He is still like that." These are statements about personality.

SIMPLE AND COMPLEX PERSONALITIES

There are simple and complex personalities. The motto of a simple personality is, "What you see is what you get." There is not too much hidden or buried. At the same time we could say, "Still waters run deep." A simple personality can be capable of great depth.

Complex personalities have many facets to their personality—many traits, quirks, idiosyncrasies, strong likes, strong dislikes, and opinions. Complex personalities have many issues to resolve. When you see an aspect of a complex personality, you are often looking at "the tip of the iceberg." Change for a complex personality can necessitate "melting much of the iceberg" and can take a long time. Often, many of the issues that a person with a complex personality has were caused by childhood trauma; therefore, complex personalities often have more challenging lives.

One personality type is not preferable to the other. They are just different. Also, there is a continuum from simple to complex— "degrees of complexity." People can also be simple in some areas of their personality and complex in other areas.

> *Point of Empowerment: Change for a complex personality can take a long time.*

> *Practice: In what areas of your personality are you simple and straightforward, and in what areas are you complex and complicated?*

APPROACH TO LIFE

Our approach to life is an aspect of our personality. Do we live life with gusto, or are we cautious and reticent? Do we forge ahead, sometimes without thinking, or are we careful and thoughtful? Do we tend to have confidence in our Self, or do we have insecurities and Self-doubts? Are we a "glass half-empty" or a "glass half-full" person? There are many variables that comprise our "approach to life," some of which we are born with.

ATTITUDES

Certain attitudes are part of one's personality. An attitude is a state of mind, or a feeling that is part of our approach to life. Attitudes are more limited than our general approach to life. We may have a belligerent and hostile attitude. We may be agreeable, cooperative, and desire to please. We may be rebellious and nonconforming. We may be compliant and seek to "blend in."

INTERESTS

Some of our interests are part of our personality. We are born with them. Other interests are stimulated by our family and other people in our life. You ask someone, "Why are you interested in that?" They cannot explain why. It comes from their personality. For example, some people are interested in history. Others could care less.

LIFE EVENTS

Our personality can start a chain of events. For example, a personality trait, like shyness, can cause conflict with others and influence the course of our life. "I was shy. My parents forced me to be social in ways that caused me constant anxiety. I rebelled, and had a lot of conflict with my parents. I left home at age 18, before I was really ready."

SUB-PERSONALITIES

We have sub-personalities. Sub-personalities are strong, repeating patterns of thinking, feeling, and behavior that occur as we respond to certain situations. For example, we may often react with anger, fear, or anxiety to certain situations. These situations may be: when we are a parent, when we face change, when we are being criticized, or when we are dealing with loss.

VULNERABILITIES

Our personality contains our vulnerabilities and our tendencies. For example, "My father and uncle were alcoholics. I have a vulnerability—a tendency toward becoming an alcoholic." Or, "Depression runs in my family. I get depressed." Vulnerabilities and tendencies are not guarantees that something will happen. Here nature and nurture both influence the outcome. In addition, personal choice is an important factor.

> **Point of Empowerment:** *If we recognize and acknowledge (see) our vulnerabilities or tendencies, we can take steps to prevent the development of unwanted situations.*

CHARACTER

Our personality, along with our conscience and developmental self, holds our values, principles, ethics, and ideals. These are the components of our character. What is our character like? How do we put it into practice in the living of our life? This is a very important question, because *every choice we make and every action we take expresses our character.*

> **Point of Empowerment:** *In formulating our Self-esteem, we evaluate our behavior, motivations, and attitudes according to the values, principles, ethics, and ideals of our character.*

> **Practice:** *Think about your character. Do you have a constructive character that helps you have good Self-esteem?*

Character and Anxiety/Depression

We tend to think that it is desirable to have a good character. Of course, being human, we have many "character flaws," like being rigidly idealistic or being opportunistic (i.e., without guiding values). Aside from questions of morality, there is a relationship between character and overwhelmingly intense feelings of anxiety and depression.

Someone who lacks character often has intense anxiety or depression, or both. Someone with intense anxiety or depression may have significant character flaws. This correlation is often overlooked. If we recognize and identify exactly how these two are related within us, we have a tool for change. We can solve some of our problems by focusing on both sides of the issue—character and anxiety/depression.

Practice: Identify a character flaw and see if you can identify the anxiety and/or depression that it causes. Observe your anxiety/depression and see if it arises out of a character flaw.

MATURITY

The rate at which we mature in life is a personality factor. Do we mature quickly or slowly, or extremely slowly? Remember that maturity is something we do not have control over. As adults we may recognize our immaturity. We can desire to become more mature, but this happens indirectly as the result of giving up childish reactions, and instituting more adult thinking and behaviors.

Practice: To mature, let go of childish personality characteristics. Focus on "acting your age" in the most constructive sense.

PERSONALITY TYPES

There are certain personality characteristics and traits that tend to come together. These tendencies define personality types. It can be interesting to explore one's personality by reading the descriptions of personality types that have been designed and researched.

TEMPERAMENT

Temperament is composed of certain personality characteristics that influence our thinking, feeling, and behaving. Temperament influences our reactions to certain situations. The discomfort caused by temperament can influence what we pursue in life and what we avoid. We are born with these patterns. They are "nature," not "nurture"; therefore, they persist throughout our life and are very difficult to change. The following characteristics of temperament have been identified by psychologists:

1. **Activity Level:** Tendencies to be more or less active.
2. **Distractibility:** Able to pay attention or be easily distracted.
3. **Intensity:** On the softer, milder, and relaxed side vs. intense, forceful, strong, and concentrated.
4. **Regularity:** Repeating, predictable, and consistent vs. irregular, unpredictable, and inconsistent.
5. **Persistence:** Once beginning an activity, how easily does a person give it up?
6. **Sensory Threshold:** Sensitive, reactive, and easily irritated by the environment vs. less sensitive, less reactive.
7. **Approach/Withdrawal:** Moving toward, or moving away, as a behavioral response to new or stressful situations.
8. **Adaptability:** Responding to transition and change with ease and comfort or with difficulty and discomfort.
9. **Mood:** Optimistic and lighthearted or pessimistic and serious.

If we understand our temperament, we can identify some of our strengths and weaknesses. We can make life easier for our

Self by anticipating situations that will cause us discomfort or anxiety, based on temperamental characteristics. For example:

- Our reluctance to travel may be a function of low adaptability.
- Our usual pessimistic response may be a function of our disposition toward pessimism.
- Our child can have difficulty in school because of distractibility.
- I may like to rest, since my activity level is low. My spouse may always be "on the go" since her activity level is high. We argue about how much we will do in a day.
- I like predictable situations. My spouse likes novelty and newness. We argue about what we will do together—new or routine activities.
- Loud noises cause my child irritation, which causes tantrums and other angry behavior. I get angry at my child for this behavior, and there is conflict between us.

There are children whose temperaments contain extreme versions of one or more of these variables. Hyperactive and distractible children are examples. They can be very difficult to raise. Medication and specialized approaches to managing their behavior are sometimes necessary. Some adults also have extreme versions of the aspects of temperament. It is important to recognize this, and adopt ways of coping with the problems that arise from temperament.

Point of Empowerment: Our temperament can make situations in life difficult for us to handle.

Practice: Identify some persistently difficult situations and consider whether or not your temperament makes it harder to handle these situations. Develop strategies to make life easier for your Self.

TRAITS

Your personality is a vast resource of traits. Three important questions to consider are:

- What traits of our personality can we put to good use to accomplish the tasks of our stage of the life cycle and to fulfill our needs?
- What traits of our personality are making it difficult for us to get what we want?
- How difficult is it going to be to change those traits?

EXPRESSING A TRAIT

Traits are aspects of our personality that are expressed through our behavior. As we express a trait through behavior, we experience our Self as having a trait. Reflecting upon our actions, we learn that we have a trait.

> *Point of Empowerment: As we express a trait in a number of different situations, we are getting to know our Self.*

> *Practice: "Know thy Self."*

USING TRAITS

Traits exist at opposite ends of a continuum. At either end of the continuum is "a lot of this trait, and none of its opposite." There is intensity. In the middle of the continuum are milder versions of each trait. The middle tends to hold a flexible use of each trait.

Trait A (Intense Version)	Trait A (Mild Version)	Trait B (Mild Version)	Trait B (Intense Version)

Available for our use are either ends of the continuum, or "the middle ground." One tendency that we have is to get stuck in an extreme end of the continuum, which causes us to refuse to use the opposite end of the continuum.

Consider, for example, the following traits:

Patient	Impatient	Remembering	Forgetting
Focused	Diffused	Agreeable	Disagreeable
Giving	Withholding	Impulsive	Deliberate
Unyielding	Flexible	Deliberate	Spontaneous
Thoughtful	Carefree	Adventurous	Cautious
Planned	Impulsive	Disciplined	Free-Flowing
Ordered	Disordered	Open	Closed
Inventive	Routine	Trusting	Skeptical
Loud	Quiet	Energetic	Calm
Extroverted	Introverted	Confident	Insecure
Intense	Relaxed	Letting Go	Holding On
Sensitive	Nonreactive	Bold	Subdued
Cooperative	Rebellious	Conforming	Non-conforming

In the living of life we are faced with many situations. To respond effectively, we need to be able to use any of the four possibilities: intense versions of trait A and trait B, or milder versions of trait A and trait B. We also need to have the *flexibility* to switch from one to another of the four choices. This makes us more adaptable to changing situations and gives us the ability to effectively respond to those situations.

For example:

- If we are skiing, we need to be intense and have *focused attention*. If we are watching a romantic comedy, we are relaxed and *diffused in our attention*. (Diffused attention opens us up to spontaneously playful reactions.)
- If we have been holding a grudge in anger, we need to *let go*. But if we are standing up for our principles, we need to *hold on*.
- In considering a vacation, we are *deliberate* with our plans. Once on vacation we can be *impulsive and spontaneous* at times.
- If we have been playing tennis for many years, we can be *confident* in our game. If we are just learning to play

tennis, we are naturally *insecure* about our game, which helps us be open to learning.

The yin-yang symbol is a fascinating way of visualizing traits. We can think of the outer circle as the context or situation, or set of circumstances. Each side within the circle is one end of the continuum that we can apply to a situation. The line down the center of the circle represents the middle of the continuum. We can easily move from one side to the other if we "live in the middle." Also, within each side is the potential for the other side. One side is not preferable to the other. Both are useful depending on the context, on the situation.

> *Point of Empowerment: We can also view the yin and yang circle as representing wholeness. As human beings, we desire wholeness and completeness, and are seeking to actualize all aspects of our Self.*

OVERUSING A TRAIT

Problems occur when we tend to always apply one trait, one side of the continuum, to all situations—when we lack the flexibility to switch between traits. For example:

- Our first response to something new being presented to us is always to be closed and to say "no." We do not open our Self up to what is new in our life.
- We keep our environment in a state of disorder. We refuse to make any effort to create order.
- We are always seeking order in everything we do. We can't tolerate disorder. We become anxious.
- Our activity level is always intense and focused. We can't relax and let go.

- We lack the ability to concentrate, as we can't effectively focus our attention.

USING THE WRONG TRAIT

Problems also occur when we apply the wrong trait to a situation. For example:

- Where we need to be open, we are closed; for example, when a friend is giving us negative feedback.
- Where we need to be withholding, we are giving; when our greedy, ungrateful sister is asking us for money and we can't say no.
- We create compulsive routines, and become bored because we cannot be inventive or spontaneous, or try something new.

Point of Empowerment: Deliberately using personality traits can make us very successful at achieving what we want in life, and can offer us enormous opportunities for change and growth.

Point of Empowerment: A personality trait can contribute to our failure to deal effectively with what life presents to us.

Practice: Identify a repeating situation in your life that causes you frustration and pain. See if a personality trait is involved. The opposite trait may be more useful.

Practice: Develop the ability to flexibly use both sides of the continuum of a set of traits.

CHANGING PERSONALITY TRAITS

1. The first step in changing a personality trait is to identify a situation that you are handling badly. We can do this by noticing the frustration and pain this situation generates. Situations that repeat themselves month after month

and year after year are situations where a personality trait is probably contributing to the difficulty we are having. For example, "I may tend to be mistrustful. My mistrust causes significant difficulty for me as I try to form intimate relationships. I have destroyed relationships by my inability to become intimate."

2. Identify the trait you want to change. "I want to change mistrust."

3. Next, identify the opposite trait in the continuum. "I want to be more trusting."

4. "Try this trait on" by imagining yourself using the trait. Does it "fit" well or poorly?

5. Is it "you" or "not you"? Stretch by imagining your Self succeeding in using your new trait. "I imagine my Self finding a trustworthy person and learning to trust him or her."

6. Put the new trait into practice. Act on it. You may meet with partial success, or you may face a real challenge. Keep trying. "I continue to work with trust in my relationships." See what issues or conflicts come up for you during this process of learning to use a new trait. What comes up for you (the issue) now becomes the focus of your attention. You are facing your resistance, what stops or slows you down, to incorporating a new trait into your personality. "When I start to trust, I feel fear and anxiety. I back away." (A parent may have frequently violated your trust.)

7. Work through your resistance. Answer the question, "What investments do I have in holding on to the old trait?" The old trait serves a purpose, has a benefit for us. Let go of that investment by finding a more constructive alternative that serves the same purpose. "By keeping me

from getting intimate, my mistrust protects me from hurt and rejection." New strategy: "If I am hurt or rejected, I will feel those feelings, and know that I can handle them by seeking support from friends whom I trust."

8. Return to putting the new trait into practice. Evaluate your success. Repeat steps 4–7, if necessary, until you are successful.

POSITIVE TRAITS

Remember the challenge for your growth: "Seek to feel good all the time." If we want to feel better on a daily basis, we can incorporate new, positive traits into our personality. We can practice using these traits each day. Traits like optimism, hopeful, happy, pleasant, generous, and caring are but a few examples.

> *Practice: You can put a positive trait into action by using the strategy outlined above. You could also try "faking it until you make it" as a temporary strategy. Deal with your resistance to being more positive by considering the investment you have in staying negative.*

RIGID OR FLEXIBLE

As we face the need to change or modify a personality trait, we face a continuum—rigid to flexible. There is a time and use for rigidity. If appropriate to the situation, this could be seen as "strength of character." Yet when a trait is not working for us, we need flexibility. We want change to be easy. We want to have the willingness and the ability to change.

In regards to personality, there are two causes for rigidity and inflexibility.

First, we can be born with a tendency toward rigidity. There is a rigidity of the personality that makes change difficult. Extreme rigidity is an aspect of what are called "Personality Disorders."

The other cause of dysfunctional rigidity in a personality is past or present trauma. As the result of trauma, a person seeks safety at all costs. He comes to believe that his safety lies in using rigidity to always keep everything in life "the same." Trauma causes a person to expect the worst. A traumatized person thinks that if he holds on to what he has at this moment, he can prevent the worst from happening. Since life is always changing, this strategy generates anxiety and fear of life.

Point of Empowerment: *Trauma creates rigidity in our personality. To obtain the flexibility that we need in our personality, we need to heal any traumas that we have experienced.*

Practice: *See if you can identify a trauma in your life that causes rigidity for you. Begin to consider ways of healing this trauma.*

Qualities

Qualities are things that do not exist in a continuum of opposites. They only exist by themselves. They are a "unity." They can't be divided, as they don't have an opposite. They are "pure." There is only more or less of a quality. We can speak of the "quantity" of a quality. Love is an example. If we say that "the opposite of love is hate," then we are talking about a trait or behavior. As a quality, there is only more or less love.

We can recognize the absence of a quality. We then give a name to the absence of a quality and place it on a continuum of opposites. As an example, consider the quality of patience. As a quality, there is patience or a lack of patience. When considering the trait or behavior of patience, we call the lack of patience, "impatience." As a trait, we have the continuum of patience . . . impatience.

As aspects of our personality, qualities are part of our "being." Remember, statements of being include: "I am . . ." For example: "I am helpful." "I am loving." "I am generous." Out of our being flows action, how we behave. If we are comfortable with the quality we are expressing, the action flows easily, effortlessly. If we have some inner conflict, some resistance to expressing the quality, our actions will reflect this. The ease will not be there.

Point of Empowerment: *As we think of the qualities we have, we can feel deep pride in our Self.*

USING QUALITIES

The word "quality" is useful because we can think of our personality, and our Self, as possessing or lacking a quality. Qualities exist as nouns and as verbs/adverbs. The nouns name a quality, the verbs are the expressions of a quality in action, and the adverbs describe a particular action. (This can be confusing, as the same word can be a noun or a verb/adverb, depending on the context.) Some examples:

Noun	Verb/Adverb
Love	Loving
Kindness	Kindly
Compassion	Compassionately
Enthusiasm	Enthusiastically
Trust	Trusting
Giving	Giving
Willingness	Willing
Hope	Hopefully
Helpfulness	Helpfully
Friendliness	Friendly
Generosity	Generously

As we are now, we possess certain qualities. On a daily basis we put these qualities into action.

Practice: Recognize some of the qualities you have as you put them into action. Experience the Self-esteem that comes with having positive qualities.

Practice: Put your good qualities into action, further building your Self-esteem.

DEVELOPING QUALITIES

To develop and incorporate (make a part of you) new qualities, we can:

- Identify a quality you possess. Work to increase the amount of that quality, "becoming more of who you are" as you do.
- Identify a new quality that you want to incorporate into your being, your personality. Use the affirmation "I am …" as you fill in the quality. Imagine a situation where you are expressing that quality. Put the quality into practice. Act on it.
- Identify the trait continuum that is derived from that quality. Incorporate the trait. Extrapolate the results to the quality. For example, if you find your Self being unreasonably impatient, seek to develop the opposite trait, patience. Then, seek to become—to be—patient, having the patience that is "beyond" the trait continuum of patience/impatience.

In this last approach we are identifying a trait and contrasting it with its opposite as a steppingstone toward identifying the quality. For example, words like hate, mean, cruel, or destructive are useful in pointing out the lack or absence of love. We then seek to adopt the quality of love.

Practice: Think about a situation that you want to handle differently. Identify a quality that would be useful. Imagine yourself using this quality. Put your imagination into action.

DISTORTIONS: TOO MUCH, TOO LITTLE, BALANCE

Distortions of a quality occur when we: take it too far; do not balance it with a different quality; or apply it indiscriminately without thinking about the appropriateness of the quality for the situation. If we are kind, we may be too gentle in a situation that demands firmness—when a child needs discipline instead of nurturing, for example. If we are always giving to our child or spouse out of generosity, we may be encouraging a lack of appreciation in the other person. If we are too agreeable, we cannot say "no" in situations where we need to protect our Self.

There are times when we do not have enough of a quality to make an impact on our Self, on a situation, or on another person. We need to increase the quantity of the quality to make a difference. For example, if we have something important to say and others are not listening, we may need more confidence in the importance of what we have to say. This confidence will enable us to speak in a louder, more forceful voice, hopefully allowing us to make an impact.

Practice: Are there distortions to your good qualities?

HIGHEST FORM OF ACTION, OF GROWTH

The distinction between a trait and a quality can be hard to see. We could say we use traits, but become or "are" qualities. We reach the ultimate form of our human potential when we say: "I am love," "I am kindness," "I am fairness," "I am generosity." We merge our being with the quality. Incorporating new qualities into our being, into who "I am," is the highest form of growth.

Point of Empowerment: Our actions flow easily, spontaneously, effectively, appropriately, and joyfully when we express the qualities of love as who we are.

Using Your Personality

We can use our personality to make our life better, more enjoyable, and more fulfilling. Here are some suggestions:

- Understand what your personality consists of. You can't use your personality without knowing what it is.
- Eliminate negative traits and create positive traits. Put the new traits into action.
- Eliminate negative, ineffective attitudes. Cultivate positive attitudes.
- Incorporate new qualities. Increase the quantity of the qualities you have. Become more effective at using these qualities.
- Make life easier by changing the aspects of your personality that make your life hard.
- Remember that our temperament and inborn aspects of our personality can be changed, but are harder to change. Understanding this will make you less frustrated with yourself.
- Identify where you are making things in your life more complex or more complicated, because of a complex personality or complex personality aspect. Complex personalities have complex lives, but there can be opportunities to make things simpler.
- It is useful to recognize if and when we are being immature. Though we can't directly change our maturity level, we can focus on being more effective at accomplishing the tasks of our life stage by working with our personality. As we become more effective in an area of our life, our maturity level will increase.
- Put the challenge to give and receive only love into practice. Include more loving attitudes, traits, and qualities in

your personality. As you incorporate loving aspects into your personality, you will spontaneously and automatically act in more loving ways.

CHAPTER 14

THE CONSCIENCE

In this chapter we will explore the human conscience, including the:

- Purpose and Nature of the Conscience
- Components of the Conscience
- Formation of the Conscience
- Limitations of the Conscience
- Malfunctions of the Conscience
- True Conscience
- New Conscience

There exists what could be called a traditional, basic conscience and a "true" conscience. Humanity has had the traditional, basic conscience for hundreds, maybe thousands, of years. It is created in a "traditional manner."

The "true" conscience exists along with the basic conscience, but it is hard to see, as it has not been clearly defined. We seek to define it clearly, and therefore, to activate it more consistently. We will also explore some ideas that could lead to the creation of an even more effective, better-functioning, loving, and supportive conscience—what we can call "The New Conscience."

Purpose and Nature of the Conscience
COMPONENT OF THE SELF

The conscience is a part of the Self. It is an absolutely necessary and indispensable component of the Self. We need a healthy, functional conscience, as knowledge about what is right and wrong is a necessary part of living. Our conscience makes demands of us, and guides and instructs us. It is also there for us to consult, to ask it questions.

In addition to the external world of the people we interact with, we have an internal world of thoughts and feelings. We want to have harmony in our internal world. In order to accomplish this, we need our conscience to tell us what thoughts and feelings are good and healthy for us ("right") and which are destructive ("wrong").

GROWTH, DEVELOPMENT, AND MATURING

The conscience grows, develops, and matures throughout the life span. The conscience of the toddler, child, and young adolescent tells the child directly what he should or shouldn't do, what the right thing to do is, and also what the wrong thing is—what not to do. For an older adolescent and young adult, the conscience has grown, developed, and matured to some degree, so that it is beginning to function more as a guide and instructor. It instructs, advises, teaches, guides, and recommends, along with making demands. Ideally, the conscience reaches maturity as we become adults, so that the demanding role of the conscience is minimal. As seniors or elders, we know and do "the right thing" naturally and spontaneously, as a result of the wisdom we have acquired.

> **Point of Empowerment:** *The mature conscience shows us what is right and wrong. It does not tell us what to do. Since we have free will and therefore choice, we take responsibility for our behavior.*

RIGHT AND WRONG

We come upon an interesting issue here. People do not agree upon what is right and what is wrong behavior. For example, there are situations where people feel it is not only permissible, but necessary, to kill another person. The fact that killing another human being is prohibited by most, if not all, of the religions of the world doesn't seem to matter. Individuals decide for themselves when killing another human being is "the right thing to do." We look to our conscience to advise us on this matter. We see that what is in the conscience, in terms of what is right and wrong, is variable.

The variation in our conscience is due to the fact that various points of view are represented in an individual's conscience. These points of view come from: an individual's society and culture, a person's family, groups that an individual belongs to, and one's country. We add our ideas about what is right and wrong, and assemble all these points of view into the unique blend of ideas that forms our conscience.

Point of Empowerment: Is "right" and "wrong" merely seen from one's point of view, or is there some standard of ethics that transcends what people think?

Practice: This is a question for you to think about. As we explore the conscience, you may have some ideas about how to answer this question.

In our discussion of conscience, we refer to "doing the right thing." What is the right thing? Ultimately, this is for each person to decide for his or her Self.

HUMAN NATURE

We make assumptions about the nature of human beings. (They are assumptions or opinions, because no one really knows what human nature is.) Many people believe that human beings are inherently evil by nature. Therefore, they must be controlled with a strong and strict conscience. If you believe that human beings are inherently good and loving by nature, you will have different ideas about what a healthy, functional conscience is. As we explore the conscience, you will have more information about the formation and role of the conscience, and therefore about the nature of human beings.

Components of the Conscience

TRADITIONAL, BASIC CONSCIENCE

The components of the traditional, basic conscience are: fear of punishment; the fear of experiencing guilt, shame, and humiliation; and the fear of deprivation (that we will not be rewarded for good deeds). This conscience also contains instruction (verbal instruction), training (rewards and punishments), and learning (behavior modeled for us by our role models) about what constitutes acceptable behavior. We learn which behavior we should feel guilt and shame about. The instruction, training, and learning become "rules for behavior." If we break these rules, our conscience punishes us with guilt, shame, humiliation, or fear (or all of these).

TRUE CONSCIENCE

> *Point of Empowerment:* The components of the true conscience are: remorse and sorrow, ideals, and a deep inner knowing of what is right and what is wrong. These components are provided to us by the wise part of You.[1] This deep inner knowing speaks to us as "the still, small voice."

---

1 Remember, we have defined "You" as the sum total of your being.

Formation of the Conscience

REWARDS AND PUNISHMENTS

The conscience is formed during the socialization process. The socialization process occurs when parents and other authority figures teach children how to function and how to fit into their society. Children must learn this in order to survive and to succeed in their culture. Children learn what is acceptable and "correct" behavior through what is called "discipline," the giving of rewards and punishments. Rewards and punishments "shape," influence, and determine behavior. Good behavior is rewarded. Bad behavior is punished. Rewards for good behavior are: praise, approval and love, privileges, money, and various kinds of gifts.

Punishment can include: corporal punishment (hitting a child), isolation ("Go to your room"), restricting a child's freedom of movement ("Sit in the time-out chair"), and depriving a child. Deprivation could include such statements as: "No TV or electronics of any kind, no friends, no fun." "We are going to withhold—deprive you of—love and approval." Verbal punishments involve instilling guilt and shame in a child, and occasionally humiliation. Additionally, there is the threat of all the above. This threat creates fear, which also becomes part of the conscience.

There can be appropriate use of punishments. They motivate good behavior to some degree, or at least compliance with parental wishes. It seems that there are some children who only respond to punishment. There is also the misuse of punishment, which is excessive and inappropriate punishment. No TV for three months for hitting your sister is excessive. Punishing a child for poor grades in school when the child has truly done the best he can do is inappropriate.

Why do children put up with all this punishment? They are dependent, and have no choice. The anger, hate, and rage that a child feels when he is punished, justly or unjustly, has to be squashed and buried, repressed. These feelings cannot be expressed for fear of punishment. The child may not even want to experience these feelings because they can feel overwhelming and frightening. Once children are older, more independent, and can "fight back," they will rebel against punishments. This can happen openly or covertly, in some hidden manner.

IDENTIFICATION

Children go through a complex process called **identification**. In identification children and adolescents (and sometimes adults) seek to, and actually do, become like another person, mostly like a parent. There can be conscious imitation: "I want to be like my mother or father when I grow up." "I want to be like my favorite rock star." However, most often, identification is an unconscious molding of the Self to be like another. Children identify with their parents because they love and fear their parents. Identification is a method of learning that helps children live and function in their world.

Identification is very useful for the child, the parent, and society. In becoming like a parent, the child adopts the behavioral standards that the parent holds. The child then rewards and punishes himself. The parent, or parental substitutes, no longer have to reward or punish the child. The conscience is forming.

> *Point of Empowerment: As adolescents, young adults, and adults, we continue to reward and punish our Self as our parents did; we are Self-rewarding and Self-punishing.*

> *Point of Empowerment: Self-punishment is a destructive process.*

> *Practice: Identify where you punish your Self. Stop!*

Identification with the Aggressor

Children experience being punished as aggression, an attack, and experience the punishing parent or teacher as an aggressor. They react with hurt, anger, fear, hate, and rage. As we said, these feelings are often overwhelming and frightening. The child denies the feelings ("I don't feel this way") and represses them (buries them in the unconscious). At the same time, the child is identifying, becoming like, the authority figures in her life. The child or adolescent becomes like the punishing parent or authority figure. This process is called identification with the aggressor.

Through identification with the aggressor, the child or adolescent feels powerful, like a parent or an authority figure. Instead of experiencing painful and terrifying emotions, like powerlessness, the child feels empowered and in control. In addition, as a punishing aggressor, the child feels justified in being aggressive, mean, and cruel toward others.

Our conscience is often harsh, mean, and cruel to us. We "beat our Self up." We often become a punishing aggressor toward our Self. We do to our Self what others have done to us.

> *Point of Empowerment:* The reason that our conscience is, at times, harsh and brutal toward us is because our conscience is partly formed by the process of identification with the aggressor.

> *Point of Empowerment:* As adults, we need to end Self-aggression and Self-punishment.

> *Practice:* Seek to soften your conscience by identifying with a "soft" mentor—someone you like who is easy on his or her Self.

Rebellion against Authority

As a formative process for the conscience, identification with the aggressor is limited at best. Even though it produces good behavior, there is ambivalence about "being good," and there is often a hidden wish to rebel by "breaking the rules." As an adolescent, young adult, or adult, we may blindly and compulsively rebel against authority. We "break the rules" just for the sake of breaking the rules. Sometimes our rebellion is based on ethics, morals, and principles. Often it is merely for the sake of rebelling. This kind of blind rebellion has many destructive consequences.

Consider the following examples. Rebellion can take the form of Self-destructive behavior. "If you (an authority figure) say you want what is good for me, I will rebel, and do what is bad for me." This statement can be made to our real parents or teachers, or to the imaginary parents or teachers who live "inside our heads." Spite, or depriving one's Self of something beneficial, can be another example of blind rebellion against an authority figure. We may "give the boss a hard time" for the pleasure of rebelling. We may refuse to learn something that is beneficial for us out of rebellion against a teacher's authority.

Displaced Aggression

As children, adolescents, young adults, or adults, we can feel beaten up by our parents or by other people in our life. We can feel beaten up by our own conscience. To lessen the pain of this feeling, we "beat up" someone else. This is called displaced aggression. "Beating up" can be physical abuse, but most often is verbal abuse. Here the strategy is, "I was beaten up, so I will beat you up, and then I won't feel so bad." This is one motivation for bullying in schools. Another example of displaced aggression is being abusive toward one's spouse.

THE PARENT'S CONSCIENCE

Through the process of unconscious identification, the child adopts, internalizes, and makes his own the healthy and functional aspects of the parent's conscience. At the same time, unhealthy and dysfunctional aspects of the parent's conscience are taken in. This is how a large portion of the conscience is formed.

As adults, we can discover, often to our amazement and displeasure, that "I sound like my mother or father." Or, "I did just what my parents did."[2] This is what the process of identification results in. (Also, as parents, we will parent and raise our children almost exactly the same way we were parented, unless we made a decision to behave differently.)

> *Point of Empowerment: For better or for worse, part of your conscience is composed of part of your parents' conscience.*

> *Practice: Sort out the healthy and unhealthy parts of your conscience that come from your parents.*

A Functional but Limited Conscience

Most human beings have a functional, but limited, conscience. Our conscience keeps us on the "straight and narrow." But there are serious limitations to the way our conscience functions. We often pay an unnecessarily high price for obeying our conscience. In the language of psychoanalysis, the conscience is called the superego. The purpose of the superego is to control the ego and the id. The id is the wild, primitive, destructive part of our Self that is considered to be extremely dangerous.[3] The instrument of the superego is guilt.

---

2   Sometimes we choose to do the opposite of what our parents did. This is often a compulsive choice, and therefore not a free choice. "I *must* do it this way" is not freedom.

3   The id lives in our reptilian brain, the primitive part of our brain.

GUILT

Guilt has been the foundation of a traditional conscience for many hundreds, perhaps thousands, of years. The message of guilt is, "You have done something wrong and you must condemn yourself for it." Guilt is a painful feeling. Our Self-condemnation causes the pain of guilt. We seek to avoid guilt's pain. If we violate the rules of our conscience, we feel guilty. In order to avoid guilt, we will "do the right thing," obey the rules, comply, and conform. We use the phrase "I beat my Self up." "I beat my Self up" is the conscious thought that accompanies inflicting guilt upon our Self. We are punishing our Self with guilt. Many people believe that guilt serves a useful purpose, and therefore we must have guilt.

Real and False Guilt

The proponents of guilt ("We must have guilt") contend that we would not have a conscience without guilt. To understand some important distinctions about guilt, let's say that there is real and false guilt. Real guilt is useful and appropriate—for example, "The punishment fits the crime." Real guilt sets boundaries and limits for many individuals' behavior. The consciousness of many people operates mainly with rewards and punishment, with guilt.

False guilt is extremely common in our everyday experience. False guilt is exaggerated guilt, guilt that is not appropriately proportional to the severity of a misdeed. Since we cannot know the "right amount of guilt," we tend to employ more guilt than necessary "to be on the safe side," to guarantee that we "keep our Self in line." "I am my own worst critic/enemy" is a common phrase that refers to exaggerated guilt. At times we may actually use exaggerated guilt as a cover-up for appropriate, genuine guilt. We feel very guilty over something minor ("I forgot to call you on your birthday") while we ignore our real guilt ("I have betrayed you by gossiping about you to others"). Or, we feel very guilty over a minor character flaw ("I am often late") while ignoring our real guilt ("I am frequently dishonest").

False guilt is inappropriate guilt, the feeling that we have done something wrong when we truly have not, and do not deserve to feel guilty. Let's say, for example, I am tired and want to stay at home while my friend wants to go out. Our desires conflict, a common and inevitable situation in life. She tells me that I have "hurt her feelings." I feel "bad," guilty that I have hurt her feelings, while in reality, I have asserted my right to have my own desires. I cannot recognize the inappropriateness of my guilt and cannot reason my way out of it. With inappropriate guilt, we cannot know whether or not we are doing "the right thing." The guilt confuses us. It does not provide a useful guideline for behavior, which is what our conscience should do for us. Inappropriate guilt is a daily experience for all of us.

> *Point of Empowerment: Guilt is not a reliable indicator of right and wrong. We need a replacement for guilt. Fortunately, as we will see, there are replacements for guilt.*

Resentment, Paralysis

Guilt automatically generates resentment. We resent being made to feel bad. We resent the punishment that guilt is. We resent Self-inflicted pain. We resent the pain inflicted upon us by other people, who manipulate us with guilt. Yet we are often vulnerable to being manipulated by the use of guilt. We can feel hate and rage about this manipulation.

There is often a feeling of being trapped by one's guilt. Guilt can paralyze us. In addition, no one likes being told what to do. This includes being told what to do by our guilty conscience. At a deep level within us, our guilty conscience does not feel like our Self. It feels like an "alien invader."

JUSTIFICATION, GOODNESS

We "misbehave" and make our Self "okay" with what we did. We create justifications for our behavior with "reasons why" (rationalizations). Human beings can justify any behavior they want to. We need to justify our behavior to feel that our behavior is "just." This points to the idea that we have a deep inner knowing of what is right and wrong, and that we cannot really do something wrong without our true conscience "nagging at us." We say, "My conscience is nagging at me." We are being asked to listen to "the still, small voice" inside.

Our need to justify our behavior can be very powerful. In the absence of a plausible justification for our actions, a person becomes depressed and Self-hating.

> **Point of Empowerment:** *At the core of our being, we need to feel that our behavior is just.*

> **Practice:** *Consider this question: Does the need for justifications (justice) point to the fact that humans are essentially good, and that behaving destructively triggers our true conscience to make itself known to us, to "nag us"?*

DOING THE RIGHT THING BRINGS LITTLE PLEASURE

We are often complying with the dictates of our conscience out of fear of punishment, fear of guilt, shame, and humiliation, and fear of deprivation of rewards. We do the right thing but get very little pleasure out of it. How can you feel pleasure or satisfaction when you act out of fear? You can't.

> **Point of Empowerment:** *We want and deserve to get pleasure—to deeply feel good about our Self, when we do the right thing.*

Malfunctioning Conscience

We have discussed the limits of the basic conscience. Beyond being limited, the basic conscience makes us vulnerable to the ravages of an extreme conscience, and to a conscience that destroys our Self-esteem.

HARSHNESS, BRUTALITY

The conscience that most human beings have is overly harsh at times. Some people have a malfunctioning conscience that is constantly and/or brutally harsh. The voice of the harsh conscience is full of guilt, shame, humiliation, and fear. It says:

- You can't do anything right.
- Why can't you do anything right? (This question is a hidden attack. It contains an assumption, a belief: "You can't do anything right.")
- You are an idiot.
- You are stupid.
- You are worthless.
- You are never good enough.
- There is something wrong with you.
- What is wrong with you? (Assumption: "There is something wrong with you.")
- You should be ashamed of yourself.
- What you have done is a great crime.
- You need to feel immense guilt about your behavior.
- You deserve punishment.
- You deserve to die.
- You don't deserve to live.
- You can't rest until you have atoned for your sins.
- Punish yourself.
- You are the devil himself.

As we have said, the conscience punishes us if we have done something wrong. A harsh, brutal conscience leads to harsh or brutal Self-punishment. A brutal conscience can kill you or drive you to kill yourself, either slowly or quickly, through suicide. It can crush you by overwhelming you with guilt.

A constant, unrelentingly brutal conscience can result in severe mental illness. It can cause drug abuse and alcoholism. It can trigger violence in a person. "Instead of beating myself, destroying myself, I will beat and destroy you."

In general, most people are excessively Self-critical. Rather than face the pain of this Self-criticism, we deny it, and project this criticalness onto others. We say, or yell, in anger at the other person, "You are so critical of me!" While this may be true, it is more important to say, "I am too critical of my Self; I now stop."

Point of Empowerment: A harsh conscience is an inevitable side effect of the way we currently form our conscience.

Practice: Instead of harsh Self-criticism, have compassion for your Self.

DESTRUCTION OF SELF-ESTEEM

Point of Empowerment: An overly harsh conscience destroys our Self-esteem. If we are overly or brutally Self-critical, we cannot feel good about our Self.

Practice: Notice how the criticism of your conscience diminishes your Self-esteem.

Remember, the process of establishing Self-esteem is that we evaluate our behavior, motivation, and attitudes according to the values, ethics, principles, and ideals we hold for our Self. As a shortcut, let's call our values, ethics, principles, and ideals the "standards we hold for our Self." If we live up to our standards, we give Self-esteem to our Self. Some of the standards set for us by our conscience are unrealistic, impossible to live up to, and demand that we be perfect. We fail to give Self-esteem to our Self because we cannot live up to these standards.

For example, if I set the standard for my Self that I will *always* "Do the best that I can," I will not have Self-esteem because this standard is impossible to live up to. We cannot always do our best. Sometimes we do and sometimes we do not. A more realistic standard is, "I will decide when I want to do the best that I can according to what a situation presents to me. Sometimes I will decide to do the best I can; sometimes I will do something less. And I will be okay with my decisions." Here we are setting the kind of workable standard for our Self that will generate Self-esteem.

Point of Empowerment: My ability to have Self-esteem is tied to having the reasonable standards of a healthy conscience.

Practice: Identify an overly harsh standard or demand of your conscience. Think about how it robs you of Self-esteem.

The True Conscience

REMORSE AND SORROW

The true conscience has remorse and sorrow as a part of it. We apologize, saying, "I am sorry that I did that to you." If it is sincere, an apology of this kind is an expression of remorse and sorrow. **Remorse** contains regret and anguish about the negative impact that our behavior has had on another person. **Sorrow** feels for and with the other person, and acknowledges the hurt or pain that we have caused in some way. Remorse and sorrow are healthy, functional feelings that communicate to us that we have done something wrong. We should not be afraid of feeling remorse and sorrow. They are cleansing emotions. We actually feel better after feeling remorse and sorrow about our behavior. (This is a very different experience than feeling guilty.) If we need to change our behavior, and take action accordingly, we feel very good about our Self.

> **Point of Empowerment:** *Remorse and sorrow are messages from our true conscience.*

> **Point of Empowerment:** *Empathy is the skill that enables us to feel remorse and sorrow. Empathy is feeling for and with another person. It includes having, or developing, some understanding of what another person is experiencing.*

> **Practice:** *Learn and practice the skill of empathy.*

THE WISE YOU

Another component of the true conscience is the wise You. How do we know that there is a wise part of you? Have you ever given advice to someone who didn't know the right thing to do? On occasion, when you did, you may have been surprised and amazed at how great the advice was, how wise it was. You had experienced, and expressed, your own deep inner wisdom. The wise place in us has an intuitive knowledge about what is right and what is wrong.

> **Point of Empowerment:** *All human beings have a place, deep within their being, that knows what the right thing to do is in every situation.*

> **Practice:** *State to your Self, "I now wish to experience the wise place within me." See how you respond to this request. Give your Self some time makes ideals into, a few days, to experiment with this.*

When the wise You is functioning as your conscience, it whispers its suggestions to you. This is the "still, small voice" whispering to you. It never shouts or dictates. Since it is whispering in a soft voice, the trick is to hear it. We want to hear it because it always has our best interests at heart. We have to be open to the idea that it exists, and make an effort to listen to it.

> *Point of Empowerment: The still, small voice loves us, and always has our best interests at heart.*

> *Practice: Try listening to and acting on the still, small voice. See what the results are. See if you feel loved.*

IDEALS

The other aspect of the true conscience is our ideals. Ideals are paths of thinking, feeling, and acting that bring us to a better place. They are paths because we actively walk along them. Honesty, goodness, love, generosity, caring, integrity, and empathy are some examples of ideals. (They are the qualities we discussed when we talked about personality.) We strive to put our ideals into action. *We don't expect our Self to achieve the ideals, but to become a better person as we reach for them.* We are not seeking to be perfect. As we strive to put our ideals into practice, we feel good about our Self. We are doing the right thing and feeling good about it.

> *Point of Empowerment: Ideals provide inspiration for taking action.*

> *Point of Empowerment: If our intention is to act only according to an ideal, we feel good about our Self because we have no hidden agenda.*

> *Practice: Try to put an ideal into practice and see how you feel about your Self. You could practice the ideal of "giving and receiving only love."*

Distorted Ideals, Practical Reality

Blind idealism is a distortion, a misuse of ideals. Blind idealism—following ideals without question—make ideals into dictators. Blind idealism ignores practical reality. We need to also consider practical reality when we chart a course of action for our Self.

People also use ideals to justify destructive behavior.

In Summary

We need to use our true conscience along with the traditional, basic conscience. Otherwise, our conscience can easily malfunction.

We can see that our conscience is partly effective in doing its job. It informs us about right and wrong, but it also inflicts unnecessary pain and suffering upon us. As we observe the behavior of human beings, we can conclude that humanity's conscience has limited effectiveness, and, at times, is an abysmal failure.

> *Point of Empowerment: Humanity needs a new conscience.*

The New Conscience

Let us consider what our new conscience would consist of. The new conscience is based on the best in You.

> *Point of Empowerment: The new conscience makes it possible to feel really good about doing the right thing.*

THE TRUE CONSCIENCE

The new conscience includes and builds upon the true conscience. Remorse and sorrow, ideals, and the "still, small voice" of the wise You currently function as a very healthy conscience.

SELF-ESTEEM

As we have discussed, there is a close relationship between Self-esteem and the conscience. When we follow the realistic standards and positive/constructive behaviors suggested to us by a healthy conscience, we build our Self-esteem. This feels good.

- Positive/constructive behavior generates good Self-esteem. Good Self-esteem generates positive/constructive behavior. Positive/constructive behavior generates good Self-esteem. This is a positive/constructive circle.
- Negative/destructive behavior generates low Self-esteem. Low Self-esteem generates negative/destructive behavior. Negative/destructive behavior generates low Self-esteem. This is a negative/destructive circle.

The negative/destructive circle is a vicious circle. A person can get caught in this loop and have great difficulty breaking out of it. A way of breaking this vicious circle is to behave better, give your Self credit for this behavior, and allow it to build your Self-esteem. Another way out is to understand how Self-esteem is obtained, and to intentionally seek to build Self-esteem.

Point of Empowerment: When we do the right thing, we want to experience good feelings. Good Self-esteem feels really good.

Practice: Choose a "do the right thing" action. As you take this action, notice how your conscience is helping you build your Self-esteem and feel good.

Self-esteem is a part of the new conscience.

DIGNITY

Human beings have dignity. Like Self-worth, dignity is a given. It is given to us when we are born. It is present within us, no questions asked. It is a guarantee. But we have to act on dignity to experience it. Dignity is a form of healthy pride combined with Self-respect. It flows out of a sense of valuing our Self and out of our Self-value.[4]

How does dignity enhance our conscience? Dignity advises us about right and wrong behavior. Dignity says, "I will not lower myself to do that." "I will not do that; it is not me, not who I am." "I will not retaliate against this person who hurt me. If I do, then I am not serving my best interests." We refrain from behavior that diminishes our dignity.

> **Point of Empowerment:** *When we act in a genuinely dignified manner, we experience our dignity.*

> **Practice:** *Choose a "do the right thing" action that flows out of your dignity. Feel the pleasure of dignity as you follow through with your action.*

Dignity is part of the new conscience.

LOVE

Remember the challenge for our growth: "Give and receive only love." This is a wonderful guideline for our conscience to adopt and follow. We can adopt "give and receive only love" as a way of life. We are not talking about becoming blindly idealistic. We balance our ideals with practical realism. Along with loving another person, we love our Self. This adds balance to our loving.

When we use love as a guideline for behavior, there will be moments when we will not know what the loving thing to do is. We can ask our wise part, "What would love do in this situation?" We then listen to the still, small voice for an answer. We may need to find a quiet place to listen to our inner voice. Meditation can help.

---

4   Self-value is my Self-esteem, Self-worth, Self-love, and Self-respect.

Point of Empowerment: As we do the right thing—act according to love—we feel great.

Practice: Try it!

Love is a part of the new conscience.

SELF-ACCEPTANCE

Self-acceptance is an extremely useful attitude to include in our conscience. It is an attitude toward our Self that expresses the following: "I am a fallible human being. I am imperfect and make mistakes. *And this is okay.* I won't criticize my Self or beat my Self up for what I do wrong. I accept my Self in this moment exactly as I am." Contrast Self-acceptance with the Self-condemnation of guilt. Which feels better?

Strictly speaking, Self-acceptance is not a component of the conscience. The value in adopting Self-acceptance as an attitude toward our Self is that it makes it easier:

- To look at our Self and our behavior
- To recognize when our behavior, thoughts, and feelings are negative and destructive
- To hear what our conscience is telling us
- To take responsibility for what our conscience is telling us
- To learn from our mistakes
- To change our negative and destructive behaviors

Self-acceptance is part of the new conscience.

THE OLD CONSCIENCE AND THE NEW CONSCIENCE

The old conscience will be with us for a while. It still serves a purpose. Many people predominantly respond to fear, guilt, shame, humiliation, and punishment. Many societies have strict and extensive rules for behavior, rules that are enforced by controlling individuals with the feelings mentioned above.

In order for humanity to have the new conscience, parents need to learn how to teach it to their children. Parents can begin by using the components of the new conscience themselves, and teaching their children by example.

Point of Empowerment: *To create the new conscience for our future, we must learn what it is.*

Practice: *Put the new conscience into practice and feel good as you do the right thing.*

CHAPTER 15

INTRODUCTION: THE SIGNIFICANCE OF IDENTITY AND IMAGE

Let's briefly consider some ideas about identity and image to get a feel for their significance:

My future is created by my destiny.

My destiny is created by what I think, feel, and do.

What I think, feel, and do is created by "who I am."

"Who I am" is my identity and image.

My future and my destiny are created by my identity and image.

Point of Empowerment: *As aspects of our Self, our identity and image create our future and our destiny.*

Statements of "I am" are statements of identity and image. These statements give rise to very significant, even crucial, aspects of a person's life.

- "Since I am a member of the Schwartz family, I am a Democrat."
- "Since I am a doctor, I am a Republican."
- "Since I am a member of the middle class, I value education and go to college."
- "Since I am a poor student, I got a low grade on my exam."
- "Since I am an unfaithful spouse, I just met the person I plan to have an affair with."

These "I am" statements of identity and image generate thoughts, feelings, choices, decisions, beliefs, attitudes, desires, expectations, and actions. In other words, aspects of being human—the tools that we use to create our lives.

Point of Empowerment: Identity and image shape the tools that we use to create our lives.

Consider these powerful "who I am" statements and notice their impact:

- "Shame is part of who I am. I feel ashamed of my Self."
- "Pride is part of who I am. I feel proud of my Self."
- "Being successful is part of who I am. I feel happy with my Self."
- "Anger is a part of who I am. I feel angry all the time."
- "Confidence is a part of who I am. I usually feel Self-confident."
- "Fear is a part of who I am. I am often afraid. I am afraid to live life."

Point of Empowerment: Aspects of our Self-image determine how we feel about our Self and how we live life.

CHAPTER 16

IDENTITY

The Formation of Identity

IDENTIFICATION

We build an identity through the process of identification.
Identification is the process of building and defining our Self by
becoming like another person. When we identify with a person,
we seek to be like him or her. The first people we identify with are
our parents. We imitate them. We copy what they do, sometimes
consciously and by choice, but mostly unconsciously, automatically, without thinking. We think, feel, and do what they think,
feel, and do—not absolutely exactly, but with great similarity.
We model our Self after who they are.

We may also identify with other family members—grandparents, siblings, aunts, uncles, and cousins.

As we grow and our world extends beyond our family, there are
other people with whom we identify. Teachers, other students, and
friends become sources of identification. Bosses, mentors, movie
and TV stars, athletes, and rock stars all become role models to
identify with.

On occasion we may say, "Wow, I admire that person; I will
be like them. I will imitate them, do what they do." This is a conscious identification. Most of the time the identification process
of forming an identity is done automatically, without thinking
or awareness. It is invisible.

THE ELEMENTS OF IDENTITY

There are numerous aspects of, and sources for, an identity.

- My stage of life: Toddler, child, adolescent, young adult, adult, senior, or elder.
- The roles I play in life: Son, daughter, brother, sister, parent, husband, wife, in-law, parent, grandparent, aunt, uncle, cousin, friend, student, worker, boss, doctor, lawyer, and any other career role I might take on.
- As a member of a specific family.
- My religious and ethnic life as a: Protestant, Jew, Muslim, Hindu, or other religious or ethnic group I may belong to.
- As a citizen of: The United States, Canada, France, Iran, China, Japan, or any country I might live in.
- In any activity I might do: Walk, run, talk, laugh, cry, paint, throw a ball, eat, or sleep.

Here are examples of what I think, feel, and do based on these sources.

- "As a child, I will play all day."
- "As a student, I will hardly study at all."
- "We Smiths don't accomplish much in life."
- "We Silvers succeed at everything we do."
- "We De Marcos are smart."
- "We Trumps are shrewd businessmen."
- "We Ryans barely make it in this world."
- "As a tennis player, I try hard, but don't win any matches."
- "I am a strict Catholic, Jew, or Protestant."
- "I am a relaxed Muslim."
- "As an emotional person like my mother, I cry easily."
- "As a man, I am tough and strong like my father."
- "I am like my sister/brother: a picky eater, poor sleeper, excellent golfer, clumsy dancer."
- "Like my grandfather, I hardly ever laugh."

These are all statements of identity: "who I am, what I think, what I feel, what I do." They are all based on being like others.

Point of Empowerment: *Through the process of identification, we are creating "I am" statements and systems of thought, feeling, and behavior. The process of identification is all-encompassing, and continues throughout our life.*

We can also identify with an idea or a set of ideas. "I am a capitalist, communist, socialist, libertarian, or conservative." We can identify with a mode of being and acting in the world. For example: a free thinker, nonconformist, rebel, independent, lover, hater, stalker, seeker, or fool.

MANY IDENTITIES, NATURAL CONTRADICTIONS

We see that we have many identities. The more identities we allow our Self to have, the more complex we become as people. Our complexity brings us richness. At the same time, we don't want to experience our Self in a fragmented way. We want to "make sense of" and have some "logical coherence to" the wholeness of our identity. We want to experience a consistent sense of Self. However, as we look at all the possibilities for our identity, we see that it is inevitable that we have contradictions in it. Some examples of the contradictions we have in our identity could be:

- "At work, as a supervisor, I am assertive and in charge. At home, as a spouse, I often just follow along."
- "In school, as a student, I am an independent thinker. When I talk to my father, as a son, I defer to his opinions."
- "As a sports fan I am wildly enthusiastic, but you will never get me on a dance floor. As a dancer I am totally inhibited."

These are just a few examples. However, if we see that we are different in different situations and contexts, we can relax and accept the variety of who we are. We need to recognize that experiencing contradictions in our identity is natural, inevitable, and even desirable if we are to become all that we can potentially be. By using the different aspects of our Self in a variety of identities, we Self-actualize.

The best way to achieve a consistent and coherent sense of our Self is to see that the personality, ego, and conscience tend to be stable and consistent. We can then allow our identities to be free to form and to reform themselves.

> **Point of Empowerment:** *If we can allow our identity to be flexible and free, we will be able to reach our full potential as people—to realize, make real, our Self.*

> **Practice:** *Consider an aspect of your identity. See if you are rigidly keeping it the same (as it has always been) and therefore limiting your Self-development.*

AN IDENTITY OF "THE OPPOSITE"

We have said that the process of identification is becoming like another person, most often like our parents. However, we may decide to be or to become the opposite of our parents. Out of anger at them for some kind of mistreatment, neglect, or abuse, or for another reason, we decide to do the exact opposite of what they did. Or, we may have a personality trait that lends itself to rebelling and being nonconforming, so we decide to "do the opposite."

- "My parents were strict disciplinarians. I will be relaxed and permissive as a parent."
- "My parents worked hard all the time, and were never home. I will not work hard. I will take it easy."
- "My parents were very religious and tried to force me to be religious. I will not have any religion."

- "My parents never enjoyed themselves. I will indulge myself."
- "My mother was depressed and lethargic. I will never rest, and will always be active."
- "My father was very conservative in his politics. I will be very radical in mine."
- "My father was withdrawn from the family. I will always be engaged."

As you read these statements, you may recognize how they express extremes. Being locked into an extreme (taking the "always" position) creates rigidity and limitation.

Here the process of identifying our Self as the opposite of a parent limits our freedom and traps us into repetitive, thoughtless behavior. In discussing personality we saw how certain traits are at the ends of a continuum. Always adopting the opposite end of the continuum from our parents limits our choices. In truth, life presents us with a wide variety of situations. We need to be able to flexibly choose our response from all the possible responses available to us.

> **Point of Empowerment:** *We have created some identities in opposition to our parents. If these identities contain rigid ways of thinking, feeling, and acting, we are doing our Self a disservice.*

> **Practice:** *See if you have created some rigid "I will be the opposite" identities. Think about how they have limited your choices in life.*

SELF-IDENTIFICATION

Since we are saying that our identity is constantly active, alive, and always influencing what we think, feel, and do, we must ask our Self this question: What part, aspect, of my Self am I identifying with at this moment in time? Who am I?

- "I am my ego. As my ego I will be judgmental."
- "I am my nine-year-old inner child, not the thirty-five-year-old adult I actually am. I am going to have a tantrum."
- "I am my adolescent self, who is feeling deprived, not the twenty-five-year-old adult I actually am. I am going to overeat."
- "I never got over being rejected as a teen. Even though I am a forty-year-old adult, I will try to please everyone so as not to get rejected again." I am identifying with my teenage self. I am seeing my Self as a teenager.
- "I was often punished as a child. Even though I am forty-five years old, I refuse to have any Self-discipline." I am identifying with my inner child, and acting as if I were that age.
- "Being a thirty-two-year-old parent, I speak to my child's teacher about his uncooperative behavior. I automatically take my child's side without knowing all the details of the conflict." I am identifying with my own inner child, and acting as though this is who I am.

In most of these examples, the older me is identifying with the younger me. I am being my younger, less mature, less capable part of my Self. I am thinking, feeling, and acting as though I were that part. This is an internal identification, an identification with a part of my Self that is from the past. Everyone does this from time to time. Some people live their entire life as though they were a part of their Self from the past. If we are identifying our Self as a child or an adolescent, we are denying our Self the use of our current abilities, skills, and power. We can see how dysfunctional this is, as it destroys our ability to act effectively in our life.

Point of Empowerment: To empower our Self, we will identify our Self with the strong, positive parts of our Self.

Practice: Notice how the disempowering aspects of your Self weaken you. Withdraw your identification by no longer considering them as "Who I am now."

UNRESOLVED ISSUES, UNFINISHED BUSINESS

In the above statements under Self-Identification, we can see that there is an unresolved issue. We will never get to resolve an issue if we identify our Self as the part that is having the issue. We need to see (identify and identify with) other aspects of our Self. If we are an adult or older, we need to state, "I am an adult, and I claim all the power that I have available to me now." We can then use our power and our skill to resolve past issues.

We don't want to limit our identity. We don't want to see our Self as our negative ego, or fearful child, or rebellious adolescent, or insecure young adult, or associate it with any other negative, inadequate parts of our Self.[1]

Point of Empowerment: We will never get to resolve an issue if we identify our Self as the part that is having the issue.

Practice: Allow unwanted parts of your Self to fade into the background of your life after you have resolved the issues attached to those parts.

LEARNING AS IDENTIFICATION

Students say, "I like or don't like this teacher." Students do better with and learn more from teachers they like. Students, and adults, identify with someone they like. Identification is a process of opening up. Refusing to identify is a process of

---

1   These parts of the Self are called the **Lower Self.**

closing down. If students like a teacher, they identify with him; they open up to him. They take in the teacher's ideas, and make them part of their Self. This is learning through the process of identification.

Frustration Tolerance, Delay of Gratification, Self-Discipline

As a toddler, child, or adolescent we acquire certain abilities and strengths through identification with our parents. Three essential life skills that are almost entirely learned through identification are: the ability to handle frustration, the ability to delay gratification, and the ability to have Self-discipline. These skills are essential for success in life.

If there is a serious parental deficiency—if the parents lack the ability to handle frustration, delay gratification, and have Self-discipline—there is little to identify with. If there is neglect or abuse by a parent, there will be interference with the identification process. If a child or adolescent is excessively rebellious and nonconforming, constructive identification with a parent is disrupted. Under these circumstances, a child or adolescent will not learn, or not fully learn, these three essential life skills.

> **Point of Empowerment:** *The ability to handle frustration, delay gratification, and to have Self-discipline is initially learned by identification with one's parents.*

> **Practice:** *Give some thought to this question: Where have you diminished your abilities, your Self, by refusing to identify/learn these three essential skills for succeeding in life?*

We now understand what our identity is and how it is formed through the process of identification. Let's get excited and take the next, very important, step.

Creating and Expanding Our Identity Consciously, by Choice

The identifications we made growing up have been necessary for us, serving as a foundation and a preparation for engaging in life. We have seen how identification is part of the process of learning. If we are to expand our abilities and continually learn through our life, we need to form new identities through new identifications. If we insist on holding on to old identities and old identifications that no longer enhance our life, that do not expand our abilities and allow us to continually learn, adapt, and change, we limit our Self-development.

> *Point of Empowerment: Growth involves expanding and changing our identity through the process of making new identifications.*

IDENTIFICATIONS WITH PARENTS

We have identified with our parents. We need to be willing and able to think about and evaluate the effectiveness of our identifications with our parents. We may resist this. We may think, "I am like my parents, and this is only good," or "It was good enough for my parents, so it is good enough for me." Or we may think that we are different from our parents, and that this is only good. In truth, we are like our parents in positive and negative ways, and different from our parents in positive and negative ways. Positive ways are approaches to life that get us what we want. Negative ways are approaches to life that do not get us what we want.

> *Point of Empowerment: Our identifications with our parents can enhance our life and can also detract and diminish our life.*

> *Practice: Give some thought to how you are like your parents and different from your parents. Consider how your identifications with them have made your life more or less fulfilling.*

CREATING NEW IDENTIFICATIONS

As we become aware of how old identifications limit us, we can decide to make new identifications and to create new aspects for our identity. We want our new identifications/identities to liberate us, empower us, and enable us to be effective in living our life.

LETTING GO OF AN OLD IDENTIFICATION, CREATING A NEW IDENTITY

- Get a clear picture of an old identity and the identification that formed it. Write it down.
- What is limiting about it? Write the answer down.
- State the affirmation, "I no longer have . . . (a thought, feeling, or behavior) as part of who I am, as part of my identity."
- Formulate an idea of what you want your new identity to be. Choose new: role models, teachers, mentors, ideas, beliefs, attitudes, or approaches to life.
- Sense the resistance that frequently arises to fight your new identity. Talk to your resistance, helping it dissolve.
- If you are working with a mentor or teacher, understand who that person is by learning about how he or she thinks, feels, and acts.
- State the affirmation, "I now make . . . (a thought, feeling, or behavior) part of my new identity."
- Imagine situations that could come up where you will act on your new identity.
- Put your new identity into action as a situation arises, or create an opportunity to practice your new identity.
- If you notice your Self thinking, feeling, or acting as the old identity, say, "No, this is no longer me." Act upon the thinking, feeling, or behavior that your new identity suggests.

Changing an aspect of our identity will be easier if it is simple and was formed with a straightforward identification. Changing an aspect of our identity can be an extensive process if the identity/identification is complicated and involves a lot of strong feelings.

To illustrate the process, let's consider a simple identity change:

- When I play tennis, I do not play as well as I know I can.
- My father told me that I should play for fun and not worry about getting better. As I identify with my father, I accepted his idea about how I should play tennis.
- I want to improve my game.
- I decide to create a new identity for my Self as a person who is continually improving his tennis game.
- "You could become obsessed with tennis; stay as you are." (My resistance.) "No, I will keep my life in balance, with tennis occupying an appropriate place." (Affirmation to respond to my resistance.)
- I take a tennis lesson from a pro I like and admire. I follow her instructions and talk to her about her approach to tennis. I understand what she thinks, feels, and does.
- I sit comfortably and imagine myself improving my game and playing better. I state, "I am a person who continually improves his tennis game."
- I put my new identity as a tennis player into action, in a real game. I know, and believe within my Self, that I am acting on my new identity as a continually improving tennis player. If my old identity pops up, I say to myself, "No, that is no longer me. I am a person who continually improves his tennis game."

Through this example, we can see how this process can work. Here are a few examples of identities that can enhance our life. They inspire us to become more of who we can be.

- I am a student who gets grades that I can be proud of.
- I do my best in situations that are important to me.
- I am effective in managing my money.
- I am a good mother, father, sister, brother, son, or daughter.
- I am a loving spouse.
- I am excited about life.
- I increase my awareness of my feelings.
- I think with clarity.
- I am a person who allows change into my life.
- I am a person who allows my identity to be free, to change, and to enrich my life.

Point of Empowerment: *To be whoever you want to be, to do whatever you want to do, and to have whatever you want to have, start by changing aspects of your identity.*

Practice: *As you work with changing aspects of your identity, modify the process so that it works best for you.*

CHAPTER 17

IMAGE

Images of the Self

An image is a picture we create for our Self. An image can be an actual scene, like a photo, or it can resemble the pictures we see in a night dream or daydream. "Image" can also mean "a collection of thoughts, feelings, attitudes, beliefs, decisions, memories, and expectations for the future, that we collect, put together, and assemble into a meaningful whole, a **gestalt**."[1] This collection has been gathered and assembled by our thinking and our imagination. **Identity** answers the questions "Who am I?" and "What should I think, feel, and do?" **Image** answers the questions, "Who do I imagine myself to be?" and "How do I see my Self?" Our mind (the conscious, subconscious, and unconscious mind) holds the images of our Self.

> *Point of Empowerment: Our images are very powerful influences on our behavior. To change your behavior, change your image. If you try out a new behavior, it must become part of your image in order to be permanent.*

---

1   In the language of psychoanalytic object relations, an image is called an "object." In the language of cognitive psychology, an image is called a "schema."

We are discussing images that belong to the Self, that are part of our Self-definition. We are not referring to a single "Self-image." Self-image has been thought of as "beliefs about one's Self." Our definition of image is more complex than a single statement of belief.

An image takes the form of "me and ____." We fill in the blank, which is some aspect of our life.

Me and success	Me and love
Me and fun	Me and my ability to think and feel
Me and my mother	Me and my father
Me and my family	Me and my ability to act effectively
Me and my role as a father	Me and my ability to be honest
Me and athletics	Me and marriage
Me and my body	Me and my spouse
Me and books	Me and having what I want
Me and God	Me and my boss
Me and my computer	Me and my car
Me and authority	Me and my clothing
Me and my sports equipment	Me and my hair

As with identities, we have an almost unlimited numbers of images. The sum total of our images is our Self-image. It is not possible to work with our Self-image; rather, we work with our individual images.

It has been said that a picture is worth a thousand words. Our images can be very complex. It might take a thousand words to describe a complex image. Despite their complexity, it only takes a fraction of a second for an image to have an impact on us. As a component of the Self, images help determine the way we think, feel, and act in any given moment of time.

An Example of an Image

Let's take a look at an example of an image to get a better understanding of what an image contains. The best way to get at the content of an image is to free associate,[2] freely writing down whatever you are thinking and feeling. Free association is just letting go, letting thoughts pop into your mind, and tuning into whatever feelings come up. We do not judge or evaluate, we just write down. Free associating—writing down an image—may take some practice. As we relax our control of our thoughts and feelings, we may feel afraid of what emerges.

MY IMAGE OF SUCCESS: ME AND SUCCESS

Sample free associations:

- Success isn't all it's cracked up to be.
- You work hard and you die, just like my father did. He didn't get much out of working hard.
- My mother didn't seem to appreciate him. But he did seem to enjoy his work.
- Others will be jealous of your intelligence and will attack you. Hold yourself back and keep quiet. Limit your success.
- Children are to be seen and not heard; it's best for them to be quiet in meetings, and with others.
- Be invisible; it's safe.
- Success exposes you.
- Don't let your full abilities be seen. Others will be jealous and envious. Don't upset people.
- About your career, it's better to be a big fish in a little pond instead of being a little fish in a big pond.
- This is what my sixth-grade teacher told me. I liked him. I guess he gave me good advice.
- The pond is my world.

---

2   Images are formed by association and explored by free association. Free association is the technique that psychoanalysis uses to explore the Self.

- How does a big fish in a little pond behave?
- I stand out. This is dangerous.
- But, I have my limits. I limit my success.
- One limitation is my rebellion, my outspokenness.
- But I find myself often outspoken and in rebellion against authority.
- Why kill yourself (work hard) if you will be unappreciated?
- Helping people is more important than making money.
- It's wrong to want money.
- I want enough money to be comfortable in life.
- I want to succeed.
- I will succeed, I guess.

An image contains thoughts, feelings, beliefs, attitudes, decisions, and memories. It also contains projections and expectations for the future. It also contains projections and expectations, which originate in the past but have powerful implications for the present and the future.

The above image would cause a person to limit his development, limit his abilities, and limit the degree of success that he would allow himself to achieve. After becoming aware of the contents of this image, the next step is to change limiting beliefs, attitudes, decisions, memories, and influences into expansive ones that facilitate greater, and even explosive, success.

Point of Empowerment: When we write out an image, we can see all its details—where it came from, and how it has influenced us. This influence can be profound and extensive.

Not all images are complex or profound. The following is an example of a simple image.

Free Associations: Me and Tennis

- I love tennis.
- But, I suck at tennis. No doubt about it.

- I will never improve.
- Why bother?

CORE BELIEFS

Profound images contain our primary (core) beliefs about our Self and about life. Core beliefs give rise to secondary beliefs, which guide all our actions. Core beliefs can be deeply buried in our subconscious minds. Some core beliefs are fundamental decisions about what our future should be. They form a plan, a blueprint, for our future.

ESSENCE OF AN IMAGE

Even though images are usually complex, with many different aspects, there can be an essence, a theme, to the image. The image can be expressed in one sentence that expresses the essence of the image.

Image	Essence
Me and Self-esteem.	"I have low Self-esteem."
Me and my role as a father.	"I strive to be the best father I can be."
Me and God.	"We have a close relationship."
Me and my ability to be honest.	"I try to be honest, but I tell many 'white lies.'"
Me and success.	"I try, but do not seem to succeed."
Me and having what I want.	"No matter what I do, I will not get what I want."

FORMATION OF AN IMAGE

Our experiences give rise to our images, but not directly. Images are formed by:

- The meaning we give to the experience: "I got punished. This means that I am a bad boy."
- Our interpretation of the experience: "I made a mistake. This shows how incompetent I am."
- What others say to us about the experience: "That was so terrible, what my friends said when my parents wouldn't let me stay out past curfew. Since it wasn't a big deal to me, I felt (am) confused."
- What we say to our Self about the experience: "That was the worst thing in the world. My parents took away the comfort blanket I had since I was three years old. I am nine years old. I am weak and vulnerable."
- The story we tell, to our Self and to others, about the experience: "Let me tell you what happened. My boyfriend hit me and I couldn't do anything to protect myself. I am a helpless victim."
- The conclusions that we draw from our experience: "I (at fifteen years old) felt devastated when my girlfriend cheated on me. You can't trust girls. I will never trust a girl again. I am mistrustful."
- The projections we make about the future, based on a difficult experience: "My pet died. I was so sad. I will never get another pet. I would be devastated by another loss."

For an experience to lead to an image, it needs to have great impact or significance, or it needs to be repetitive. Singular, unimportant events and experiences do not lead to the formation of an image.

Assembling an Image

As we live our life, we generate bits and pieces of information: our thoughts, feelings, memories, and the stories we tell about our experiences. Our thinking and our imagination assemble all the bits and pieces of information into a coherent whole in the form of "Me and ____." This is the image. The assembly process involves associating (connecting) whatever seems relevant. Associating is like gluing something together. The pieces become attached to each other. *This is not a logical process.* Things that are "next to each other in time," happening simultaneously, get connected.

For example, my father was yelling at me and my sister was laughing. I assumed that the two were connected. I thought, "My sister is laughing at me and is happy that I am being punished. I now hate my sister." In reality my sister might have just been happy that she wasn't getting punished, and not really happy that I was suffering. She might have been fearful and laughing nervously. However, in my mind, she was glad that I was suffering, and I hated her for it. This experience is now part of the "Me and my sister" image.

Over time, we have additional experiences that strengthen, weaken, or change the nature of an image. Whatever is relevant gets associated, connected. In our example, if I seek revenge on my sister and she retaliates, my image of "Me and my sister" now has additional hurt, anger, and hate. I am also building an image of my sister as a person, "Who my sister is." (Hopefully I also have some positive experiences with my sister so that the image is not just negative.)

This example also shows how feelings are involved in image formation. I was angry at my father. If I could not fully express my anger at my father, my anger at him spread (was "displaced") to my sister. My hurt, anger, and hate toward my father got connected to, associated with, my sister. She may or may not have deserved the degree of venomous feelings I felt toward her.

Point of Empowerment: *If I have an investment in holding on to negative feelings toward my sister, I will nourish the negative image of her and of "Me and her." I will repeatedly replay memories of "how mean she was to me."*

Practice: *Consider this question: Are you keeping alive, nourishing, negative and painful images by replaying painful memories?*

Point of Empowerment: *We can consciously (by choice) change, revise, or eliminate an image.*

Practice: *Identify images that you want to change, revise, or eliminate.*

The Influence of Parents and Other Authority Figures

What our parents and other authority figures say to us as we are growing up becomes part of our images. These messages may be explicitly verbal, or implied by a parent's behavior.

- "You are just not a student." Image of my Self as a student.
- "Girls are pretty, not smart." Image of appearance and my intelligence.
- "You will never do as well as your sister or brother." Image of my ability to succeed in the world. Image of "Know your Self through comparison."
- "You will never amount to much." Image of how far I will get in the world.
- "Just get by in the world—that is good enough." Image about my potential for achievement.
- "You can get better grades." Image that my accomplishments are not good enough.
- "Children are seen and not heard." Image about communication. Image of low Self-worth.

- If a parent does not put any limitations on what a child says, this teaches him, "You are free to say whatever you want; don't worry about the consequences." Image about what I can communicate. Image of "It's okay to ignore the impact and consequences of my statements."
- "You can't do anything right." Image of low Self-esteem.
- "You are angry all the time." Image of me as an "angry person."
- If a parent ignores what a child says, the message is, "What you say is not important." Image of me as unimportant, not mattering.
- If a parent pays attention to everything a child does, the message is, "What you do is the most important thing in the world." Image of me as having exaggerated importance.
- If a parent rarely buys anything for the child, the message is, "You are worthless." Image of me as lacking Self-worth.

Of course the opposite is true. If a parent gives a child positive messages about his Self, the child builds positive Self-images.

- "You did a great job cleaning your room." Image of effectiveness, high Self-esteem.
- "I am pleased with the grades you got on your report card. How do you feel about them?" Image of "I make my parents happy with my accomplishments. I can be happy with my accomplishments. My opinion counts." Image regarding accomplishment, and the importance of my ideas.
- "Tell me how you feel about the fight with your friend?" Image of "I am important. My feelings are important. I matter, beyond what I do."
- "Here is your birthday gift. Hope you like it." Image of "I am worthy."

- "I understand that you feel justified in being late, but this is the third time this week. No going out to play with your friends after school for a week." Image of "I am important. What I do matters."
- "Good night. I love you." Image of "I am lovable."

Practice: What negative and positive messages did you hear from your parents that got incorporated into positive and negative images?

How an Image Affects Us

NEGATIVE IMAGES

- If I have an image of me as an angry person, I will have the feeling of anger inside me much of the time. I will look for things to be angry about so I can express that anger through my behavior. In looking for things to be angry about, I will distort my perception of another person's behavior. I will be very sensitive to criticism and feel criticized often. I can then justify my angry behavior.
- If I have an image of low Self-esteem, I will experience my Self as less than others. I will continually try to please others and make them happy. I will deny my own needs and put others first. Or, I will become excessively demanding and feel entitled to having my needs met all the time. This way I can feel important. I think I can build my Self-esteem this way.
- If I have an image of, "I am the most important person in the world," I feel entitled. I expect the world to cater to my needs. I am incapable of giving to others.
- If I have an image of, "I will never get ahead in the world," I will not see opportunities that come my way for success. I may sabotage a good job and get fired. I will underachieve.

These are examples of how destructive images play out in our experience. We can see that the influences of images can be complex.

POSITIVE IMAGES

- If my image is, "I am good at sports," I will feel excited about participating in a sport. I will utilize my athletic abilities. I will perform well at sports.
- If my image is, "I am a good student," I will apply my Self to my studies. I will feel good about my accomplishments. I will learn from the feedback of poor grades. I will do well as a student.
- If my image is, "I succeed at anything I do," I will use all the resources I have at my disposal to accomplish my goals. I will feel confident as I take action. I will be thoughtful about my approach to a project. I will learn from my mistakes. I will value my efforts.
- If my image is, "Girls like me," and if this image is consistent with my experiences, I will approach women with confidence. I will be friendly and attentive. My behaviors will be what women generally like. I will be liked by the women in my life.
- If my image is, "I have healthy ambition," I will apply my Self to my work. I will look for opportunities to get ahead. I will dedicate my Self to being productive. I will succeed.

Point of Empowerment: Acting on negative images leads us to frustration and failure. These feelings alert us to negative images that we will want to change. Positive images lead to satisfaction and success. We want to acknowledge the existence of positive images. In doing so, we reinforce them. We will then create more success for our Self.

THE SELF-FULFILLING PROPHECY

We have been discussing how our images create our life, our future, and our destiny. This process of creation is called the **Self-fulfilling prophecy**. I *expect* and *fear* a future event. Or, I *expect* and *hope* for a future event. In anticipation of that event (before the event occurs), I behave (think, feel, and act) in ways that bring it about. After the event I say, "I was right. I knew this would happen. My opinion about my Self (my image) is correct." We have confirmed the "truth" of our image. We start out with an image (positive or negative; containing expectations, fears and hopes) created by our thinking and imagination. After the event, we end up with "the truth." Of course if we change our image, we will create a new "truth."

> *Point of Empowerment: The Self-fulfilling prophecy is an extremely important process in our lives. We create a desired or feared event. What we expect generates behavior in anticipation of a future event. This behavior creates the event.*

> *Point of Empowerment: It is through the Self-fulfilling prophecy that our images create our future, our destiny.*

For example, let's say I have an image of a fear of rejection. To prevent the rejection, I constantly try to please a certain person in my life. This excessive "pleasing" behavior provokes him to disrespect and devalue me. The disrespect and devaluing gets me angry. My anger creates a lot of conflict with the other person. My friend or romantic partner wants to end our relationship because he does not like the conflict. I am rejected. I have created the rejection that I fear.

My image of vacations—"Me and vacations"—is that I have great fun with my vacations. In anticipation of the event (a vacation), I enjoy planning it. As I go on my vacation, I look for ways to have fun. I find ways of enjoying my vacation, even if the weather is bad. If undesirable events occur on my vacation I "make the best of them." After my vacation I have memories of "another great vacation." My positive image of vacations is reinforced.

All the above examples of the effects of positive and negative images are examples of the Self-fulfilling prophecy at work.

> *Practice:* Work with the Self-fulfilling prophecy. Examine a desirable or an undesirable event that occurred. What had you expected to occur? Identify what you did in anticipation of the event happening. Explore the underlying image that is at work.

> Examine an event that has not yet occurred. What do you expect to occur? What will you do, in anticipation, to bring this event about? Explore the underlying image that is at work.

DISTORTED PERCEPTIONS

Let's say I have an image that contains the thought, "I can't do anything right; therefore I am not deserving of compliments." When someone likes something I did, and gives me a compliment, I will either tell him he is wrong, or just silently think that he's wrong. I may think that he has an ulterior motive for giving me a compliment. I am suspicious of his motive. In reality, I am mistaken in my perception of him. I have a distorted perception.

In addition, I am being presented with evidence that says, "You can do something right."

If my image is strong and I want to hold it in place, I will deny any evidence that contradicts it. I distort my perceptions of the world around me with denial. I say, "No, this isn't true. I can't do anything right." My image stays in place.

Let's say my image contains, "My opinion doesn't matter." If I'm at work and someone asks for my opinion, I may say that I have no opinion, even though I do. I say to myself, "This person isn't really interested in what I think." I have distorted my perception of that person, believing that he is not telling me the truth when he asks for my opinion. If I repeatedly say, "I have no opinion," the other person will stop asking me what I think. I say to myself, "You see, I am right—no one is interested in my opinion; my opinion doesn't matter." My image stays in place. The Self-fulfilling prophecy is at work.

Point of Empowerment: Our images distort our perception of the world around us. We filter our perceptions through the eyeglasses of our images.

Practice: See if you can notice a distorted perception, and try to connect it with an image.

CONFLICTING IMAGES

We can have conflicting images of our Self. I have an image that contains the thought, "I am a caring, giving person." Yet I often behave selfishly. Since I deny that I behave selfishly, my Self-perception is distorted. That I am a giving person is my conscious Self-image. However, my selfish behavior is driven by an unconscious image. The unconscious image may hold the belief, "There is not enough to go around. Take what you can get for yourself now."

As the world gives me feedback about my behavior, as I am called selfish by others, I start to feel inner conflict, tension, frustration, and anxiety. I may start to think that people do not see me as I am. I feel angry about this. If I am getting this feedback from my spouse, problems arise in my marriage.

Point of Empowerment: Conflicting images of the Self are normal, but painful.

Practice: See if you can notice the pain of conflicting images. Remember, pain shows us where we need to pay attention.

IDEALIZED SELF-IMAGE

Formation of the Idealized Self-Image

As children, expressing certain aspects of our Self through our behavior got us into trouble. We did not have the ability to constructively express our anger, for example. Or we selfishly expressed our desires. We were punished, sometimes severely. We were not able to modify these aspects of our Self, changing them into constructive forms of expression. We felt frustrated and angry with our Self. We turned against our Self, did not like our Self, and experienced Self-hatred.

We felt that aspects of our Self caused us to lose our parents' love. We hated these aspects and converted them into something else. Our anger, rage, hate, stubbornness, cruelty, or rebellion got sanitized. In addition, our passivity, shyness, eagerness to please, or fearful aspects also got converted into something else. We imagined perfect, ideal versions of all these aspects. Each new idealized aspect became a component of our idealized Self-image. We than presented this idealized version of our Self to the world.[3]

> *Point of Empowerment:* Creating the idealized Self-image helps a child keep her sense of Self intact. However, beyond adolescence, the idealized Self-image becomes dysfunctional.

---

3   The idealized Self-image has also been called the persona, or the false Self.

Idealized Image Distorts Us

Point of Empowerment: Idealizing parts of the Self distorts the Self. We pretend to be something that we are not.

Let's say I was six years old and was extremely jealous of my newborn sibling. I hated him, wanted him dead, and from time to time I expressed these feelings by hitting him. This got me into serious trouble. I denied and repressed the hate, and substituted love for it. I now behaved in a loving manner toward my sibling. The feeling/image of hating my sibling was replaced with the feeling/image of loving him. I presented this image to the world, and believed in the image myself. I was a loving brother or sister. This didn't mean that I didn't also love my sibling, but the hating side of me got transformed into a loving, idealized Self-image.

Losing Aspects of the Self; Recovering Lost Aspects

Point of Empowerment: The idealizing process causes us to lose parts of our Self that need to be recovered in the future.

Here are some examples of starting out with an ability, trait, desire, or need that was of great value, misusing it, experiencing negative consequences, losing it, and substituting a distorted aspect of my Self in its place.

- I was extremely friendly. I got hurt and withdrew. My friendliness got me into trouble. The surface-level "outer me," as presented to others, was still friendly, but inside, I was judgmental and withdrawn. Though I buried my friendliness, it was still there as an aspect of my true Self. I need to recover my true friendliness and drop my judgmental attitude.

- I was sensitive, shy, and withdrawn. I got teased. I forced my Self to be tough and outgoing, but was resentful and angry inside. I presented a false Self-image of being tough and outgoing. The positive quality of sensitivity got lost and needs to be recovered.

- I was never appropriately disciplined for my destructive behavior. I knew my behavior was wrong. I decided to deny my needs and to please others instead. I lost my ability to know and to pursue what I need. I need to recover that ability.

- I loved learning and loved school, but was not as smart as my sister, who got our parents' approval for her accomplishments in school. I buried my love of learning and dedicated my Self to accelerating at sports, getting approval this way. My love of learning still exists within me, but needs to be recovered.

- I was a bully and got severely punished by my parents. I became weak and submissive, always walking around with a smile on my face. I buried my aggressiveness, losing healthy power and assertiveness. My power and assertiveness need to be recovered.

- I was left alone often and felt lonely. I became overly Self-reliant, presenting an image to the world of "not needing others." I buried my desire for contact and closeness. Now I can't connect fully with others. I need to recover my desire and ability to connect with others in intimate ways.

Practice: *What aspects, parts, and abilities have been diminished or lost as you formed your idealized Self-image? Seek to recover them.*

Destructive Impact of the Idealized Self-Image

"I have never changed my childhood idealized Self-image regarding my sibling. It has had a destructive impact on my life as an adult. Part of my ability to love was tainted and lost by the idealized Self-image that covered hate with love."

As an adult, it is normal to occasionally hate the person you love. If you cannot admit this feeling to your Self because of your idealized Self-image, you again deny the feeling. You repress it and substitute love for hate. You express behavior dictated by your image. This doesn't mean that you don't love, but you substitute a false feeling of love for an honest feeling of hate. However, this hate inevitably "sneaks" out in some other form, like low sexual desire toward your partner. As a result you have a less satisfying love/sexual relationship than you are capable of having.

Practice: Where are idealized Self-images disrupting your capacities and your relationships? Seek to free your Self of these images.

Idealized Image and Others

Point of Empowerment: The idealized Self-image often brings us into conflict with others who have a different or opposite image of us.

For example, I see my Self as easygoing and agreeable. However, when others ask me to do something, I make a face, say no, and give an excuse. In my mind, my excuses are reasonable and justify saying no. The excuses allow me to maintain my Self-image of easygoing and agreeable. Since this happens often, other people see me as difficult to get along with and disagreeable, which contradicts my Self-image. My Self-image is idealized, as it is mistaken and blind.

As a child I was often criticized and punished for saying no. I became "agreeable," repressing (burying) my desire to say no. I developed the idealized Self-image of being easygoing and agreeable. As an adult I often find excuses to say no. Actually I deny, disown, and refuse my right to say no because I got punished for saying no as a child. In the place of saying no I developed the Self-image, and the behavior, of "easygoing and agreeable." I have carried that image into adulthood. In my interactions with others, they perceive me as "difficult." My idealized image has brought me into conflict with other people.

To resolve my image problem, I need to reclaim my right and my ability to say no appropriately. As I constructively assert my Self, I will find that I can handle conflict with others, and, in the long run, be in harmony with them.

Practice: Where does your view of your Self conflict with how others see you? Seek to resolve these conflicts by examining and changing your idealized Self-images. Examine your childhood experiences and the beliefs that formed as a result of these experiences. See how these beliefs resulted in the formation of idealized Self-images.

IMAGE AND IDENTITY INTERACT

Images and identities can be in conflict with each other, or they can reinforce each other. When they are in conflict, we feel torn inside. We feel confused and anxious. Where they reinforce each other, we feel secure and confident. We know that we are doing what we want, and that we will be successful.

- For example, since I identify with my father, I think that I should like baseball the way he does. I also have an image that says, "I should be truthful with my Self, and be faithful to who I am." The truth is that I do not like baseball.

Being truthful with my Self requires that I acknowledge this. Acknowledging that I do not like baseball (being true to my Self) conflicts with my identification with my father. My image and identification conflict.

- Consider the example of the image about tennis. I love tennis, but play poorly. I also have an identity that says, "Men are good at sports." This identity leads me to take tennis lessons and to practice my game. I improve my game and feel happy about this. My image and my identity have worked together, and enable me to create greater satisfaction and happiness for my Self.

- In identifying with my older brother, I want to be a good student like him. My parents told me that they are proud of my school accomplishments. Their compliments helped me create an image of my Self as a good student. I do well in school. My identification with my brother and my image as a good student reinforce each other, and I am a successful student.

- My image is that I am an independent thinker, who is ethical in the way I behave. I like my boss, consider him to be a mentor, and identify with him, wanting to be like him. However, my boss begins to ask me to do dishonest things. I feel very confused and agitated, and experience conflict inside. As an independent thinker and ethical person, I know that what my boss asks of me is wrong and is "not me." Yet I like my boss and want to be like him. My image and my identification are in conflict.

Practice: *Consider situations where your image and identity are working together, and situations where they are in conflict. Think about changing your image or your identity, or both, so that they complement each other and work together.*

CHANGING AN IMAGE

We can see that we have images we want to change. These are negative, destructive, or conflicting images that we have formed in childhood, adolescence, young adulthood, or adulthood. Images exist on a continuum from simple to complex. Changing a complex image is an involved process and has numerous steps. Changing a simple image can be straightforward and can go quickly. Below is the process to change an image—to collapse the old image and install a new one.

Finding an Image to Work With

1. You are seeking a statement: "Me and ____." (See the examples listed above.)

2. To find out what you want to fill in the blank with, use any one (or all) of these three approaches:

   a. Identify a behavior that is not getting you what you want, that causes you pain, that repeats, or that you have not been able to change. Identify what situation the behavior is connected to. Fill in the blank with that situation.

   b. Identify painful feelings. Connect them to a situation. Fill in the blank with that situation.

   c. Identify thoughts that are disturbing to you, that create painful feelings. Connect the thoughts to a situation. Fill in the blank with that situation.

3. Free associate, writing down the *elements* of an image: the thoughts, feelings, beliefs, attitudes, decisions, memories, and expectations of the future. Write until you feel that you have included all the relevant information.

Working with the Image

4. Look for patterns in the image. See how it was formed and where it came from. Look for insights into your Self. This creates a context of understanding, which will facilitate your image work.

5. Take a piece of the image to work with. A piece could be aspects or elements of the image that seem to go together in a logical manner. Some examples: a memory, the thoughts and feelings of the memory, and what you decided about the future based on the memory. A piece could also be a constellation of thoughts, attitudes, and beliefs that go together, or one or more expectations about the future. Write that piece down on a separate sheet of paper.

6. Pick an element of the image to work with. Be clear about what that element is.

   a. We don't work with feelings directly, as they flow from the other elements of an image.

7. To change an element, close your eyes and state the old thought, attitude, belief, decision, or expectation. Say to your Self in a loud voice, "No! I no longer think this way, or hold this attitude, belief, decision, or expectation."

8. Next, formulate new thoughts, attitudes, beliefs, decisions, or expectations.

9. Imagine your Self acting on these new aspects of the image. Feel positive emotions: being pleased with and proud of your Self, and feeling happy, enthusiastic, and excited as you work in your imagination. You are creating new associations.

10. Put the new elements of your image into action. Act on them.

11. Observe your behavior and the results of your new actions. Do they fit your new image?

Working with Painful Memories

12. Work through and let go of painful memories that may be present in your image. (Get help with traumatic memories!)

   a. Select a memory. Review it.

   b. Within your comfort level, experience the feelings contained in the memory *with the intention of experiencing and letting go of those feelings.*

   c. See how you got through the situation using whatever coping mechanisms you had available to you. See the strength contained in those coping mechanisms.

   d. Seek to let go of the past through a process of forgiveness—*forgiveness for your own benefit.*

13. Discover any decisions about your Self and about your life you might have made as a result of this painful experience. See if there are expectations for the future flowing out of these decisions.

14. Make new decisions. Create new expectations.

15. Use steps 9–11 above.

Continue to Work with Pieces of the Image

16. Work with a number of aspects of the image until you sense that the whole image has changed. You may or may not have to work with every part of the image.[4]

Live Your New Image

17. Live your new image. As you use the image, it will become part of your Self.

---

4   If you persist, the image may "change on its own" through the mechanisms of cognitive dissonance, and the subconscious mind's desire to have consistency.

Point of Empowerment: You can follow the above process start to finish. Alternately, you can modify and adapt the above process to suit your needs.

Practice: Play with your images and with the change process. Have fun while you succeed in changing your images.

In Conclusion

We have explored the profound impact that identity and image have on us. As you work with them, you will see how your life will change. This is a powerful way to work with your Self to bring greater fulfillment to your life.

CHAPTER 18

DISTURBANCES OF THE SELF

Disturbances of the Self: Definition

We have said that we, as human beings, have abilities that we use to satisfy our needs by fulfilling life's demands and tasks. We also use our abilities to create new things for our Self. Some abilities are fully functional at birth, some develop naturally over time, and some are developed as we discover that we need them.

The same can be said about the other aspects (parts) of the Self: the developmental self, the ego, the personality, our conscience, and our identity/image. We are born with some of the aspects fully functioning and develop other aspects over time.

Yet as we live life, abilities and parts of the Self become distorted (poorly functioning), damaged (barely functioning), and lost (not functioning at all) through disturbances of the Self.

Consider, for example, our ability to express and communicate our thoughts, ideas, feelings, desires, and needs. As young children we express our Self. However, over time, we may be told directly (verbally) or indirectly (through nonverbal behavior) that:

- Our ideas are stupid
- Our thoughts are confused
- Our feelings are unjustified

- Our desires are unreasonable
- We do not deserve to fulfill our needs

As a result, our ability to express our Self, to communicate to others about these aspects of our Self, becomes diminished, inhibited, damaged, or lost. We have sustained a disturbance of an ability, a disturbance of our Self.

Point of Empowerment: *Disturbances of the Self are distortions, damages, and losses of our abilities to live our life effectively and to reach our full potential. Disturbances of the Self are also distortions, damages, and losses of the parts of the Self: our ego, personality, developmental self, conscience, and identity/image.*

Practice: *As you begin to think about the disturbances of your Self, seek to develop kindness, empathy, and compassion toward your Self.*

Recognizing Disturbances of the Self

PAIN

We experience various kinds of pain. Pain and painful feelings are usually thought of as negative and unwanted. However, one of the most important purposes of painful feelings is to give us the message that we are experiencing a disturbance of our Self. Short-lived, brief painful feelings are not indicative of a disturbance. For example, the feeling of frustration tells us that we are not accomplishing a task, or fulfilling a need or a desire. This is useful, important information. However, it is the *prolonged and chronic* feeling of frustration about an aspect of our life that asks us to examine our Self for disturbances.

Often, we cannot identify a specific disturbance of our Self on our own. We need the help of family, friends, teachers, mentors, counselors, and professionals. Yet we must begin the search by looking inward and experiencing painful feelings. We usually react to painful feelings by avoiding them, and by defending our Self against them. Avoiding pain may be a natural response in the short run, but in the long run, this avoidance is very harmful to our Self.

Point of Empowerment: Painful feelings contain important messages for us about disturbances of our Self.

Practice: Recognize that your initial response to pain is to avoid it. Practice approaching pain instead by tuning in to a physical pain and asking for the message it has for you. Say, "Pain in my _____, what message do you have for me?" Listen for an answer.

OTHER INDICATORS

Other indicators that we are experiencing a disturbance of our Self are:

- We chronically make the same mistakes and experience the same failures. We do not learn from our mistakes or failures.
- We never seem to satisfy a specific need or desire.
- We rarely reach our goals.
- We are ineffective in fulfilling our roles.
- We are thinking, feeling, or behaving the same way, year after year. We are failing to mature in one or more areas of our life.
- We feel excessive anxiety, depression, worry, doubt, frustration, or guilt.
- We experience periodic or constant crises in our life.
- We lack Self-esteem, Self-confidence, Self-worth, healthy Self-love, Self-respect, or Self-awareness.

- We are not a child or an adolescent, but we frequently "act childishly" or "like an adolescent." We often use a child's or an adolescent's coping mechanisms, or problem-solving approaches. We refuse to "grow up," to mature.

If, as adults, we use a child's or an adolescent's coping mechanisms, or problem-solving approaches, we will not get the results we want. We often get the opposite of what we intend to create for our Self. We create unnecessary difficulties for our Self. A disturbance has left part of our Self stuck at a certain age, a certain developmental stage. It has not grown, developed, or matured. This part then becomes active and seeks to deal with the situation we are faced with. If we, as adults, agree to let the child or adolescent part of our Self cope with the situation, we get that child's approach, that child's strategy, and our actions express it.

A common example is the situation of wanting to be loved. The child's or adolescent's approach to getting love is to pressure or force a parent, relative, or friend to love him by using anger, intimidation, threats, guilt, helplessness, manipulation, dependency, illness, or Self-destructiveness. While these strategies may have been partially successful in the past, using them as young adults, adults, seniors, or elders will inevitably get us the opposite. We will get rejection and anger. (A more effective strategy to get love would be to give love, knowing that we will get love in return.)

Point of Empowerment: Disturbances of the Self cause us to get the opposite of what we want for our Self; they make our lives more difficult than they have to be.

Practice: Try to identify a situation where you wanted something and tried to get it, but got the opposite of your desire.

Causes of a Disturbance of the Self

DISTURBANCES CAUSED BY JUST BEING A CHILD OR AN ADOLESCENT

Some disturbances of the Self are guaranteed to occur, as they are the inevitable results of having been an infant, toddler, child, or adolescent.

The ways in which this can happen are:

- As young people we have a limited understanding of the world. We misinterpret the meaning of events. We then respond to events based on misunderstandings. Our behavior can lead to inappropriate and intense negative feedback from others, which results in a distortion of and damage to our Self.

- Because of their limited understanding of the world, children and adolescents mistakenly blame themselves for problems that they aren't responsible for. At other times children and adolescents deny responsibility for their behavior. If the Self-blame, or denial of healthy responsibility, is chronic and/or severe, a disturbance of the Self can occur.

- Children are dependent and relatively powerless. This creates fear, frustration, and anger. Sometimes coping with these feelings involves inhibiting, distorting, and damaging our Self, and therefore creating disturbances of the Self.

- Children or adolescents can be excessively aggressive, selfish, Self-centered, immature, Self-important, and dramatic. These behaviors are bound to get them into trouble with family, friends, teachers, and other people in their lives. In the conflict that ensues, they get hurt and feel pain. If that pain is severe or chronic, or both, there will be a disturbance of the Self.

- Growing up, we experience a normal and necessary process called socialization. Socialization is the process by which infants, children, and adolescents learn to become productive members of the society they live in. We experience limitations, restrictions, negative feedback, and punishment. Consequently, we turn against our Self with Self-blame, Self-inhibition, Self-hatred, and Self-destruction. These create disturbances of the Self.

Point of Empowerment: No one completes the stages of infancy, toddlerhood, childhood, and adolescence without some disturbance to their Self. In the process of correcting these disturbances as adults, we grow and become stronger.

DISTURBANCES CAUSED BY A CHILD'S OR AN ADOLESCENT'S SEVERE PROBLEMS

Disturbances of the Self occur if infants, toddlers, children, or adolescents have severe problems of their own. Children can:

- Have physical illnesses and deformities
- Be in severe, chronic physical pain or discomfort
- Have inadequate intelligence
- Be unable to function in school due to learning difficulties
- Be extremely willful, angry, and aggressive
- Be excessively timid, shy, fearful, or anxious
- Be excessively demanding of themselves
- Lack common sense
- Lack the ability to learn from mistakes

If the child's caretakers are unable to respond constructively to these problems, the problems will get worse.

DISTURBANCES CAUSED BY MISTREATMENT

The next grouping of the causes of the disturbances of the Self occurs when infants, toddlers, children, and adolescents are on the receiving end of ineffective, inadequate, and inappropriate parenting. In these cases the parents are misguided and uninformed. Parents can also be destructive, neglectful, and abusive. Children and adolescents can also be hurt by the destructive behavior of siblings, extended family members, peers, friends, teachers, coaches, and neighbors.

Often, a "mistreated" infant, toddler, child, or adolescent:

- Has his needs misinterpreted or neglected, or both.
- Receives excessive criticism.
- Doesn't receive constructive criticism.
- Experiences excessive limitations to age-appropriate freedoms and privileges.
- Doesn't receive any limits, rules, or structure.
- Is constantly told what to do and how to do it.
- Doesn't receive enough guidance, support, and encouragement.
- Receives excessive and harsh discipline.
- Doesn't receive appropriate discipline.
- Receives excessive "nurturing" in the form of getting everything he asks for.
- Doesn't receive enough nurturing and love.
- Receives "discipline" by excessive manipulation. This could be through guilt or by a parent's excessive withdrawal of love.
- Is excessively punished and limited for the slightest misbehavior.
- Is not taught right from wrong in a constructive manner.
- Receives excessive expectations.
- Doesn't receive any expectations.

- Has too many demands placed on him.
- Has no demands placed on him.
- Doesn't receive enough attention because a parent is ill, preoccupied, or physically absent.
- Doesn't receive enough attention because a parent is emotionally absent.
- Receives emotional, mental, and/or physical violence and abuse.

Point of Empowerment: We can see that disturbances of the Self occur if a child experiences:

- *Extremes—either too much or too little—of the right thing, such as love or discipline.*
- *Too much of the wrong thing, such as verbal or physical abuse.*
- *The right thing at the wrong time, such as nurturing when discipline is called for, or discipline when nurturing is called for.*

We do not expect parents to be perfect. Mistakes in parenting are inevitable, and generally do not cause excessive damage to a child or adolescent. A parental mistake or failure can actually be a constructive challenge for children and adolescents. Mistakes can be corrected. Hurt can be healed. Forgiveness can be given. Learning can take place. Usually, parents give enough loving and caring, and children and adolescents have enough of their needs met. However, severe parental failure and mistreatment by others cause damage to both the child's and the adolescent's Self.

TRAUMA CAUSES A DISTURBANCE OF THE SELF

Trauma causes a disturbance of the Self. The severity of the disturbance is related to the severity of the trauma. Trauma is caused by a situation that severely threatens our survival, or by a situation that persistently and chronically threatens our physical, emotional, and/or mental safety and security.

Under traumatic conditions we experience extreme emotions that we cannot cope with. We split the emotions off and stop feeling them, separating them from our Self. We lose a part of our Self. We also split off and repress (bury in our unconscious) some or all of the memories of a traumatic experience. We lose abilities. These split-off parts of the Self remain stuck in the developmental period where the trauma occurred. Aspects of the Self do not develop in a normal manner, nor do they mature.

For example, say we were four years old, and our mother was hospitalized for a week. During this time we didn't get to see or speak to her. No one explained to us what was happening. We felt very alone and abandoned. This situation caused great fear and anxiety. To cope with this situation and our feelings, we might have retreated into our Self, becoming quiet, withdrawn, and passive. If we didn't get a chance to speak about our fears and anxieties, and about what happened to us, this experience would have become a trauma. A piece of our ability to express our Self and be active in the world would have been lost. A piece of our Self would have gotten frozen in time. This is an example of the lost Self. This trauma would need to be healed, and the lost abilities would need to be reclaimed and recovered.

Point of Empowerment: *The effects of trauma never go away unless the trauma is healed. The psychiatric diagnosis for this condition is called Post-Traumatic Stress Disorder.*

Faulty Coping Strategies

Many of our coping strategies that originally worked to get us through a trauma become dysfunctional. They cause new problems and new pain. Some examples of previously useful coping strategies are:

- Extreme use of denial and repression
- Using anger and aggression to keep people away
- Withdrawal and isolation
- Passive submission
- Manipulation and control
- Overachievement or underachievement
- Self-destructive behavior
- Obsessive thoughts and compulsive behaviors

Point of Empowerment: We usually outgrow the need for past coping strategies. If we continue to use them, they create new problems for us.

Practice: Think about difficult, painful, or traumatic experiences that you have lived through. What strategies did you use to cope with these situations? Are you continuing to use these strategies? Are they causing problems? Decide to let them go.

Disturbances Create New Disturbances, Vicious Circles

A disturbance of the Self takes on a life of its own, and causes further disturbances, resulting in a vicious circle. For example, we may abuse drugs to deal with the pain caused by a disturbance of the Self. Our drug use causes more problems. This generates new pain, which may result in more drug use. We therefore have a vicious circle that continues until the pain that accompanied the disturbance-causing events is dealt with. We need to interrupt the vicious circle by stopping one of the steps along the way. In our example, we must first stop the drug use, then heal the pain we feel.

Correcting Disturbances of the Self

Correcting disturbances of the Self is a worthy quest. The quest is a healing journey that accomplishes many tasks, and consists of the following:

- The pain of the past is gone.
- The pain of the present is gone.
- We have corrected distortions to our Self.
- We have repaired damage to our Self.
- We have recovered the lost aspects of our Self.
- We have strengthened our Self, enabling us to create a better future for our Self.

Methods we can use for healing are: introspection, journaling, meditation, prayer, turning to religion/spirituality, walks in nature, travel, reading, going to movies and plays, dancing, playing sports, participating in workshops, talking with family and friends, and professional counseling. Working with a professional is often an essential part of the healing process.

Point of Empowerment: If you have detected a disturbance of your Self, seek healing.

Practice: Set an intention to heal through decision and choice. Find and use activities and modalities that will serve you on your healing journey.

Preventing Disturbances of the Self

In life, some trauma and disturbances of the Self are inevitable. In healing these disturbances we gain experience, skills, and knowledge about the Self.

We can prevent some disturbances of the Self through effective parenting. We cannot automatically blame parents when there are disturbances of the Self. We know that children have their own problems, and their own faulty ways of coping. At the same time, what a parent does is important, and has an impact on his or her child. Parents love and take care of their children. They also respond to a child's behavior. What parents do is important and matters.

Evil

Human evil is extreme, destructive behavior. Remember, behavior arises from our thoughts and feelings. If our thinking and feeling is distorted, twisted, faulty, out of touch with reality, perverse, excessive, obsessive, angry, enraged, or hurt, the behavior that arises out of these thoughts and feelings will be destructive.

> **Point of Empowerment:** *When a human being behaves in an evil manner, his or her goodness has become a prisoner of an extreme disturbance of the Self.*

CHAPTER 19

THE PROCESSES OF LIFE

Throughout *The Operating Manual for the Self* we have looked at the "big picture" of the Self. Here we will look at the "big picture of the big picture."

As we have explored the Self, we have talked about living. There are some processes of life that the Self participates in. These are:

- Using abilities to fulfill needs.
- Fulfilling our needs to allow for the unfolding of the developmental self.
- Turning our abilities into skills, capabilities, then into mastery, then into artistry.
- Using the abilities of each stage of the developmental self.
- Accomplishing the tasks of each stage of the life cycle.
- Gaining experience and knowledge about life.
- Using our abilities to create our issues.
- Using our abilities to resolve our issues.
- Resolving our issues to explore themes in life.
- Exploring themes in life to learn life lessons.
- Learning life lessons to develop wisdom.
- Using our abilities to live our life.
- Seeing how living life brings us experience.
- Seeing how living life bring us knowledge about life.

- Using our abilities to integrate experience and knowledge, which then produces wisdom.
- Using our abilities to make choices in life.
- Making choices to see what the consequences of our choices are.
- Evaluating the consequences of our choices to understand what works to get us what we want.
- Learning how to use our freedom.
- Creating and having life experiences.
- Exploring the themes of life.
- Growing, developing, maturing, and evolving.
- Reaching for our full human potential.

CHAPTER 20

FINAL THOUGHTS

A few final thoughts:

The Self as a System

We have explored the wide variety of the aspects of the Self, and what it means to be human. As you look at all the aspects of the Self, you can see its **complexity**. Even with all those "moving parts," the Self can act as a single entity. It is truly magnificent.

Systems Thinking

In thinking about the Self, we need to use systems thinking. This involves considering how all the parts of a system are unique, and at the same time intimately related. Their relationship to each other allows them to work together as a whole.

Systems thinking suggests a thought process of "both/and" instead of "either/or."

Our world today is infinitely more complex than the Self. We need to apply systems thinking if we are to understand how the world functions, and how to change it. Systems thinking teaches us how to solve problems.

Human Potential

As human beings at a specific moment in time, we are who we are. We also have a potential—who we can become in the future. Through the development of our Self, we can reach our potential. *The Operating Manual for the Self* has explored all the "moving parts" of the Self, and has given us choices for our Self-development.

Point of Empowerment: The Self is worthy of our deep appreciation and amazement.

Practice: Develop a deep appreciation for your Self.

MAP OF THIS BOOK, MAP OF THE SELF

Part One: Groundwork

1. How to Use This Book
   a. A Reference Book, Manual, and Self-Help Book
   b. The Glossary
   c. Charts
   d. Book Map, Map of the Self
   e. Familiar and Complex Ideas
   f. Brief or Deep
   g. A Self-Help Book
      1. Recognize Yourself
      2. Points of Empowerment, Practices
      3. Change
      4. Resistance
      5. Self-Acceptance
      6. I Don't Understand. I Don't Know How to Do a Practice.
   h. Special Contributions of *The Operating Manual for the Self*
   i. In Conclusion: Wrestle, Persist, Companionship
2. Why Do We Need an Operating Manual for the Self?
   a. Operating Manuals

Part Two: Being Human

2. Consciousness
3. Energy
4. Self-Awareness
5. The Observer
6. Foreground and Background

b. Being, Doing, Having
1. Being
   i. Existing
2. Doing
3. Having
   i. Ownership, Responsibility

c. Thinking, Feeling, Acting (Taking Action)
1. Thinking
   i. Freedom
   ii. Errors in Thinking
2. Feeling: Our Experience of Life
   i. The Messages of Feelings
   ii. Defenses against Feeling
3. Acting
   i. Behavior Follows Thinking and Feeling
   ii. Our Actions Show Us Who We Are
   iii. All Behavior Is Purposeful
   iv. Destructive Behavior

d. The Mind
1. The Conscious Mind
2. The Subconscious Mind
   i. Holds Our Belief System; Seeks Consistency
   ii. Seeks Coherence
   iii. Holds, Organizes, and Screens Information
3. The Unconscious Mind

e. The Mind and the Brain

5. Ability, Will, and Choice

b. Self

c. Parts of the Self

d. Life Span

e. Developmental Self

f. Self and the Life Span

g. Human Needs

h. Self and the Mind

i. Growing, Developing, Maturing, Evolving

    1. Growing

    2. Developing

    3. Maturing

    4. Evolving

7. Human Needs

a. Not Knowing How, Doing Our Best

b. Unfulfilled Needs

c. Survival Needs: Physical, Emotional, Mental, and Spiritual

    1. Physical Survival

    2. Emotional Survival

    3. Mental Survival

    4. Spiritual Survival

    5. Physical Survival Throughout the Life Span

d. Safety and Security

e. Belonging and Loving

    1. Belonging

    2. Loving

f. Self-Esteem

    1. What Is Self-Esteem?

       i. Liking and Valuing Our Self

      ii. Knowing and Feeling Your Right to Exist

     iii. Permission and Authority: Ability and Willingness to Assert Your Rights

2. Life Lessons
3. Increasing Abilities
4. Themes
5. Issues
    i. Ambivalence: Wishing for and Fearing at the Same Time
6. Self-Esteem, Self-Worth, and Self-Love
    i. Becoming an Adult Through Self-Esteem
    ii. Self-Love
7. The Child's and Adolescent's Coping Mechanisms

k. Senior (65–80 Years Old)
1. Continue the Work of the Adult: Self-Esteem, Self-Actualization, Health
2. Deepen and Enrich Relationships: Belonging and Loving
3. Expansion into New Areas
4. Completion of Unfinished Business
5. Experiencing Loss
6. Beauty, Mystery, the Transcendent: Religion and Spirituality, Wisdom
7. Ending Suffering
8. Look to the Future
9. Celebrate Life

l. Elder (80+ Years Old)
1. The Work of a Senior
2. Elder: The Best Stage of Life
3. Conscious Dying

12. The Ego
a. Purpose and Abilities of the Ego
1. Protection and Survival
2. The Self's Interface
3. Fulfilling Needs

    1. Component of the Self

    2. Growth, Development, and Maturing

    3. Right and Wrong

    4. Human Nature

b. Components of the Conscience

    1. Traditional, Basic Conscience

    2. True Conscience

c. Formation of the Conscience

    1. Rewards and Punishments

    2. Identification

        i. Identification with the Aggressor

        ii. Rebellion against Authority

        iii. Displaced Aggression

    3. The Parent's Conscience

d. A Functional but Limited Conscience

    1. Guilt

        i. Real and False Guilt

        ii. Resentment, Paralysis

    2. Justification, Goodness

    3. Doing the Right Thing Brings Little Pleasure

e. Malfunctioning Conscience

    1. Harshness, Brutality

    2. Destruction of Self-Esteem

f. The True Conscience

    1. Remorse and Sorrow

    2. The Wise You

    3. Ideals

        i. Distorted Ideals, Practical Reality

g. In Summary

h. The New Conscience

    1. The True Conscience

    2. Self-Esteem

3. Dignity
4. Love
5. Self-Acceptance
6. The Old Conscience and the New Conscience

15. Introduction: The Significance of Identity and Image

16. Identity

   a. The Formation of Identity

     1. Identification
     2. The Elements of Identity
     3. Many Identities, Natural Contradictions
     4. An Identity of "The Opposite"
     5. Self-Identification
     6. Unresolved Issues, Unfinished Business
     7. Learning as Identification

       i. Frustration Tolerance, Delay of Gratification, Self-Discipline

   b. Creating and Expanding Our Identity Consciously, by Choice

     1. Identifications with Parents
     2. Creating New Identifications
     3. Letting Go of an Old Identification, Creating a New Identity

17. Image

   a. Images of the Self

   b. An Example of an Image

     1. My Image of Success: Me and Success
     2. Core Beliefs
     3. Essence of an Image

   c. Formation of an Image

     1. Assembling an Image
     2. The Influence of Parents and Other Authority Figures

WISDOM FROM *THE OPERATING MANUAL FOR THE SELF*

The following statements contain some of the wisdom of *The Operating Manual for the Self.*

- All growth and change begins with self-acceptance. Self-acceptance states: As a human being I will make mistakes. It's ok to make mistakes. I can learn and forgive myself.
- There is always resistance to change. Resistance is natural and necessary.
- All behavior (thinking, feeling, acting) has the purpose of fulfilling our needs.
- Knowledge is power when you put ideas into practice.
- Self-worth is an innate part of who we are. We have self-worth by virtue of being human. We only need to uncover it.
- Self-esteem is created. We create self-esteem for ourselves by evaluating our behavior, motivation, and attitudes. The criteria for our evaluation is our principles, ethics, values, and ideals. We ask, "Are we putting our principles, ethics, values, and ideals into practice?"
- We have self-esteem when we do the right thing for the right reason and feel good about it. We also experience a quality of our Self, our goodness.

- A healthy conscience allows us to feel good as we do good, for the right reason.
- You cannot have healthy self-esteem without a healthy conscience.
- Your destiny is your destination, where you are going. To change your destiny, change your identity and image.
- To expand your personality adopt new traits. To expand your being adopt new qualities.
- The Self is a system, like the human body, that functions automatically, unless you take charge of it.
- Our boundaries are sacred.
- The ego lives on the surface of our boundaries.
- Wisdom is learning what works and what does not work in life. We learn by making a choice and experiencing the consequences of that choice.
- A challenge for your growth is to: Think about every thought you have. Seek to feel good all the time. Give and receive only love.
- Our actions flow easily, spontaneously, effectively, appropriately, and joyfully when we express the qualities of love as who we are.
- At the core of our being, we need to feel that our behavior is just.

GLOSSARY

Ability: A skill that we can use to accomplish a task.

Artistry: Using a mastered skill in creative and novel ways.

Attitude: Consists of a set of strong feelings generated by our beliefs. Attitudes govern our approach to some area of our life. (E.g., "He has a belligerent attitude toward authority.")

Autonomy: Being a separate and unique individual. Being in charge of one's life. Having and exercising freedom of choice.

Awareness: An ability that allows sensation to register in our consciousness. Our sensations can be simple ("My toe hurts") or they can be complex, existing over time ("I am aware of dissatisfaction in my marriage").

Belief: A persistent thought that we hold over time. Beliefs can be about "the way things are," the nature of our Self and others, or life.

Belief System: A collection of beliefs about how life operates, and about how we operate or think we should operate. These ideas are usually firmly held by a person. They are "believed in." We invest our Self in our belief system.

Boundary: A barrier that separates.

Capability: An ability that I have confidence in. I know that I can rely on and depend on this ability. I know that it will be there when I need it.

Change: The process that makes the next moment in time different from the present one.

Choice: Weighing alternatives by using our ability to think. After giving consideration to our alternatives, we make a decision for one and against the others. We have made a choice.

Complexity: A quality inherent in systems. Each part retains its separate identity, but works with the other parts of the system to function as a whole.

Conscience: Part of us that guides us in our journey through life, telling us what's right and wrong.

Conscious Learning: Identifying an aspect of our Self that we consciously, with awareness, choose to learn about and develop further.

Consciousness: The ability to think, feel, and be aware. Consciousness has intelligence and creativity, intention, and purpose. All our abilities come from pure consciousness.

Consciousness (Collective): The ideas and beliefs held by humanity as a whole.

Coping Mechanism: A strategy we employ to get through a difficult, challenging experience. Coping mechanisms can be mental/thinking, emotional, or behavioral.

Creator: The creator is the creative part of the Self; present in every human being.

Damaged Self: Part of the Self that got injured and therefore damaged, a part we still use but not up to its full potential. Damage to the Self occurs mostly during childhood and adolescence, but can happen during adulthood also.

Defense Mechanism: A coping strategy to deal with a moment of an unbearably painful experience. The strategy starts with denial—a statement that what's happening isn't happening. Denial is followed by an action that manages the painful moment of the experience. Some examples of managing strategies are: numbing, distracting, substituting, pretending, distorting, burying/repressing, and projecting. Defense mechanisms have positive and negative uses.

Desire: Something we want for our Self. In contrast to a need, a desire is "optional," something that we choose to pursue.

Developmental Self: Stages of the Self during the life span: infant, child, adolescent, young adult, adult, senior, elder.

Ego: The part of our Self that is our interface with the external world beyond our skin. It has many abilities that enable it to fulfill its purpose.

Ego Defense Mechanisms/"Ego Defenses": Defense mechanisms employed by the ego to manage unbearable or overwhelming pain from a threat to our well-being. The ego uses these mechanisms to keep us stable and functioning in our world.

Emotion: The synergy (combining into a whole) of a thought and a feeling. Also, a feeling put into motion by a thought. The energy of an impulse to take action.

Empathy: The skill that enables us to feel remorse and sorrow. Empathy is feeling for and with another person. It includes having, or developing, some understanding of what another person is experiencing.

Empowerment: The authority and permission to be powerful, to exercise our power.

Errors of Thinking:

> **Catastrophizing.** A sequence of thoughts that begins with a particular event and ends with an expectation of a catastrophe. (E.g., "My spouse is late getting home. He must have gotten into a car accident.")

Disqualifying or Discounting the Positive. If something is positive, "It doesn't count." (E.g., your boss says that you did a good job. You think that this isn't true, that he must be planning to take advantage of you.)

Imperatives. You or another person *must* behave in a certain manner. There are no alternatives.

Labeling. Putting a rigid, absolute label on a person or event. (E.g., you made a mistake. You call yourself an idiot, convinced that you're stupid.)

Mind Reading. The other person hasn't expressed his thoughts, but you think you know what he's thinking.

Restricted or Tunnel Vision. You only see the negative in a person or event.

Feelings: Our experience of life. Also, an experience in and through our bodies of a certain kind of energy. This energy contains information, a message for us, that we need to interpret. Negative feelings are feelings we want less of. Positive feelings are feelings we want more of.

Functioning: The ability of the Self to accomplish the tasks of living according to our stage of life.

Gestalt: A physical, biological, psychological, or symbolic pattern of elements so unified that its properties cannot be derived from the sum of its parts. A synergy (whole) with foreground and background.

Grow, Develop, Mature, Evolve: To grow is to become larger in size. To develop is to increase our ability. To mature is to grow and develop in a way that enhances who we are. To evolve is to Self-actualize in a way that increases the richness and depth of our being.

Healing: The restoration of health and well-being. A process of change that occurs through indirect action.

Identification: The process of building a Self by becoming like another person. Usually done unconsciously.

Identity: A part of our Self that answers the question, "Who are we?" Contains information about how we should think, feel, and act in all the situations that we encounter in our lives.

Image: A collection of thoughts, feelings, attitudes, beliefs, decisions, memories and expectations for the future that we collect together and assemble into a meaningful whole, a gestalt.

Incorporation: To grow and develop our Self through the process of taking aspects of other people into our Self. These aspects are then assimilated and made our own, adding to our uniqueness.

Intuition: Knowing something without knowing how you know it. The knowing can be a feeling, a thought, a sensation, or an impulse to act.

Issue: A distorted belief or system of beliefs about the way the Self or the world operates. It is often generated in childhood, and causes either internal conflict within the Self or external conflict between the Self and others. It can also do both simultaneously.

Life Span: The years of our lifetime, from birth to death. The Self changes throughout our life span.

Lost Self: Parts of our Self that we disowned, buried in our unconscious, and forgot about, mostly during childhood and adolescence, but also during adulthood.

Lower Self: Less functional and immature, negative, inadequate parts of the Self. For example, negative ego, fearful child, rebellious adolescent, or insecure young adult.

Mastery: Ability to use a skill with ease and spontaneity. Practicing mastery leads to artistry.

Mind:

Conscious Mind. Our usual day-to-day ordinary awareness. We think, feel, act, perceive, remember, and make decisions and choices with the conscious mind. It operates in the foreground of our consciousness.

Subconscious Mind. The mind that stores and helps us use information, knowledge, and memories of all our experiences. It seeks consistency and coherence. It operates in the background of our consciousness.

Unconscious Mind. The mind that stores bits and pieces of the Self that we have disowned, discarded, and buried/repressed. The unconscious mind operates beyond our awareness, in the "underground" of our consciousness.

Motive: The reason we take action.

Needs: Something we feel intense motivation to fulfill for our Self. Our needs are: to survive, to have safety and security, to experience belonging and loving, to have Self-esteem, to create/produce/know, to actualize the Self, and to pursue beauty, mystery, and the transcendent.

Personality: Part of the Self. The personality constitutes much of what makes us individuals. It contains our temperament, character traits, our life challenges ("issues"), and our approach to life in general.

Perspective: How a person sees things from his or her point of view. Gaining perspective: Looking at a situation in a way that includes a larger point of view.

Power: The willingness and ability to act.

Protector: The protector is an aspect of our Self whose function/job is to protect us, arising partly from our survival instincts.

Remorse: The regret and anguish we feel about our behavior's negative impact on another person. A function of a healthy conscience.

Repression: A common defense mechanism, especially of childhood, that results in parts of our Self being lost.

Resistance: Anything that prevents movement from starting, or slows something down that's already in motion. Resistance is often "the reason why not."

Responsibility:

1. The capacity (ability and willingness) to see that our actions always have consequences and that we own the consequences of our actions. The consequences belong to us.

2. The capacity to respond to the consequences of our actions, and to cope with the effects of our actions on the world of people and events.

3. Response-Ability. The ability to respond to something that impacts us, to a trigger or an event.

Self (with a capital S): The sum total of all our aspects and parts, as human beings.

self (with a small s): The developmental self. A component of the Self.

Self-Acceptance: An attitude toward our Self that expresses the following: "I am a fallible human being. I am imperfect and make mistakes. *And this is okay.* I won't criticize my Self or beat my Self up."

Self-Awareness: The ability human beings have to step outside of their Self and look at their Self.

Self-Confidence: The belief that I have the ability to cope with situations that come my way.

Self-Discipline: An ability that enables us to pause between thinking/feeling and acting. An ability to focus our attention on an important activity, and to accomplish the tasks involved with that activity, even though we do not feel like doing it at the moment.

Self-Esteem: Self-esteem is having a fundamental and deep, good feeling for, and about, our Self. Having a deep, positive regard for our Self.

Self-esteem is the knowing, conviction, and certainty of your right to exist.

Self-esteem is based on the evaluation of your behavior, motivations, and attitudes according to the values, ethics, principles, and ideals you hold in your character/personality, conscience, developmental self, and identity/image (your Self, excluding the ego).

Self-Fulfilling Prophecy: A process of creation where we expect an event (usually unwanted) to occur in the future and bring it about with behavior that we are not fully aware of.

Self-Love: Love that we have for our Self. Love that we give to our Self. Different from narcissism.

Self-Realization: To realize, make real, the potentials of the Self. To use potential abilities.

Self-Respect: The admiration we have, and the honor we hold, for our Self. Generated as we live up to the standards we hold for our Self.

Self-Worth: The sense of our worth that is innate, that we are born with.

Shame: The feeling that accompanies the belief that our Self is flawed and defective.

Skill: An ability that I can use with consistent competence to accomplish a task.

Sorrow: Feeling for and with, the pain of another person whom we have hurt in some way. A function of a healthy conscience.

Synergy: Combining elements so that the whole is greater than the sum of its parts.

System: A collection of parts that work together to accomplish a task.

Truth: An accurate description of what is.

Unfinished Business: Experiences from the past where there is emotional disturbance, turmoil, or pain still attached to them. They continue to influence current functioning. Also, experiences where there was no closure or completion.

Vicious Circle: A negative interaction among two or more parts that mutually reinforce each other in a circular process. The circle continues to affect us until we consciously or accidently end it.

Will: The expression of desire. Our ability to generate and sustain movement toward the accomplishment of a goal or purpose. The force that moves. A "will/energy current" that generates momentum.

Willingness: A commitment to use my will.

Willpower: The power generated by my will.

You: The sum total of your being. Includes all aspects of the Self, plus aspects that are beyond the Self that we are most familiar with.

BIBLIOGRAPHY

Bailey, Becky A. *Easy to Love, Difficult to Discipline* (New York: HarperCollins, 2000).

Beck, Judith S. *Cognitive Therapy: Basics and Beyond* (New York: Guilford Press, 1995).

Branden, Nathaniel. *Six Pillars of Self-Esteem* (New York: Bantam Books, 1994).

Buber, Martin. *I and Thou* (New York: Charles Scribner and Sons, 1958).

Chetkow-Yanoov, B. *Social Work Practice: A Systems Approach* (New York: Haworth Press, 1992).

Covey, Stephen, R. *The 7 Habits of Highly Effective People* (New York: Free Press, 1989).

Erikson, Eric H. *Identity: Youth and Crisis* (New York: W. W. Norton and Company, Inc., 1968).

Freud, Anna. *The Ego and the Mechanisms of Defense* (New York: International University Press, 1966).

Freud, Sigmund. *The Problem of Anxiety* (New York: Psychoanalytical Quarterly Press and W. W. Norton and Company, Inc., 1936).

Ginott, Haim G. *Between Parent and Child* (New York: Avon Books, 1961).

Ginott, Haim G. *Between Parent and Teenager* (New York: Avon Books, 1969).

Grinker, Roy R. *Psychosomatic Concepts* (New York: Jason Aronson, Inc., 1973).

Hendrix, Harville. *Getting the Love You Want* (New York: Henry Holt and Company, 1998).

Hendrix, Harville. *Keeping the Love You Find* (New York: Pocket Books, 1992).

Henry, Jules. *Pathways to Madness* (New York: Random House, Inc., 1965).

James, Muriel. *Techniques in Transactional Analysis* (Reading, Massachusetts: Addison-Wesley Publishing Company, 1977).

James, Muriel, and Dorothy Jongeward. *Born to Win: Transactional Analysis with Gestalt Experiments* (Reading, Massachusetts: Addison-Wesley Publishing Company, 1971).

Jeffers, Susan. *Feel the Fear and Do It Anyway* (New York: Fawcett Columbine, 1987).

Kernberg, Otto. *Object Relations Theory and Clinical Psycho-Analysis* (New York: Jason Aronson, Inc., 1976).

Langs, Robert. *Unconscious Communication in Everyday Life* (New York: Jason Aronson, Inc., 1983).

Madanes, Cloe. *Sex, Love, and Violence* (New York: W. W. Norton & Company, 1990).

Mahler, Margaret S. *Separation-Individuation* (New York: Jason Aronson, Inc., 1979).

Maltz, Maxwell. *The Psycho-Cybernetics* (New York: Prentice Hall Press, 2001).

Maslow, Abraham. *A Theory of Human Motivation* (Psychological Review: 1943).

Peck, M. Scott. *The Road Less Traveled* (New York: Touchstone Books, 1978).

Pierrakos, Eva. *The Pathwork of Self-Transformation* (New York: Bantam Books, 1990).

Popkin, Michael. *Active Parenting* (New York: HarperCollins, 1987).

Pursel, Jach. *Loving* (NPN Publishing, 1986).

Pursel, Jach. *Self-Esteem* (NPN Publishing, 1986).

Pursel, Jach. *The Secrets of Empowerment: Loving Beyond Self* (NPN Publishing, 1997).

Robbins, Anthony. *Awaken the Giant Within* (New York: Summit Books, 1991).

Schwartz, Richard. *Internal Family System Therapy* (New York: The Guilford Press, 1995).

Talbot, Toby, ed. *The World of the Child* (New York: Jason Aronson, Inc., 1967).

Turecki, Stanley, with Leslie Tonner. *The Difficult Child* (New York: Bantam Books, 1985).

Young, Jeffrey E. and Janet S. Klosko. *Reinventing Your Life* (New York: Plume Books, 1994).

INDEX

A

Ability, 55-57, 62-64, 67-70, 103, 287-288, **321**
Absolutes, 163
Abuse, 234, 293
Accomplishments, 80, 99-100
Acting. *See* Behavior
Actions, 67-70. *See also* Behavior
Actualization, 102-106, 178, 254
Actualizing Potential, 103
Adolescents
and boundaries, 140-142, 148
and the conscience, 228, 232, 234
and the developmental self, 162-165, 176-178
and disturbances of the Self, 290-294
and ego, 190, 197-198
excessive demands placed on, 197-198
and identification, 162-163, 258
stages of life, 117-120
Adults
and boundaries, 142-144, 148
and the conscience, 228, 232, 234
and the developmental self, 167-178
and disturbances of the Self, 290
and identification, 235
love and hate, 280
stages of life, 120-124
and temperament, 213
Aggression
boundary violations, 147-148
as a coping mechanism, 176-177
displaced, 234, 269
identification with aggressor, 233
misuse of will, 58-59

Alcohol Abuse, 240
All-or-Nothing Thinking, 43-45
Alternatives, 66
Ambivalence, 136, 173-174
Anxiety, 211
Approach/Avoidance Conflict, 136, 173-174
Artistry, 55-57, **321**
Assertiveness, 95-96
Associations, 265-267, 269, 283
Attitude, 8, 209
Authority, 63-64, 95-96
Authority Figures, 270-272. *See also* Mentors; Parents
Autonomy, 97-98, 140, **321**
Awareness, 16, 27, 45-48, 51, 66-67, 168, **321**. *See also* Self-Awareness

B

Beauty, 106, 181-182
Behavior, 48-50, 319-320
Being, 37-38
Belief Systems, 51-52, 155, **321**
Beliefs, 17, 158, 163, 173, 195-196, 239, 267, **321**
Belonging, 90-93
Boundaries
generally, 134-137
adolescents, 140-142, 148
adults, 142-144, 148
autonomous Self, 140
blurring of boundaries, 143
children, 140-142, 148
confusion of boundaries, 143-144
created and defended by Self, 138-146
defined, **321**
differentiation, 141

ABOUT THE AUTHOR

Jeffrey Bryan is a licensed clinical social worker and a Board Certified Diplomate in Clinical Social Work. He obtained his master's of social work in 1978 from the Adelphi University School of Social Work, specializing in clinical social work. Since entering the field of mental health, he has been a practicing psychotherapist and a supervisor. When he wrote *The Operating Manual for the Self*, he had conducted over 40,000 clinical interviews. The information gained from clients and patients, combined with extensive reading, has resulted in the theory and practice of *The Operating Manual for the Self*.

In 2014, Mr. Bryan established the International Institute for Self-Development. The institute has a broad mission and utilizes *The Operating Manual for the Self* as one of its theoretical foundations.

To learn more about the institute and about Mr. Bryan's work, visit: jeffreyibryan.com, manualfortheself.com, and IIFSD.org.

ABOUT THE INTERNATIONAL INSTITUTE FOR SELF-DEVELOPMENT

The International Institute for Self-Development was founded by Jeffrey Bryan in 2014. The institute has broad goals, as expressed in the following vision and mission statements.

VISION STATEMENT:

- To awaken and further our human potential through Self-development.

MISSION STATEMENT:

- To facilitate and empower Self-development by providing a theory of the Self, and by providing practices to put the theory into action.
- To develop leadership training based on the idea that who a leader is as a person is the most important factor in the effectiveness of a leader.
- To explain what Self-esteem truly is and to teach individuals how to have and raise their Self-esteem.
- To help parents develop the Self-worth, Self-esteem, and Self-love of their children.
- To explain the basis for a new conscience; a new conscience founded on the idea that a person can and should feel good for doing the right thing.
- To explain what personal boundaries are and how to create and protect them.

Website: IIFSD.org

CPSIA information can be obtained
at www.ICGtesting.com
Printed in the USA
LVHW051033050222
710245LV00010B/218